Study Skills for
International Postgraduates

Palgrave Study Skills

Authoring a PhD
Business Degree Success
Career Skills
Critical Thinking Skills (2nd edn)
e-Learning Skills (2nd edn)
Effective Communication for
    Arts and Humanities Students
Effective Communication for
    Science and Technology
The Exam Skills Handbook
The Foundations of Research (2nd edn)
The Good Supervisor
Great Ways to Learn Anatomy and
    Physiology
How to Manage your Arts, Humanities and
    Social Science Degree
How to Manage your Distance and
    Open Learning Course
How to Manage your Postgraduate Course
How to Manage your Science and
    Technology Degree
How to Study Foreign Languages
How to Study Linguistics (2nd edn)
How to use your Reading in your Essays
How to Write Better Essays (2nd edn)
How to Write your Undergraduate
    Dissertation
Information Skills
The International Student Handbook
IT Skills for Successful Study
Making Sense of Statistics
The Mature Student's Guide to Writing (2nd edn)
The Mature Student's Handbook
The Palgrave Student Planner
The Personal Tutor's Handbook

The Postgraduate Research Handbook (2nd edn)
Presentation Skills for Students (2nd edn)
The Principles of Writing in Psychology
Professional Writing (2nd edn)
Researching Online
Research Using IT
Skills for Success (2nd edn)
The Study Abroad Handbook
The Student's Guide to Writing (2nd edn)
The Student Life Handbook
The Study Skills Handbook (3rd edn)
Study Skills for International Postgraduates
Study Skills for Speakers of English as
    a Second Language
Studying Arts and Humanities
Studying the Built Environment
Studying Business at MBA and Masters Level
Studying Economics
Studying History (3rd edn)
Studying Law (3rd edn)
Studying Mathematics and its Applications
Studying Modern Drama (2nd edn)
Studying Physics
Studying Programming
Studying Psychology (2nd edn)
Teaching Study Skills and Supporting
    Learning
The Undergraduate Research Handbook
The Work-Based Learning Student Handbook
Work Placements – a Survival Guide for
    Students
Writing for Nursing and Midwifery Students
Write It Right
Writing for Engineers (3rd edn)

Pocket Study Skills

Series Editor: Kate Williams

14 Days to Exam Success
Blogs, Wikis, Podcasts and More
Brilliant Writing Tips for Students
Completing Your PhD
Doing Research
Getting Critical
Planning Your Essay

Planning Your PhD
Reading and Making Notes
Referencing and Understanding Plagiarism
Science Study Skills
Success in Groupwork
Time Management
Writing for University

Study Skills for International Postgraduates

Martin Davies

Associate Professor in Higher Education,
Faculty of Business and Economics,
University of Melbourne, Australia

palgrave
macmillan

First published 2011 by
PALGRAVE MACMILLAN

Palgrave Macmillan in the UK is an imprint of Macmillan Publishers Limited,
registered in England, company number 785998, of Houndmills, Basingstoke,
Hampshire RG21 6XS.

Palgrave Macmillan in the US is a division of St Martin's Press LLC,
175 Fifth Avenue, New York, NY 10010.

Palgrave Macmillan is the global academic imprint of the above companies
and has companies and representatives throughout the world.

Palgrave® and Macmillan® are registered trademarks in the United States,
the United Kingdom, Europe and other countries

ISBN 978-1-4039-9580-3   ISBN 978-0-230-34553-9 (eBook)

DOI 10.1007/978-0-230-34553-9

This book is printed on paper suitable for recycling and made from fully
managed and sustained forest sources. Logging, pulping and manufacturing
processes are expected to conform to the environmental regulations of the
country of origin.

A catalogue record for this book is available from the British Library.

A catalog record for this book is available from the Library of Congress.

10 9 8 7 6 5 4 3 2 1
20 19 18 17 16 15 14 13 12 11

To Jackson, who has a lifetime of learning to enjoy

Contents

Preface

Obtaining an international education in an English-speaking country is becoming more important in the globalised world in which we live. In Australia, international students, especially those from Asia, made up roughly 40 per cent of the total student body in 2007. Education of international students is a $16 billion-a-year industry, the third largest industry in the country after coal and iron ore exports! In some Faculties, international students comprise more than seventy per cent of the student body and the number is growing. Tertiary institutions in other western countries are facing similar upward trends. However, despite the growing demand for educational services by international students, there are few study skills textbooks written specifically for international postgraduate students. This book tries to meet this need.

The book can be read from cover to cover, or dipped into as the need arises. It is designed to be practical, clear and comprehensive. It includes all the main skill areas required for successful postgraduate study. As a quick guide, the book has seven main parts:

1 Being a Postgraduate Student
2 Basic Survival Skills
3 Perils and Pitfalls: Tips for New Players
4 Standing on the Shoulders of Others: Doing Research
5 What About Me? Criticising and Analysing
6 Putting Pen to Paper: Writing for Assessment
7 Being Heard: Speaking for Assessment

As part of the writing chapters, I have included some material on learning English as a Second Language (ESL). The advice given in this chapter is information I find myself giving to almost every student I see. But I stress that this is not an ESL book, and I am not an ESL teacher. For additional resources on ESL, you should consult specialist ESL texts. Similarly, I have not dealt with broader issues of social or cultural transition. This too is covered comprehensively in other books in the Palgrave series (e.g. Cotterill, 2003).

Each of the chapters has been written in a style that allows for independent study. None demand preparatory reading. Activities are provided within boxes, but they are certainly not mandatory. If the book is used in a classroom situation, the activities will be useful for consolidating learning.

The book has had a long gestation period. The first draft was helpfully edited by Roger McCart at the Australian National University. The second draft received helpful input from Susan Harris, and considerable input from my colleague Tim Beaumont from the University of Melbourne. Palgrave Macmillan provided editorial assistance on the penultimate version. I particularly want to thank Suzannah Burywood from Palgrave, and several anonymous readers assigned to evaluate the book for publication. I would also like to thank Penelope Goodes for her last-minute help with shortening the manuscript. The Office of Teaching and Learning in the Faculty of Business at the University of Sydney provided a congenial environment in which to prepare the penultimate draft. I also wish to thank St. John's College at the University of Sydney for their pleasant hospitality and the use of the 'Gatehouse' while I was a Visiting Fellow during the autumn of 2007. Most of the material herein was developed as 'Help Sheets' for students at the Faculty of Business and Economics at the University of Melbourne, and are still in use in that format there and in equivalent Faculty at the University of Sydney. It only became clear to me after using this material with students over many years that the material might be useful in book form.

MARTIN DAVIES
University of Melbourne

Acknowledgements

The author and publishers wish to thank the following for permission to use copyright material:

Asia Pacific Press for the figure on p. 24, from A. Bartlett, S. Holzknecht and A. Cumming Thom, *Preparing Students for Graduate Study: To Hit the Ground Running* (1999).

D. J. Clarke (source), for the table on p. 92, from *Research Methods in Education*. Unpublished manuscript, Melbourne (2003).

D. Taylor, for pp. 220, 226–7, from *Writing in Health Sciences: A Comprehensive Guide*, 1:1 (2008).

Pearson Australia for the table on p.14, from B. Ballard and J. Clanchy, *Studying in Australia* (1988).

R. Hurworth for the figure on p. 92, used in Subject 481812 University of Melbourne: Introduction to Qualitative Methods (2010, based on an original cited in 2003).

The Taylor and Francis Group for pp. 171–2, from C. Johnston, *Higher Education Research and Development*, 20:2 (2001).

The editors of the *Australian Agribusiness Review* for pp. 221–2, from *Australian Agribusiness Review* 1 (1993).

The University of Melbourne for pp. 288–9, from *PhD Handbook* (2011).

Every effort has been made to contact all the copyright holders, but if any have been inadvertently overlooked the publishers will be pleased to make the necessary arrangements at the first opportunity.

Part I

Being a Postgraduate St

Part I

Being a Postgraduate Student

1 Getting Started as a Postgraduate

● 1 Introduction

Perhaps you are reading this book because you plan to study overseas. Perhaps you have just been accepted into a university as a postgraduate. If so, congratulations! Postgraduate study is exciting and stimulating if it is approached in the right way. It can lead to increased employment prospects, and it can change your life.

It is also true that postgraduate study brings significant challenges. As a postgraduate learning specialist, I regularly see students who say that postgraduate study is more difficult than they had expected. This is a natural reaction. The western education system demands increasingly more from students as they move to higher educational levels. The higher you go, the more independent and self-reliant you are expected to be.

The demands of postgraduate study are not simply in terms of a greater workload. One of the major challenges is to realise that your success as a postgraduate is entirely up to you. Few people will hold your hand and tell you what to do. Postgraduate study demands independence and self-reliance, qualities that are highly valued by employers. Naturally, the transition from a semi-dependent undergraduate to an independent postgraduate brings considerable challenges.

Before commencing postgraduate study in a western tertiary institution, you need to be aware of three things:

- ● the **outcomes** expected of you during your course of study;
- ● the **types of assessment** used in your intended Faculty;
- ● the **expectations** of you in terms of your **oral** and **written work**.

Awareness of these three is important for all students, but students from non-western backgrounds also need to understand a little about the western education system itself and what it means to be a postgraduate student within it.

● 2 Getting to know yourself

Activity:
Getting to know yourself

The western academic environment values the ability to discuss and express one's point of view. Students should not be afraid of expressing their point of view as often as possible. Usually a postgraduate class will begin with an 'ice-breaker' ice-breaker to encourage free exchange of ideas, and to allow you to meet fellow students. The following is an example of such an activity.

Imagine yourself in a classroom consisting of students from mixed backgrounds – i.e. western and eastern, male and female, of different ethnic and religious backgrounds. Imagine some of your fellow students as well-dressed, professional people who are very confident in English. Spend a moment imagining a class in which you are a participant. Write down and practise your responses to the following discussion questions:

- Why have you come to a foreign country to study?
- What do you hope to learn?
- Why didn't you consider studying in an institution in your own country?
- What is different (or special) about a western university education?
- How do western countries differ in general from your own country?
- How does the western education system differ from the education system in your own country?
- What do you like or dislike about the western education system so far? (If you have not yet started your course of study, what do you *expect* to like or dislike?)

If it helps, rehearse your answers in front of a mirror. Try to present a coherent verbal **argument** for each question (i.e. don't just answer the first question with 'I don't know' or 'I wanted to experience something different').

Let's take the first question. Consider starting with a general introductory phrase that shapes your answer: 'Well, there are really three main reasons why I chose to come to a foreign country to study: the first, and most important reason, was . . .' (use different introductory phrases for each reason). Then, narrow this down to your detailed answer: 'For these three reasons, I particularly wanted to see whether I could survive on my own in another country. I am not used to living away from my family, and not used to cooking and cleaning for myself. So, I thought it might be a good challenge to study overseas.' End with a concluding sentence: 'So these are the reasons why I wanted to study overseas.' Your answers should be shaped like this:

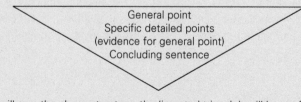

General point
Specific detailed points
(evidence for general point)
Concluding sentence

As we will see, the above structure, the 'inverted triangle', will be useful in many ways. It is a structure that is logically satisfying to the western mind, and it has many applications in writing as well as in speech.

● 3 Academic learning skills outcomes

As postgraduates you will be required to do exams and assignments. However, most of your assessment work as a postgraduate will consist of some or all of the following assessment tasks.

Typical postgraduate assessment tasks at university
1 Exercises to test information literacy and exercises to demonstrate research skills.
2 Empirical reports, business reports or business plans.
3 Critical reviews and literature reviews (either as part of a thesis, as stand-alone documents or as part of essays or reports).
4 Research essays.
5 Case studies and/or analyses of case studies.
6 Exercises to test academic reading skills.
7 Seminar and tutorial presentations.

In addition to content knowledge, i.e. understanding of subjects, and a high degree of skill in computer literacy, postgraduate students are expected to demonstrate skills in a broad range of areas. These are listed below, along with the chapters in which they are covered. See the website for an activity where you can assess your skills in these areas:

- academic expectations, time and **information management** (chapters 1, 2 and 3);
- reading skills (chapter 4);
- referencing and citation systems (chapters 5–6);
- research skills (chapter 7);
- critical thinking (chapter 8);
- writing skills (chapters 9 and 15);
- writing critical reviews/literature reviews (chapters 10 and 14);
- writing empirical reports (chapter 11);
- writing research essays (chapters 12–13);
- seminar presentation and speaking skills (chapters 16–17);
- writing research proposals and starting a Ph.D. (chapters 18–19).

At the end of the book we will revisit these skills in relation to future studies and gaining employment. Before you move on, try the more general checklist at the end of this chapter. How confident do you feel in each of these areas? You will feel much more confident by the time you reach the end of the book than you did at the beginning.

● 4 The academic expectations of postgraduates

It is important to understand what the academic expectations are in western universities, as they may conflict with those of your home university. The advice in this chapter is based on broad generalisations, which are applicable to most – but not all – western universities. Western universities have a common tradition stemming from ancient Greece. While academic writing and speaking styles may differ between the different western language groups, this common tradition means that the academic culture of western universities is broadly similar. Thus, much of the advice here may be known by an international student who has studied in Spain or Germany, but may be new for a student whose previous university was in Saudi Arabia or Thailand.

This is not to say that education in western countries is intrinsically 'better' than education in other countries. Rather, the advice here is given to help you to adapt to what is expected of you at a foreign university, so that you can succeed. This will prepare you for the globalised workforce beyond the university, which is still largely dominated by English and western traditions.

1 Adult learning in western countries

Adult learners in western countries are expected to demonstrate the following skills:
- they should take an **active** role in their own learning;
- they should seek, hold, express and justify **opinions**;
- they should be willing to **participate** in organised discussions;
- they should **contribute** to team-work assignments when requested to do so;
- they are expected to **approach** academic staff for assistance when they require help;
- they should **follow** strict assessment **procedures and guidelines**, e.g. due dates for assignments, examination times;
- they should always express ideas **in their own words** when writing being careful to acknowledge the originator of the ideas;
- they should **support** ideas and opinions with **evidence** from a variety of peer-reviewed academic sources ('peer-reviewed' will be explained in a later chapter);
- they should be expected to think and write **critically**.

(Based on *The Integrated Bridging Program*, University of Adelaide)

2 Key aspects of the western academic tradition

1 Active learning

In Western countries, university students are not expected to passively accept as true the information provided by the lecturer. Students' own ideas are valued and respected, and students are expected to contribute to the class. Questioning and critical thinking are also key to active learning; information and ideas should not be simply accepted by students. It is quite acceptable for students to question or even correct the lecturer.

At postgraduate level, students are expected to be active learners: to find things for themselves, think for themselves, disagree with the lecturer's point of view (when this is appropriate) and do their own planning, timetabling of their workload and preparation for assignments. Thus, the lecturer–student relationship is viewed somewhat differently to what you may have experienced in your home university. This is one of the greatest adjustment difficulties that international students face.

Many students, especially those from Asian countries, are used to a more 'passive' approach to learning where lecturers 'give information' and students simply write it down. This approach is very different from the western academic approach where lecturers give minimal direction, make students arrive at the 'answers' themselves, and expect students to argue with them! **Active learning** and **initiative** in **problem-solving** are important skills, particularly in the workforce. In western countries this learning starts in universities. The quicker a student adapts to this study environment, the quicker they do well.

> ### But is this education?
>
> A natural reaction by many international students to the 'active learning' approach of western universities is to feel that they are somehow 'sold short', i.e. that they are not *being educated* as much as *educating themselves*. Some students find this hard to accept, especially when they pay such high tuition fees. 'What am I getting for my money?' is an understandable reaction. 'Why don't lecturers just tell me the answer?', 'Why don't they tell me what I need to know for the exam?'

Lecturers often keep a record of the verbal contributions of students in the class, particularly in tutorials and seminars. Some lecturers keep a grade book for this purpose, ticking off students' names or assigning 'points' for intelligent comments or critical responses to ideas raised in class. At the end of semester, they calculate the points and arrive at a 'participation' grade. If students have not participated or engaged actively with the material being discussed in classes, they receive 'zero' for participation.

Surprisingly, this expectation to contribute verbally and to be an 'active' and critical learner is not often made clear to students. The reason for this is historical. Many people regard active learning as the *essence* of a western tertiary education. These historical traditions go back to ancient Greece, the birthplace of the university system. (Sometimes active engagement is known as 'Socratic dialogue' after Socrates, one of the early Greek philosophers.) It is one of the main functions of the university to provide this opportunity for active learning and engagement, and students are expected to participate in it. It is good practice, therefore, to act and respond in class *as though* the teacher were silently giving students participation grades, because often they are (even though they may not have told the students)!

Opportunities are provided for active learning and interaction in all postgraduate classes. These may take the following forms:

- in-class **groupwork** assignments;
- pairwork discussions;
- whole-class discussions;
- formal debates in class;
- problem-based learning;
- student presentations followed by critical peer feedback.

There are many other variations, all involving active learning by students. In the western university there is less emphasis on **teacher-centred learning** (where the teacher 'gives' information and students sit passively absorbing it) and more emphasis on **student-centred learning** (where students learn by *doing* something themselves). Student-centred learning allows opportunities for discussion, clarification of ideas and concepts and disagreement on the material being discussed. This has many benefits, not least of which is the development of English language skills. There is evidence to suggest that students learn better when they are actively involved in something.

The most common form of information delivery in universities are, of course, **lectures**, which are large-group, teacher-directed and teacher-centred classes. These are usually supplemented with **tutorials**, which are small-group, student-centred discussions. This practice is still common at undergraduate level, where hundreds of students attend a lecture followed by a smaller tutorial of 15 to 20 students. The purpose of the lecture is to impart information. The purpose of the tutorial is to discuss and **critically analyse** the material given in the lecture.

At postgraduate level, however, it is increasingly common to have a *blend* of the two formats in medium-sized classes (around 50 or more students in Australia; fewer in the US). This is called a **seminar**. At a seminar, students receive *some* lecturer-directed content and then are expected to discuss issues, either as a large group or in smaller 'break-out' groups. Break-out groups later reconvene in the larger group to present their ideas.

In seminars and tutorials 'active' participatory learning is crucial. Students need to demonstrate that they have read and understood the material being discussed, and they need to show that they have ideas and opinions of their own. This is not just appreciated or encouraged; it is the *purpose* of the seminar or tutorial discussion groups. If students are not contributing actively, they are simply not doing what is expected of them. In large seminars, it is particularly important to make verbal contributions as – if you stay silent – often the lecturer does not know that you understand the material, or have done the reading. In a sense, you need to 'show off' that you are keeping up with the reading and that you understand it. Again, it is good practice to treat every class discussion group *as though* the tutor or lecturer were silently assigning grades for participation. If you approach your classes in this way you can be sure that you will gain an acceptable participation grade.

2 Asking questions
Many international students are used to learning situations in which asking questions is considered to be inappropriate. In contrast, asking questions is encouraged in western

countries because this shows a desire for knowledge and also that the student is intelligent and willing to question things and seek clarification. If you are having trouble understanding something, it is likely that other students do not understand it either.

If you ask the lecturer to repeat or explain what you do not understand this helps the lecturer to understand what your problem is. They then know how to help you.

Remember too that lecturers feel that students have experiences to contribute to class discussions. For example, you may have had experience working overseas. This kind of knowledge is invaluable and very much welcomed by lecturers. Do not be afraid to **voice your views** or **opinions**. It will make a good impression and possibly advance the class discussion. The opinions and perspectives that you bring as an international student can be particularly valued and can enrich the learning environment.

Asking questions is another aspect of active learning. Tutors and lecturers want to see evidence that students have *engaged* with the material being discussed. The best way to demonstrate this is by asking intelligent and relevant questions.

3 Seeking, holding and expressing opinions

In postgraduate education, you will succeed best if you are capable of seeking, holding and expressing opinions: preferably your own **well-argued** and **justified** opinions. You will be most likely to succeed if you are **critical** of information presented to you. 'Critical' can be defined in two ways: either as 'finding fault' (e.g. 'She was criticised for not attending class') or as 'judging the merits or faults of something'. It is the second meaning that we intend when we use 'criticise' and 'critical' in the academic context of western countries. It is very important to understand this, because great value is placed on thinking about, questioning and analysing information at university. At the postgraduate level emphasis is given to the skills of **criticising**, **being critical**, and on **thinking** and **writing critically**. This is quite different from what is expected of undergraduate students at university. Undergraduates often simply accept information as being correct or true. By contrast, postgraduates are expected to be able to challenge received wisdom and come to their own conclusions.

You must endeavour to seek, hold and express opinions at all times on all topics. This means, on occasion, being critical of information presented to you. As noted earlier, some tutors will *deliberately* say something untrue in class, just to see which students in the class are being critical, and which are simply passively accepting everything they are being told.

Note this carefully now, as your success in being critical will – to a large degree – determine your grades. You will *not* get good grades by simply copying what the teacher tells you. Often lecturers and tutors are *more* impressed with students who **actively disagree** with the views presented in class (including their own). Of course, you cannot disagree with your tutor simply by finding fault with them or judging their views severely ('critical' in the first sense above). You must be critical in the second sense above, by weighing the **pros and cons** of an issue and giving compelling **reasons** for why you disagree with what the tutor is telling you. Your ability to demonstrate critical thinking is a vital part of your assessment as a postgraduate.

Critical or critique?

Sometimes you will hear the word '**critique**'. You may be asked to *critique* something for assessment. What does this mean? To 'critique' means to outline what is good **and** bad about something, i.e. the positive *and* negative aspects. In critiquing, you are required to give your *judgement* about the positive and negative aspects and come to a balanced conclusion. You are not simply meant to make a *list*. You must **argue the case** for what you think is positive and negative. This requires critical thinking.

For example, if you are asked to *critique the role of television in society,* it would be easy to give a list of positive and negative points. However, what arguments would you give for each point? How would you support the point that television is a source of entertainment and relaxation, can promote fundraising for good causes, but also is a source of moral decay, can promote laziness and spread misinformation? How would you adjudicate between the positive and negative points and evaluate them? How would you reach a conclusion? What *emphasis* would you put on the good points and the bad points? How would you argue for one side or the other?

4 Participation

Some international students find it uncomfortable to participate actively. Education in most western countries encourages active participation by students, even in primary school. With practice and training, however, international students can participate very well. It is all a matter of good advice, deliberate practice, and confidence. Importantly, it is a matter of preparation and knowing what to expect.

Participating actively involves asking questions of the lecturer, but it also involves actively playing a role in assignments and tasks. This means that you are expected to take the initiative, lead discussions, offer comments, and criticise the views of others. If you do this politely and respectfully, this is not considered rude or aggressive.

5 Contributing to team-produced assignments

Contributing to team-produced assignments may constitute a large part of your assessment. **Group work** has become a vital part of assessment in most western universities. Team-produced assignments receive a team grade, sometimes with grades for each team member and an overall grade for the group. Many students do not respond well to group-work tasks, as they feel that they can do these assignments much quicker, and often better, individually. Some also complain about 'lazy' group members who drag down the group's marks. There is some basis for these concerns. It is not easy to organise a team of people to produce a clearly argued and well-researched team assignment. Some students are unreliable, some are not interested in working hard, others have trouble with English writing skills, and so on.

However, the educational rationale for including group work as an assessment exercise is a sound one. Graduate students should acquire the skills of managing other people and themselves, such as delegating work, and setting and achieving team objectives. These are important skills for employment, as most jobs involve teamwork. Most teamwork assignments fail or do badly not because of the task itself, but because the individuals in the group were unable to manage the team to achieve the objectives that were set. In group work, you are being assessed on these skills. Students *themselves* are responsible when teamwork projects do not go well. The point of the exercise is in managing the group, as well as performing the set task.

You may be paired to do group work with western students. You will be expected to contribute, verbally and in writing. If you don't, you may be viewed by others as lazy or incompetent.

6 Approaching staff for guidance

You will be expected to take the initiative and ask your lecturer to explain if you do not know or understand something. In western countries it is not considered rude to ask a question during a lecture. Indeed, it is ruder not to seek clarification when a lecturer invites questions during a lecture and then later admit that you did not understand what was required. You should always ask even if you want only a minor clarification. Nothing is lost by asking, and much can be gained. You are expected to be *proactive* in terms of your own learning.

It is best to go straight to your lecturer or tutor with your questions, rather than asking your friends. It demonstrates that you are thinking about the material, are assertive and confident, and are eager to get it right. Other students can often be wrong or misinformed – if you don't understand something, it is likely that your friends don't understand it either. Again, it is important to note that, as a postgraduate, you are being assessed on these skills. Rather than laugh at you for asking a question, your lecturers will be impressed by your proactiveness, your interest and your dedication.

7 Following assessment procedures

In western countries, deadlines are final. Online submission is possible at many universities, and assignments are rigorously checked to ensure they are submitted on time. Lateness is unacceptable. There is no equivalent notion in western countries as the Indonesian concept of 'rubber time' (*Jam karet*), where a deadline is treated as a vague commitment to something that can be 'stretched out'. In western universities you will lose marks (usually 5 to 10 marks per day an assignment is late) unless you have a medical certificate. Often international students from Asia are surprised at how strict deadlines are in western countries. Work is due by 5 pm on the deadline day; submitted work will receive a date and time stamp to show whether it was on time or not.

Deadlines are important for reasons of equity. Strict deadlines mean that all students have the same amount of time to complete the assignment. Deadlines and strict timetables are also a cultural feature of western societies. In western society it is culturally unacceptable to be late, unless you have a valid reason.

> **Note:** If you need an extension of time for a legitimate medical reason, normally university procedures will require that you must ask the lecturer first *at least two weeks before* the due date (there are variations on this in different universities). If you are sick on the day, you must submit medical evidence if you are unable to hand in work on time. **Failure to consistently hand in work on time will result in overall failure for your course of study.**

8 Expressing ideas in your own words
Students who do not express ideas in their own words, but instead copy other people's words and ideas without acknowledgement are considered *plagiarists*. **Plagiarism** often demonstrates that a student is lacking in ideas and imagination or cannot understand the material given to them. In a worst-case situation, it demonstrates a student willing to 'steal' words and ideas from others. Sometimes plagiarism demonstrates that a student is genuinely unfamiliar with the cultural expectations of the western tertiary environment. It is essential that you learn how to express yourself in your own words. You must also understand plagiarism and its implications.

9 Supporting ideas with evidence
Postgraduates must provide **supporting evidence** for the statements and opinions expressed in their assignments. Your marks depend on your ability to back up your arguments with suitable evidence.

10 Thinking and writing critically
Critical thinking is central to university education in western countries. Thinking and writing critically allow you to argue your position in your essays, research papers and presentations. In your assessments, you will have to present your argument as a series of statements which lead logically to a conclusion, or as a series of partial conclusions leading to a final conclusion (see diagram below).

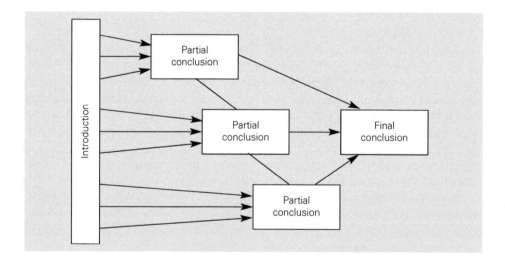

Consider the previous example of television. One *partial conclusion* is that television is entertaining owing to the large number of popular comedy and lifestyle shows that are available. You might argue that statistics show that this outweighs the number of programmes that are violent and in bad taste; and that, despite the popularity of such programmes, on balance there are more good than bad programmes. You might say

Activity:
Comparing the western and non-western academic environments

Summarise what is required to be a successful postgraduate student in the western academic environment and contrast it with what is required in the universities in your home country. Make particular reference to:

- student attitudes to study in both countries;
- lecturer expectations of students in both countries;
- assessment procedures in both countries.

that television is, on balance, a good thing. Another *partial conclusion* is that television can promote good causes, such as fundraising for the victims of natural disasters. You could argue that this influence is greater than the ability of television to mislead and damage children. Adult programmes are only screened late at night, when children cannot see them, and as adults can clearly distinguish between fact and fiction, they are less easily led astray. Another *partial conclusion* weighs up the points that watching television is both relaxing and can promote laziness. You can argue that people who do not own a television set can also be lazy (that laziness is a state of mind), and that, on balance, television can be a positive source of relaxation if watched for only a few hours a day. These points lead to an *overall conclusion* that despite some bad points, television is a good thing for society.

● 5 The aim of postgraduate education

The ultimate aim of a western postgraduate education is to teach students how to *think for themselves*. Students make a significant adjustment in their learning styles, shifting their attitudes along a continuum of learning from **'conserving' attitudes to knowledge** (reinforcing what can be summarised and described as being 'correct') to 'extending' **attitudes to knowledge** (where students themselves begin to pose their own speculative questions and make original contributions). There is also a need to move from 'reproductive' learning (simply repeating what you are told) to 'analytical' learning (being critical of what you are told) and, finally, 'speculative' learning (where students add their own original ideas). The extent to which students can make this transition largely determines how well they perform as a postgraduate. See the diagram on the following page (from Ballard & Clanchy, 1988).

In the 'conserving' and 'reproductive' style of learning, students are concerned with getting the 'right' answer and asking 'what?' questions: e.g. *What is the answer to this problem?* In western countries this kind of learning is common in school-level education and, to a lesser extent, in undergraduate education. There is a need to *memorise* and apply formulas. This is sometimes called **surface learning**.

| Attitudes to knowledge: | Conserving | ←————————————————→ | Extending |

| Learning approaches: | Reproductive ←——— Analytical ———→ Speculative |

Type	*Memorizing*	*Critical thinking*	*Deliberate search for new possibilities and explanations*
Activities	Summarising Describing Identifying and applying	Questioning, judging and recombining ideas and information	Speculating and hypothesising
Characteristic question	What?	Why? How? How valid? How important?	What if …?
Aim	'Correctness'	'Simple' originality, reshaping material into a different pattern	'Creative' originality, totally new approach/new knowledge

At higher levels of education, especially in postgraduate studies, **critical thinking** becomes more important and students are expected to be more **analytical** in their approach. In postgraduate-level education there are often no 'correct' answers, only more or less plausible (believable) theories or views. Instead of being 'correct', students are expected to be able to *argue the case* for a particular position, or – even better – to *add something new* to a discussion on a topic. Moreover, students are expected to *question* information given to them, *assess* its validity and critique the assumptions lying behind the information. This is sometimes called **deep learning**.

At even higher levels of education (i.e. doctoral studies) students are expected to be *more* than merely critical and analytical; they are expected to be *speculative* as well: to come up with their own theories, or developments of a theory, and to ask speculative and *challenging* questions ('What would happen if this was done/if this was changed? Would I get the same result?'). In other words, they are expected to be intellectually **creative** and add to scholarship and knowledge at the highest levels.

Few students have the chance or opportunity to enter the world of speculative and **extending knowledge**. However, all intelligent postgraduate students should be able to perform well in the centre column of the above diagram, and frequently they can do even better than this. In general, the closer that a student *moves toward the right* in the diagram above, the better! At master's degree-level original scholarship and creative knowledge are *not expected* of students. However, they are very welcome and encouraged. Students who demonstrate some degree of creative originality are often approached by academic staff to continue their studies by completing a research degree or even to begin a doctoral degree.

6 Summary

This chapter outlined the main skill areas needed for postgraduates. It does not cover more specific skills for ESL students. Other texts deal specifically with ESL study-skill issues and I recommend that students consult texts such as Lewis and Reinders (2003). Reinders, Moore and Lewis (2008) also provides useful information in relation to improving your language skills and vocabulary.

This chapter has also looked at the key elements of the western education system. In particular, it has discussed the expectations placed on postgraduates. The more quickly students can adjust to these expectations, the better are their chances of success.

7 A Confidence Checklist

Organization

Confidence
Low – High

☐☐☐☐ Determining goals
☐☐☐☐ Managing time
☐☐☐☐ Seeking help
☐☐☐☐ Collecting and organising materials
☐☐☐☐ Identifying and following guidelines and deadlines
☐☐☐☐ Preparing for exams
☐☐☐☐ Performing in exams
☐☐☐☐ Maintaining motivation and managing stress

Teamwork

Confidence
Low – High

☐☐☐☐ Collaborating on team assignments
☐☐☐☐ Determining team roles
☐☐☐☐ Managing different approaches and adapting your own
☐☐☐☐ Assisting others
☐☐☐☐ Maintaining and monitoring progress
☐☐☐☐ Resolving problems and conflict
☐☐☐☐ Reviewing other students' work and providing and receiving feedback

Research and reading

Confidence
Low – High

☐☐☐☐ Finding and retrieving sources

☐☐☐☐ Skimming and scanning texts

☐☐☐☐ Evaluating texts for relevance and reliability

☐☐☐☐ Reading and analysing texts carefully

☐☐☐☐ Going beyond the set readings

☐☐☐☐ Understanding and employing a range of theoretical models,
      methodologies and methods in your research

Critical thinking

Confidence
Low – High

☐☐☐☐ Selecting relevant and reliable texts

☐☐☐☐ Evaluating arguments

☐☐☐☐ Analysing, comparing and synthesising ideas

☐☐☐☐ Applying concepts, theories and models

☐☐☐☐ Predicting outcomes

☐☐☐☐ Developing questions and hypotheses

☐☐☐☐ Developing or selecting approaches to problems

☐☐☐☐ Developing opinions, solutions and recommendations

☐☐☐☐ Being curious, flexible and willing to change positions

Speaking and listening

Confidence
Low – High

☐☐☐☐ Giving oral presentations

☐☐☐☐ Using communication technologies

☐☐☐☐ Participating in seminars

☐☐☐☐ Listening actively and respectfully

☐☐☐☐ Taking notes

☐☐☐☐ Arguing for and against ideas and agreeing and disagreeing

☐☐☐☐ Expressing and supporting positions

☐☐☐☐ Asking and answering questions

Writing

Confidence
Low – High

Writing clearly, accurately and persuasively

Following appropriate text conventions

Referencing appropriately

Paraphrasing, summarising and quoting directly

Referring to other texts critically

Presenting and supporting arguments

Editing and proofreading

Information technology

Confidence
Low – High

Using research databases

Using Endnote

Using Word and Excel

Using a range of communication technologies (PowerPoint, Wikis, email, the Learning Management System of your university.)

Part II

Basic Survival Skills

2 Time Management, Getting Organised

● 1 Introduction

The best way to succeed in higher education is to manage your time effectively and to keep weekly and yearly planners. Very few students do this, however, and as a result they sometimes forget to do important tasks, or waste time doing unnecessary ones.

From personal experience, I am convinced **intelligence** is of less importance than **planning** when it comes to success in postgraduate studies, and also in the world beyond university. Employers look at university grades not so much as evidence of intelligence, but as an indication of diligence and planning and organisational skills.

At postgraduate level, no allowance will be made for lateness – time management is your responsibility. There are many strategies for good time management, some of which are described here. For more detailed discussion of time management issues associated with tertiary study, other dedicated texts are available such as Becker (2003, 2004).

● 2 A weekly planner

Make a personal **weekly timetable** after you complete the following exercise: Look at the extract from a university student's timetable below. What criticisms would you make of it?

Time	Monday	Tuesday	Wednesday	Thursday	Friday	Saturday	Sun
7–8							
8–9	study	study	study		study	study	study
10–11	study	study	study		study	study	church
12–1	study	study	study		study	study	church
1–2	study		study		study		
2–3	study	study	study		study	study	
4–5	study	study	study		study	study	study
6–7	study	study			study	study	study
8–9	study					study	study
10–11	study				study	study	
12–1	study	study	study		study		study
1–2	study	study	study		study	study	study
3–4	study	study	study		study	study	

There are several things wrong with it:

- study periods are far too long. The average concentration span is about 30–40 minutes, which is why lectures are seldom longer than 40–50 minutes, including breaks;
- no lecture or tutorial times are given;
- one day is completely free of commitments, showing that study patterns are not regular;
- it is not clear when the student wakes up, travels to university, does the shopping, and so on.

Now look at this excerpt from a timetable:

Time	Monday	Tuesday	Wednesday	Thursday	Friday	Saturday	Sun
7–7.30	breakfast	breakfast	breakfast	breakfast	breakfast	breakfast	sleep
7.30–8	study	study	study	study	study	study	sleep
8–8.30	travel	travel	travel	travel	travel	study	sleep
8.30–9	study	study	study	study	study		sleep
9–9.30	lecture 1	TLU	lecture 2	library	lecture 3		travel
9.40–10	study	study	study	lab session	study	study	library
10–10.30	tute 1	study	tute 2	lab session	study	study	study
10.30–11	study	study		lab session	study	library	study
11–11.30	study	study				library	study
11.30–12						study	
12–1	LUNCH	LUNCH	LUNCH	LUNCH	LUNCH	LUNCH	LUNCH
1–1.30	study	study					
1.30–2	study	study	study				

It has some improvements. The following things are scheduled:

- there are realistic study periods with breaks in between. You shouldn't study for longer than two hours without a half-hour break in the middle of the hour, plus short 5–10-minute breaks in between each study period);
- times are scheduled for classes, lab. sessions, tutorials and library research time;
- time is allocated for visiting the University Learning Skills Unit or Teaching and Learning Unit (TLU);
- times are scheduled for social events;
- **free periods** are scheduled;
- realistic waking and travel times are given.

It can be surprisingly difficult to design a timetable that you can keep. First you need to work out a few things about yourself.

3 Knowing yourself

A timetable you cannot keep is no use at all. A study timetable has to reflect your personality and habits. Assess your own shortcomings as well as your own strengths. If you work best early in the morning, study then; not late at night when you cannot concentrate. This is very obvious but it is frequently forgotten. Don't be influenced by your friends and their habits. A study timetable is an *individual* matter.

You can learn about yourself by trying different study routines and identifying which ones are the best for you. Assess when you are **most productive**, when you concentrate best, and when you get the best ideas. Use these productive times to do your most important work. Play to your strengths. If you are not good at efficient study during the evening, use this time to do tasks that don't require critical thinking skills, such as editing an assignment or checking references. Use your more efficient study times to do the detailed conceptual work.

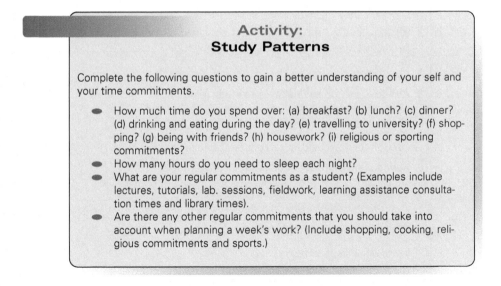

Activity:
Study Patterns

Complete the following questions to gain a better understanding of your self and your time commitments.

- How much time do you spend over: (a) breakfast? (b) lunch? (c) dinner? (d) drinking and eating during the day? (e) travelling to university? (f) shopping? (g) being with friends? (h) housework? (i) religious or sporting commitments?
- How many hours do you need to sleep each night?
- What are your regular commitments as a student? (Examples include lectures, tutorials, lab. sessions, fieldwork, learning assistance consultation times and library times).
- Are there any other regular commitments that you should take into account when planning a week's work? (Include shopping, cooking, religious commitments and sports.)

Now do the following quiz to learn more about your study preferences.

Activity:
Time-management quiz

Answer the questions below honestly. You should be able to answer them without thinking too much!

1. When are you most alert:
   (a) early in the morning?
   (b) in the middle of the day?
   (c) early in the evening?
   (d) late at night?

2. Do you prefer to study:
   (a) by yourself, in complete silence?
   (b) with a group of people who are also studying?
   (c) by yourself, but listening to music?
   (d) with a friend?
   (e) never?

3. Do you study best:
   (a) for long uninterrupted stretches? How long are these?
   (b) in shorter bursts with regular breaks?
   (c) after exercising?
   (d) before exercising?
   (e) horizontally, i.e. in bed?

4. When you study, do you like:
   (a) to drink water, coffee or tea?
   (b) to eat?
   (c) neither?

5. At home, do you have a place to study which is:
   (a) quiet and not in one of the household's busy areas?
   (b) big enough to hold everything you need to study?
   (c) bright and well-lit?
   (d) well-ventilated and at the right temperature?

6. How do you motivate yourself to complete tasks:
   (a) giving yourself rewards for small and/or big achievements?
   (b) giving yourself punishments for 'failures'?
   (c) trick yourself into starting and continuing?

7. How do you organise your work:
   (a) using a long-term plan?
   (b) to meet short-term goals?
   (c) in whatever way things come up?

8. How do you solve any study problems:
   (a) ask your academic adviser?
   (b) speak to your friends?
   (c) do nothing and panic?

(Based on Bartlett, Holzknecht & Cumming Thom, 1999, pp. 117–23)

● 4 Establishing a daily routine

1 Regularity

Efficient study is all about regularity. But, unless you are an exceptionally organised person already, *you need to train yourself to be regular.* You need to train your brain to work at peak performance. This means you need to subject it to a regular rhythm. This is why you need a weekly planner that works for you.

Studying at different times of the day will mean you will be *distracted.* You know you are distracted when you find yourself staring at the same page for 20 minutes when you are reading. This is not efficient study. I often see students doing this convinced that they are studying. They are confusing 'busy' work with 'study'. This can be corrected easily. Make sure your brain is operating at peak capacity when you study by treating study as a regular job. This will allow your brain to get into a **productivity routine**. To teach yourself to be regular *make sure you work at the same times every day*. When you sit down your brain will get the idea that it is **study time**. This will help you overcome the tendency to daydream.

2 Location

You also need to establish a connection between *location* and study. It does not really matter *where* you study. Some people actually study best when there is some noise around them; others prefer quiet. Some people like background music; others don't. Your brain needs to know that *this* location is where you work and think and write assignments. When you sit down at this location your brain goes into 'study mode'. Your brain needs routine in order to work at maximum potential. You need to study in the **same place** as often as possible.

> **So you want to be an expert?**
>
> Most experts become experts through long-term, deliberate and dedicated practice. One study estimates that competence at any skill requires around ten years of practice at four hours per day (Ericsson & Charness, 1994).
>
> Suppose you want to be an excellent tennis player or musician. What would you do? How would you practise to reach your aim? Irregular and occasional practice would not give the desired results. Practising very hard one day and resting the next day would not work either. Taking a few weeks off before 'cramming' prior to an important deadline would be out of the question. Regularity and routine are best: *a little bit each day.* Giving yourself rest periods *in between* practice sessions is critically important too. An expert tennis player or musician would never 'cram' prior to a major tournament or concert. Why should a university study routine be any different?
>
> Good study habits are similar to other kinds of skill. Whenever you think of your study skills remember the expert tennis player or musician and do what they would do.

Ask yourself: which are the places where you work most effectively? What is it about these places that appeals to you?

3 Study periods

Schedule study periods of no more than two hours. Make sure you take a 20-minute break in between. Take a 5–10-minute break within each hour period. Take a short walk to refresh yourself during the breaks. You may find that it is when you are taking a walk, having a bath or riding your bike that your best ideas jump into your mind. Creativity feeds on variety. The brain cannot study efficiently for longer periods without rest. Regular daily sleep patterns are, of course, critical as well. The number of hours of sleep needed by individuals varies, but a *regular* sleep pattern is important. If you need more than 8 hours' sleep make sure you get them regularly.

4 Give yourself a break!

If you have been studying efficiently all week it is reasonable to give yourself a holiday. You should schedule leisure time into your weekly timetable: see a film; visit a friend. Your brain needs relaxation time too, otherwise you cannot perform at peak capacity. It is important to reward yourself. Do this after completing a section of work, finishing an important exam, or after reading a long article.

Activity:
Personalised weekly planner

You should now be ready to make up your personalised weekly planner. You may need to do it several times before you get one that is right for you. The *activity* of designing a personal weekly planner is as important as the plan eventually designed. Make sure you think carefully about your regular commitments and allocate times for all of them. Then *stick to your plan*. If you can't follow it there is something wrong, and you need to rework the plan. See the website for a weekly timetable template.

● 5 Setting goals

Limit your study to things that you can *easily* complete. **Set achievable sub-goals**. This way you will always finish what you set out to do, and you will feel happier with your progress. This provides incentive to keep going.

I often see students who have trouble reading academic articles and writing assignments, because they feel overwhelmed by their tasks. It's no good thinking: 'I have to finish reading this 90-page article today'. Think: 'I have to finish this 10-page section today'. Reward yourself when you finish it. Similarly, it's no good telling yourself that you will 'finish this 8000-word assignment today' when you haven't started it yet. But it is quite reasonable to complete a section of the assignment, e.g. section 2.1. This is certainly achievable. Have a break. Reward yourself by having a rest. Then set another goal.

March	1 Research for marketing essay	2	3	4
5	6	7	8 Start marketing essay	9
10	11	12 Start macro-essay		
	29 Edit macro-essay	30	Marketing essay due	
April	1 Prepare for finance test		3 Plan for presentation	4 Read book chapter for eco tute
5	6	7	8	9
10	11 Finance test	12 Macro essay due	13	

6 Design a yearly planner

In addition to designing a weekly planner you need a **yearly (or semester) planner**. Begin by buying yourself a yearly **wall calendar**. It's a great investment. Record all your assignment deadlines. Then work back about 3 to 4 weeks for each assignment and write: 'Begin Assignment X now', which allows time to do research for each one. Wall planners are better than hand-held diaries as you can *see at a glance* when assignments are due and when you need to start each one. Generally lecturers for different subjects don't talk much to each other about exam deadlines, so often assignments for different subjects are due on the same day. Recording start and submission days helps you juggle multiple commitments. Remember that as a postgraduate you are being assessed on how well you can manage yourself and your study commitments. An excerpt from a yearly planner is given above.

Keep the following in mind:

- Use a **wall planner**, not a pocket planner, so that all deadlines are on a single page and can't be overlooked.
- Put the wall planner where you see it every day, e.g. above your desk. (Consider putting a second one in the toilet!)
- Plot in all assignment deadlines, presentations, and other academic commitments.
- Work back 3 to 4 weeks and write 'Begin assignment 1 NOW'. Do this for **all**

assessed tasks. Enter sub-tasks for each assignment, e.g. 'edit essay for Music'; 'redraft essay for Economics'.

- **Work to the plan**. If you cannot keep to the plan, start another one that does work for you.
- Tick off tasks as you accomplish them.

> **Note:** Computer programs such as Outlook Calendar (for PCs), iGTD and iCAL (for Macintosh) can also be highly useful planning tools. Learning how to use them before your commence your studies is a good idea; however, this can take a lot of time. Having a plan is more important than the technology used to do it.

7 Strategic planning

You need to be *strategic* about your planning. Almost all students wait to receive an essay topic from their lecturers before beginning research. This is bad planning and leads to the following issues:

- problems gaining access to some references in the library;
- trouble accessing student services (e.g. learning assistance or support);
- the need for **'extensions'**;
- the production of substandard work.

You can start research for essays *even before a semester begins.* All it takes is a little planning and resourcefulness. This means you can use mid-semester and pre-semester breaks productively.

Look at the subject handbook or reading pack before lectures start. Summer semester packs and reading packs from the previous year or semester are often available in the **reserve collection** of the library before the new semester's packs are accessible to students. Many of the reading packs have a list of assignment subjects. By reading these in advance, you will be well ahead of the students that start reading only when the semester starts.

Sometimes, the research assignment topics and essay questions are also included in the reading packs. The topics in any year are normally the same or very similar, even though the essay questions vary. Thus you can **start on your preliminary reading and research** before the semester starts. This research can in turn be used to complete the different assignments as soon as they are assigned, your preparatory work being well under way. It also results in you being able to contribute intelligently to class discussions from day one. You are there to study, after all, so why wait until teaching commences? Begin now and learn more – before everyone else starts! (If previous semester's reading packs are not available ask students who have completed the subject before you about the assessment tasks, or ask the Faculty or department for a copy.)

Activity:
Personalised yearly planner

Look at an academic calendar carefully. You will notice that the academic year is quite short, with only about 12 weeks in each semester. Put a line around these months on your yearly planner. This is when you have classes and see lecturers and tutors. In your weekly planner, put a line around the days and hours when you have classes. This is known as **contact time**. In the remaining time there are no classes. This is called **non-contact** time. You will see there are very large periods in the academic week and year when there is no contact time. Your time is 'free' … well … not exactly.

If you are wise, you will use this intervening time very carefully. You should also have leisure time, see friends and carry out **fixed commitments** such as shopping. Make sure that non-contact time is used efficiently. Be prepared. As a postgraduate, success in your studies is in *your* hands.

Another useful strategic tip is to make a time to see the lecturer during the presemester break before classes start. Academics are often busy doing their own research during these times, or they may be away at conferences. Make an appointment time when it is possible. Doing this marks you out as a different student, one who is genuinely interested in learning and willing to take the initiative in regard to your own learning. Here is a suggested strategy to take with lecturers (more advice is given in chapter 17).

- Make an appointment with a lecturer for a subject you plan to study.
- Explain that you intend to study their subject in the following semester.
- Tell them why you are interested in taking the course, then ask them about course content.
- Tell them you are interested in the details of the subject (even if this may not be true!) and that you want to begin your research for assignments before classes start.
- Ask them for a subject outline or, even better, an idea of the topics for the first assignment. Look genuinely interested.

This will make a very good impression on lecturers. They will probably advise you on the general assignment topics they are thinking of setting (they may even be more specific than this), and will remember you as being a keen student. It may also allow you to gain other useful insights about the subject content before the semester starts.

Strategic planning at postgraduate level allows you to use the long period between semesters and prior to the start of the academic year very efficiently. This means that you can begin the semester's work months before lectures start, giving you an 'edge' over other students.

A note on procrastination

Planning problems often arise when writing assignments. Most students experience problems getting words on paper. They put things off until it is too late. This is called **procrastination**. Here are some tips for overcoming it.

- Aim for 200 words of *quality work* per day. That's easy! (This equals 1400 words per week). In two weeks you have enough for a standard-length essay.
- Don't stop writing until you have reached your target. Finish a small section before stopping for a break.
- Write without structure to get ideas down on paper.
- Leave your work for a week then edit it ruthlessly (see chapter 15).
- Form study groups and swap work. This gives you the motivation to write.

In her book *The Postgraduate Research Handbook,* Gina Wisker makes some useful points about strategic planning, including the following.

- See your productivity routines for assignments in terms of a series of stages: (1) planning for action, (2) completing activities, (3) assessing and evaluating the activities and (4) reflecting on, and improving your ideas. This process is repeated again and again beginning with pre-planning.
- Distinguish between long-term and medium-term planning (what needs to be done in the next few weeks or the next few months).
- Draw up a 'critical path analysis'. This is similar to a yearly planner except it is used for larger and longer-term projects (e.g. a research report or dissertation). Each stage in the project (fieldwork, data collection, first draft, second draft, editing, and so on) is listed at various points in your plan and checked off as they are completed. (Wisker, 2008)

Recall the 'inverted triangle' in chapter 1. One of its applications is in planning your time. This chapter has discussed the importance of planning and organisation skills, but the *order* of planning your time was not discussed. How to plan your planning skills is an issue of strategic planning. What should you do first?

Strategic planning

Knowing yourself

– Planning for the year
– Planning for the semester
– Planning for the week
– Planning each day

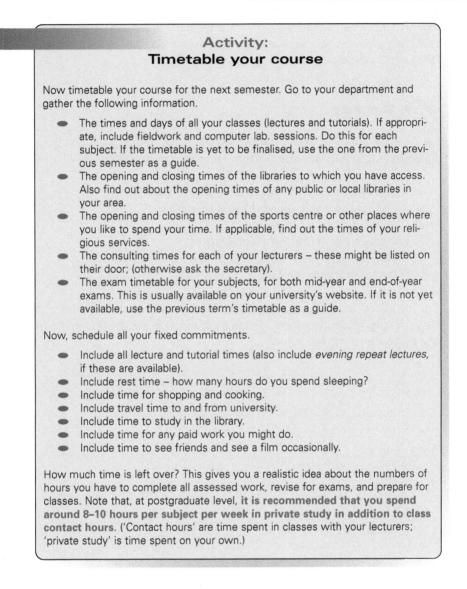

Activity:
Timetable your course

Now timetable your course for the next semester. Go to your department and gather the following information.

- The times and days of all your classes (lectures and tutorials). If appropriate, include fieldwork and computer lab. sessions. Do this for each subject. If the timetable is yet to be finalised, use the one from the previous semester as a guide.
- The opening and closing times of the libraries to which you have access. Also find out about the opening times of any public or local libraries in your area.
- The opening and closing times of the sports centre or other places where you like to spend your time. If applicable, find out the times of your religious services.
- The consulting times for each of your lecturers – these might be listed on their door; (otherwise ask the secretary).
- The exam timetable for your subjects, for both mid-year and end-of-year exams. This is usually available on your university's website. If it is not yet available, use the previous term's timetable as a guide.

Now, schedule all your fixed commitments.

- Include all lecture and tutorial times (also include *evening repeat lectures*, if these are available).
- Include rest time – how many hours do you spend sleeping?
- Include time for shopping and cooking.
- Include travel time to and from university.
- Include time to study in the library.
- Include time for any paid work you might do.
- Include time to see friends and see a film occasionally.

How much time is left over? This gives you a realistic idea about the numbers of hours you have to complete all assessed work, revise for exams, and prepare for classes. Note that, at postgraduate level, **it is recommended that you spend around 8–10 hours per subject per week in private study in addition to class contact hours.** ('Contact hours' are time spent in classes with your lecturers; 'private study' is time spent on your own.)

The inverted triangle method requires moving from the general to the specific or from the macro to micro level. Assess your **personal study habits** first (*when* you study most efficiently, *where* you like to study, etc.), then think logically about your preparations for the academic year. Begin by planning what you will do during the **next semester** on a yearly planner. Note your assignment deadlines, if necessary using the previous semester's workload as a guide. Then think about what you need to do during each week to meet these semester deadlines. Make a weekly planner to suit these aims. Then think about the **daily tasks** you need to do to meet the weekly deadlines: 'Today I need to: (1) photocopy and read an article for Biology; (2) make notes for the essay in marketing; (3) meet my classmates to prepare for our class presentation.' Tick these daily tasks off as you do them.

8 Summary

It is expected that you have acquired self-discipline, self-reliance and good planning skills as an undergraduate. Postgraduate study tests these skills.

- Don't wait for the lecturer to tell you to do something.
- Don't wait for your friends to start something.
- Don't wait to the last minute.
- Find out your assessment requirements.
- Find out what you will/might need to do and start work.
- Design your own schedule.

If you follow these suggestions you will be well planned and organised, and a highly successful postgraduate student. A little bit of planning will make a lot of difference to your postgraduate experience.

3 Managing Information Collected

● 1 Introduction

Over the duration of your postgraduate studies, you will amass hundreds of resources including books, journal articles and articles from websites. It is all too easy for this collection to become out of control very quickly – to the extent it can become almost impossible for you to find what you need.

In order to stay on top of your studies, you will need to develop an effective way to manage information, that is, you will need to develop an effective **file-management** system.

Good file management saves time in the long run. You will often find that the material you use for a particular literature review or research essay will be useful for other assignments later on in your course. The same articles can be used for different subjects in different ways, even in different discipline areas altogether. It is even possible that you will need these texts for work purposes after you graduate.

This chapter outlines some suggestions to help you to quickly devise a workable file-management system.

● 2 Managing information

Most students quickly find themselves unable to manage databases comprising hundreds of personally collected resources. What do you do with all these resources? Keeping them on a 'favourite' list on the computer is one way, but this makes it hard to search for something specific when you need to find it again. One has to trawl through lists of potentially thousands of resources, which is inefficient and takes time.

A simple thing to do is to categorise the resources somehow. But how?

A good postgraduate student will quickly see the need for their own personal cataloguing system. This can be very informal (cards or pieces of paper in a shoebox) or more sophisticated (a filing cabinet of papers with a card catalogue). Sometimes it is very sophisticated (an electronic management system). Whichever way is chosen, a sorting procedure has to exist. Here are some tips for creating one:

- Create a list of subject headings. This list will vary in length and rigidity, depending on the research purpose. How many headings and sub-headings do you need? This will depend on your area of study.

- Avoid having a variety of terms for a single concept, which would make retrieving material later very frustrating. Decide early on what concepts you need. Stick to your list and don't change the terms for the concepts.

- Read each paper or article *as soon as it is collected.* Don't make the mistake of photocopying or downloading articles, printing them, and leaving them on your desk. You will find that you forget what you have printed, and may print it twice! Reading things as you find them ensures that there is a memory trace of the article.

- File the paper away immediately after you have read it. Add the paper to the cataloguing system immediately. Make this a daily routine.

- Enter citations into the file-management system in a conventional referencing style used by your Faculty and university.

- Ensure a minimum of author and subject access are available to you. Title access is also useful. When you are searching for the same resource again (possibly years after you first read it) you need to be able to find it a number of ways, by name, title or subject area.

- Organise your files by authors. Often using the title of papers is preferred over author access; however, in a card file this becomes very clumsy once you have 50 references or more. As a postgraduate, your sources over the course of a two- or three-year degree will vastly exceed 50 references. In contrast, electronic files automatically provide a variety of possible access points.

- Note the author details in your card system or electronic system immediately you obtain a source, e.g.

Davies, Martin

(being sure to record the surname and given name correctly)

Add the citation details. If you are using a card system, this can go on the back of the author card. Then have another card for the citation details under a different category, e.g. title:

Study Skills for International Postgraduates. Basingstoke, Palgrave

(being sure to format the title in the required style)

Record the citation details here as well, or use a coding system to find the citation details on the author card, e.g. AC: 136 (author card number 136).

Create another card for the details under another category, e.g. subject (in this case 'Study Skills'). Make sure that the reference is filed under the correct sub-category of the subject list.

- Documents such as journal reprints and conference papers need to be arranged systematically and linked to the file-management system. It is critical that documents can be located quickly and easily. A filing cabinet is ideal

for this purpose. Avoid merely putting papers on your desk – within a few weeks you will not be able to find anything!
- Documents may be usefully arranged by author, broad subject categories, number, or year. If using broad subject categories, there needs to be further arrangement within each category, such as by author or by numbering each document. Arranging documents by year can be effective where a historical treatment of the literature is required.

Here are some further suggestions for information management:

- Keep track of what you need to read, especially inter-library loans (borrowing from another library). It can take weeks to get a source from a library in-country or overseas. Note when (1) you request the item, (2) when it arrives, (3) when you read it and (4) when you file it away.
- Maintain a diary of what you request, when you request it and from where it is coming, to avoid requesting material twice.
- Ensure you have absolutely correct bibliographic information for everything you read (see chapter 6).
- Begin compiling your assignment bibliography as soon as you start reading. Add everything you read and delete as necessary later.

Volumes and issues

Many international students are not clear on the difference between volumes and issues in journals. Journals publish collected papers or articles in 'issues'. A 'volume' comprises a number of issues bound together. Journals publish articles first in bound issues. When there are a suitable number of issues, they are bound together as volumes. When you look for a certain article in a journal, you not only need the title of the article and the **name** of the journal, but the **volume number** and **issue number** in which the article appears. This is usually expressed as follows: 'title of article', *Journal name,* Volume 2 (5).

The number of volumes and issues varies from journal to journal. For example, some journals have an issue each month; volumes could be published each quarter (some US journals have volumes called: 'Fall', 'Summer', etc.). Alternatively, the issues might be published each quarter, and the volumes are published each half year, and so on. You need to check each journal to be sure.

Different numbering systems are used for volumes and issues. Sometimes issues are identified with an Arabic number (1, 2, 3, etc.) and volumes with a Roman number (I, II, III, IV, etc.). But usually, Arabic numbers are used for both volume and issue number.

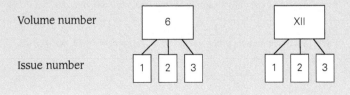

● **3 Computer-based file management**

During the course of a postgraduate degree the volume of information that needs to be managed can be very large. Using bibliographic file-management software, such as EndNote, Procite, Filemaker Pro, Notebook or Reference Manager can simplify this process greatly.

Some universities offer freely available electronic systems under a site license arrangement. Be aware that computer-based systems take time to learn and often it is better spending your time doing other important things. (Learning such systems is best done before you *begin* your studies as part of your strategic planning.)

● **4 Indexes and abstracts**

Journal indexes and abstracts are published at regular intervals, with each issue listing the most recent articles on a particular subject.

Journal **INDEXES** provide the bibliographical details (author, title of article, name of the journal, volume, year of publication and page numbers) for articles. This information allows you to find the journal in the computer catalogue and on the library shelves.

Journal **ABSTRACTS** also give the bibliographical details but also provide a short summary of the article to help you decide if it's relevant.

What follows is an example of an abstract from the database *EconLit*. Study it and think about its format.

TI:	Title **Privatisation** Initial Public Offerings in Malaysia: Initial Premium and Long-Term Performance
AU:	Author Paudyal, K; Saadouni, B; Briston, R J
AF:	Affiliation Glasgow Caledonian U; Centre for International Capital Markets Research, U Hull; Centre for International Capital Markets Research, U Hull
AV:	Availability http://www.elsevier.com/inca/publications/store/5/2/3/6/1/9/index.htt Publisher's URL
SO:	Source Pacific-Basin Finance Journal, vol. 6, no. 5, November 1998, pp. 427–51
IS:	ISSN 0927-538X

AB:	Abstract
	This study addresses four major issues related to **privatisation** initial public offers (PIPOs) and other initial public offers (**IPOs**) in Malaysia. First, an analysis of initial excess returns suggests that, on average, Malaysian **IPOs** are underpriced and PIPOs offer significantly higher initial returns than other **IPOs**. Second, regression based analysis reveals that over-subscription, market volatility, proportion of shares sold, underwriters' reputation, and ex ante risk together explain over three-quarters of the variation in the excess returns offered by Malaysian PIPOs. However, this model can only explain 10% and 36% of other **IPOs** and the whole sample respectively. Third, the analysis of secondary market performance suggests that neither PIPOs nor other **IPOs** significantly outperform/underperform the market over three years. Further analysis reveals that the **IPOs** with higher initial return underperform the market while those with low initial return outperform. Finally, the paper confirms that **IPOs** underwritten by reputed underwriters are significantly better long-term investments as compared to the **IPOs** underwritten by less reputed underwriters.
PY:	Publication Year 1998
PT:	PublicationType Journal Article
DE:	Descriptors
	Asset Pricing (G120); Economic Development: Financial Markets, Saving and Capital Investment (Financial Intermediation) (O160); Boundaries of Public and Private Enterprise, Privatization, Contracting Out (L330); Capital Markets—Empirical Studies, Including Regulation (3132); Capital Markets: Theory, Including Portfolio Selection, and Empirical Studies Illustrating Theory (3131); Business Investment (5220); Economic Development Models and Theories (1120); Public Enterprises (6140); Malaysia; IPO; Privatization
UD:	Update 199903
AN:	Accession Number 0485054

5 Information literacy

Information literacy is the ability to know when information is needed, and the ability to locate, evaluate and use information efficiently. Good students will demonstrate information literacy. There is a bonus chapter on information literacy on the website.

> **Note:** Use the information experts. Ask a librarian! Librarians are paid to help you, so make use of their experience.

Subject librarians
You can meet subject librarians regularly to discuss your research and keep up-to-date with publications in your field.

Information desk librarians
Information desk librarians are available to help you with using electronic databases. Find out who they are, and where and when they are available.

Note: *Never leave the library with your questions unanswered.* Asking for help is a sign of competence!

Search strategy

Don't search for things randomly. Have a search strategy or plan. This is vital to save time and ensure you don't miss vital information. See the website for a bonus chapter on using libraries.

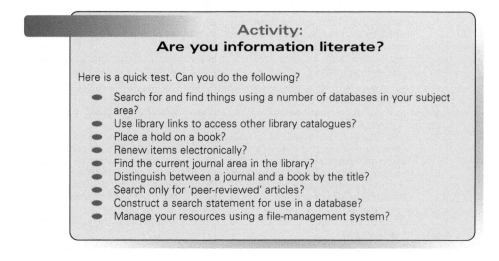

Activity:
Are you information literate?

Here is a quick test. Can you do the following?

- Search for and find things using a number of databases in your subject area?
- Use library links to access other library catalogues?
- Place a hold on a book?
- Renew items electronically?
- Find the current journal area in the library?
- Distinguish between a journal and a book by the title?
- Search only for 'peer-reviewed' articles?
- Construct a search statement for use in a database?
- Manage your resources using a file-management system?

It is difficult to convey detailed information about information literacy in a book such as this. You should consult specialist sources for further information.

6 Summary

This chapter has looked at the issue of file management, which is a critical skill for postgraduate students. Finding information is one thing; being able to keep it organised for later retrieval is another. Good habits and planning are essential.

4 Reading: A Complex Skill

● 1 Introduction

Many new postgraduate students complain about how much reading they have to do. Students often forget that there are *different kinds of reading for different purposes*. They falsely assume that every word is important, leading them to break the flow of their reading to look up a word's meaning in the dictionary. Non-native speakers of English can also get into bad habits by reading words aloud and/or using their finger to trace words as they read. This kind of reading is very slow and inefficient, as your brain operates faster than your mouth. It is unlikely that you will be able to finish your reading or be able to identify the main idea of the text using this kind of reading style, and you are more likely to fall behind.

This chapter outlines the different kinds of reading and gives some tips for reading complex academic articles. In this chapter I have greatly benefited from reading ELBC (Academic Communication Skills) Booklet (1994). Godfrey (2009) is also worth a look.

● 2 General advice about reading

1 Record the publication details
Always note the publication details of any text you use. Record such things as the title, author, date, publisher, place of publication, URL and page numbers.

2 Preview the text before you take notes
Scan, skim and 'surface read' the text first, to identify the important points (see below). Taking notes of everything is slow, boring and ineffective.

3 Maintain a central place for your notes
Some people prefer using a computer to keep their notes, while others use **flashcards**, folders, or exercise books. What is important is that you will be able to find the notes and understand their layout and content a few weeks or months later.

4 Paraphrase and summarise ideas
There will be times you need write things word for word (use quotation marks ['…'] when you do this!) but better understanding will come through putting things in your own words. Not sure how to do this? Say the key points in your own words out loud and

then write them down. Finish by checking that your paraphrase is clear and accurate. (See chapter 5).

5 Note your thoughts
Don't just note what is said in the text. Write down your ideas, points you agree or disagree with, relevant experiences, questions, examples, and relationships with other texts. Those initial thoughts may be of great use later.

6 Be creative
Consider how you should note different *parts* of texts as well as just *what* you should note. The process of thinking about how to note can aid understanding as well as the ability to remember information and reflect. Use spider diagrams, concept maps, titles, columns, dot points, numbers, symbols, colours, pictures or columns to suit the nature of the information.

7 Review your notes
Always look back at your notes and check that they are accurate, readable, contain full reference details, and that you will be able to understand them later.

What **you read at university**
You may be expected to read a wide range of texts, including the course reading pack, lecture slides, books, journal articles, internet articles, practical reports for scientific experiments, newspapers, research reports, literature reviews, case studies and strategic plans.

Why **you read at university**
You may read to prepare for lectures and tutorials, review information addressed in lectures and tutorials, conduct research for assignments, or revise for exams.

What reading *abilities* you need
Beyond being able to simply understand texts, you will need to critique them, evaluate them, compare and contrast them, and apply the information you find useful.

The following advice may seem obvious, but is important.

- Consider where you read. Always read in a well-lit and quiet place that is free of distractions, and don't get into the habit of reading study materials in bed (unless you want to go to sleep).
- Don't vocalise as you read. This will slow you down, it won't help concentration, and it will lead to bad reading approaches (see section 3).
- Read at times when you can concentrate, and maintain concentration by taking regular short breaks, perhaps every 30 or 45 minutes.
- Set yourself reading tasks: 10 pages, 1 chapter, 1 section of a chapter, and so on.

● Remember that reading often takes longer than you expect and you often need to go beyond set texts. Give yourself enough time!

● 3 Different kinds of reading

1 Purposeful reading

If you tend to begin reading like this: '*I need to read chapter 6 – here goes!*', you need to rethink your approach. You need to create a purpose for reading. You can create this purpose if you:

refer to:

● assessment tasks
● lecture slides
● tutorial questions
● textbook questions

create:

● questions based on lectures or tutorials
● questions based on a skim of the text (contents, headings, subheadings, diagrams, introductions, and so on)

consider:

● what you already know
● related knowledge or experience.

Be very clear about what you are looking for. Don't just read aimlessly. Perhaps you will look for answers to questions, a general understanding of a topic or issue, detailed knowledge, a range of perspectives, identification of a writer's position, evaluation of a writer's position, arguments that support your position, arguments that oppose your position, examples, statistics, definitions, explanations or quotes. Try to have the purpose in writing nearby so you maintain focus. Purposeful reading of this nature (sometimes called 'brain-on' reading) can help you read faster and more selectively. It can also help your concentration and your ability to remember.

2 Scanning

Scanning is looking through articles or books very quickly to find a very *specific* item. Examples:

● looking up a word in a dictionary;

- looking up a number in a telephone directory;
- finding a postcode.

When scanning you ignore anything that is not directly relevant to the item you are searching for. You can 'read' up to **1500 words a minute** with this style.

Scanning is used for 'open-book' exams or when you need to find the answer to a specific question. When writing an assignment, quickly scan to find information that you have read before. You are looking for:

- facts;
- dates;
- key points;
- statistics;
- trends.

3 Skimming

Skimming is used when you are not looking for anything specific, but glancing through to get the main idea of the book or article. You are not interested in details, just the gist or main point. To do this, you read in full only selected parts of the material:

- the title;
- the subheadings;
- the opening and closing paragraphs;
- the first line in a paragraph (usually the topic sentence);
- pictures that catch your eye.

The average reader can skim at roughly **1000 words a minute**. You need to be very good at skimming when reading academic articles. You are looking for:

- main arguments;
- key points;
- overall thesis/position of the article or chapter;
- objectives;
- relationships.

To skim:

- first look at the conclusion or concluding section;
- then look at the abstract or summary, followed by the introductory paragraphs;
- read each section heading, then the first sentence in each paragraph;
- look for key phrases such as: 'Firstly ...', 'Secondly ...', etc. These words are clues to the main points;
- finally, look at pictures, graphs or diagrams.

Take notes as you read. If you need to, repeat the process several times, taking more comprehensive notes. Only then do you read the entire article or analytically read sections that are difficult or decipher words that you do not know.

4 Surface reading
Surface reading is fast, but not as fast as skimming. You read everything in full, but you do not stop to think about it. It results in an overall though *superficial* view of the material.

You might read a novel at the airport like this, or a magazine while waiting to see a doctor. You read every word but you often cannot explain what you have read when someone asks you. This is the reading equivalent of sitting in front of the television and not taking everything in.

The average reader surface reads at about **250 words a minute**. With 10 minutes' training a day for one month, you can boost this quite easily to **over 300 words a minute**. Surface reading is useful in academic study to establish whether an article is likely to be useful for your research purposes.

5 Analytical reading
Analytical reading (or study reading) is needed when you want to make sure that you *fully grasp* and appreciate what you are reading. You may have to read statements several times, stop to think about what you are reading and take comprehensive notes. Analytical reading can be very slow, falling well **below 100 words a minute**.

While analytical reading might be needed for *certain passages* in an academic article, it is not normally needed for the *whole* article. (Usually skimming is sufficient.)

6 Deciphering
When you encounter unfamiliar words and phrases you need to slow your reading down. This style is deciphering. For example, your brain and eyes have no problem in making sense of the 36 letters in:

- MelbourneisthecapitalcityofVictoria

but it will take you much longer to establish the pronunciation and meaning of the word:

- Pneumonoultramicroscopicsilicovolcanoconiosis

(a kind of lung disease).

A single unfamiliar word or phrase can sometimes take more than a minute to decipher.

If English is not your first language you will need to decipher some words in academic articles; however, this needs to be done efficiently. One of the best ways is to keep a personal **glossary**. Write down new words and their meanings in your glossary as soon as you discover them. The *act of writing a word down* helps to commit it to memory. Keep the glossary in your pocket and read it regularly, e.g. on the bus or when waiting for someone. Use the glossary to remind yourself of new words and phrases. Avoid the use of highlighter pens.

> ### The use of highlighter pens
>
> Highlighter pens have some uses but they are not a substitute for *writing words down*. Many students routinely highlight words and phrases when they are reading, thinking that this action is helpful. The best way to commit something to memory is to *write it down.* If you are noting an important point, write it down in your own words! This is harder but it requires you to think – this is the best way. Only *key points* or *new words* need to be committed to memory.

7 Phrase reading

When you read, your eyes move along each line of print in a series of jerks. Watch someone else read to see this. The pauses between the jerks are known as *fixations.* Your eyes take in words at each fixation. Good readers have long eye fixations that cover entire phrases. Bad readers have short eye fixations that are limited to one or two words only.

> | Only a | poor reader | reads | this slowly.
> | Their | eyes | fixate | too regularly. |

A good reader, on the other hand, takes in several words in each fixation:

> | A better reader extends | the length of their | eye fixations as much as | possible.

8 Focusing

Try covering a sentence with an opaque ruler, so that only the bottom half of the letters show. Can you read the sentence? Now try covering the same sentence showing only the top half of the letters. Can you read it?

Chances are that you could read the sentence if the *top* half of the letters were shown, but not when the *bottom* half of the letters were shown. This demonstrates that the top half of letters contains more information clues than the bottom half. This shows that when phrase reading you should concentrate your attention at the top of letters.

See the website for exercises in reading phrases.

9 Eliminating backtracking and vocalisation

Backtracking is the practice of going back to passages you have already read. *Vocalisation* is the practice of silently voicing the words as you read. Both are bad habits because they slow down your reading.

To avoid backtracking, cover the article you are reading with an **opaque ruler** or piece of paper and move it down as you read, *forcing yourself* to *always read forwards.* You can return to the start of the article and phrase read it again from start to finish as often as you like.

Your mouth moves much slower than your eyes and brain, which is why vocalisation slows down your reading. To avoid it, focus on the noun phrase you are phrase reading and say: 'duh' – or some other nonsense word – each time you move to a new noun. (You can also *count silently*: 1, 2, 3 ..., etc.) Eventually, when you break the habit of voicing every word in an article, you can drop the voicing altogether and just read the noun.

> **Note:** Some people do learn better by *hearing* texts as opposed to *reading* them. For such students vocalising is helpful to learning. However, it is not helpful for learning to read efficiently.

Activity:
Reading first and last letters

Read the following. What does it tell you about reading?

Aoccdrnig to rscheearch at an Elingsh uinervtisy, it deosn't mttaer in waht oredr the ltteers in a wrod are, the olny iprmoetnt tihng is that the frist and lsat ltteer is at the rghit pclae. The rset can be a total mses and you can sitll raed it wouthit a porbelm. Tihs is bcuseae we do not raed ervey lteter by it slef but the wrod as a wlohe.

It tells us that the spelling of words is not centrally important to visual processing of words. Many of the words do not matter to reading (only nouns and verbs are really important) and the spelling does not really matter either!

10 What to read when reading academic articles

I frequently see international students trying to *read everything* using the *same reading technique.* They usually try to *analytically read* everything, stopping to *decipher* words they don't know.

Before you read complex academic articles you first need to answer the following questions:

- What is your purpose?
- How much time do you have?
- How thorough do you need to be?
- What are you preparing for (essay/tutorial/exam)?
- Does the article/book *need* to be read, or can you find the information in a better article?

If your purpose is *preparing for a tutorial* (or you do not have a lot of time to read) you should **skim read**. If you are *preparing for an exam* you should:

- **scan read** articles for specific facts;
- **scan read** the textbook for things you may have missed just prior to the exam.

A tip for exam reading

It pointless trying to reread entire textbooks shortly prior to exams. This reading becomes aimless, pointless and inefficient, and leads to needless stress and anxiety. It's impossible to read a textbook in a short time period.

It is critical that you read and take notes *regularly* during the semester and *regularly reread* these notes. Skim for main points and scan for details that you need to find.

It is best to take notes on small cards that you can carry with you every day and read when you have a spare moment. Staple the cards together under main topics and sub-topics for easy access. Catalogue the cards alphabetically under subject. Revise your cards on a regular basis throughout the academic year.

If you are *reading for an essay* you should follow these steps:

- If you are not sure if you need to read an article (e.g. if you are finding resources for an essay) you can **surface read**.
- If you find a particular **primary source** that's too difficult, find a **secondary source** to help you understand it. Read the secondary source first (see below).
- Once you have found a suitable article you can **skim read** for the main points or arguments.
- After skimming, use the **phrase-reading** technique described earlier for reading the entire article.
- You should then **analytically read** selected passages and **decipher** when needed.
- As you write the essay, **scan** the article for main points (quotations, etc.) that you recall reading earlier (e.g. quotations, facts).

Primary and secondary sources

Often lecturers give student **primary sources** to read. The reason for this is as follows:

- they are seminal (important) articles, the first time a particular idea has been published;
- they are written by academics who are famous for being influential in the field of study;
- they are professional academic articles, written by experts *for experts.*

Unfortunately, many international students find these articles too hard to read and understand. A good strategy is to use the library to find a **secondary** source that **discusses or summarises the primary article**. Read and understand this before reading the primary source article.

This is not cheating. It is good sense. These articles can be difficult for students to understand, because they are written for academics. Not all ideas will be made explicit, because the intended audience will make connections between the ideas. You should read these important articles, and by starting with a secondary source, you are being strategic in your reading: reading something easier to help you read something that is harder.

Reading is like cooking. You don't need to make the same thing all the time. If you are in a hurry you need to cook something fast! Similarly, use different reading techniques for different purposes.

11 Note-taking and reading
Note-taking is an essential skill that can help you gain deeper understanding and reflection, a better ability to remember and good exam preparation materials for later. When taking notes, keep in mind the following principles discussed in the first section of this chapter:

1 record publication details;
2 preview the text before you take notes;
3 maintain a central place for your notes;
4 paraphrase and summarise ideas;
5 note your own thoughts;
6 be creative;
7 review your notes.

● 4 Reading for research essays

Research essays are probably the most important assessment task in postgraduate education. Here are some practical steps to take in preparing for your essay when reading. This section only deals with reading for the essay, not planning or writing the essay. For these, see chapters 12 and 13.

Reading for an assignment: a plan of action
Reading for an assignment needs to be efficient but it also needs to be strategic. The following plan of action is suggested.

Step 1: Skim and scan for your topic
First decide upon your topic via consultation with your lecturer, extensive literature searching and skimming and scanning for relevant texts. As noted in chapter 2, you can

begin that process long before the due date. A good idea is to start with very general textbooks. Use these to narrow your topic down more precisely. After deciding on a topic, move on to **refereed journal articles**. List what you read under one of the two columns below. You first need to decide if the reading is *directly relevant* to your essay or assignment topic. If it isn't *directly* relevant, discard it.

Useful	Not useful

Step 2: Make a note of the reference details
Note the bibliographic details of every reference and add it to your filing system *immediately*. See chapter 6 for the formatting of references.

Step 3: Keep a filing system and bibliography
Update the **bibliography** file on your computer or your card system *every time* you read a relevant article or book (see chapter 3).

Step 4: Distinguish quotations from your ideas
When taking notes, carefully distinguish quotations and paraphrases taken from the text. Don't confuse these. **Quotations** are *someone else's* words. Paraphrases are someone else's ideas, but *your* words (see chapter 5).

Distinguishing quotations and paraphrases and ideas

A simple way is to put single inverted commas ' ... ' around the quoted passages, followed by a page number. Follow *paraphrases* with a reference and a page number, but don't use inverted commas. (A paraphrase is someone else's idea expressed in your own words.)

You will need to use your own convention to distinguish notes that you personally have added – i.e. your *own* thoughts, not those of the writer. You might just write 'ME', 'My idea', or something similar.

It is important to get these reference details right. You may find that you will reuse the information you have found for your essay for another assignment later on in your course. Using the correct reference details makes it easy to relocate the information in the years – even decades – ahead. It is also important for avoiding plagiarism (see chapter 5).

Step 5: Note the main point and your conclusion about it
When you read, remember that the main idea in each paragraph will be found in the

topic sentence. The rest of the paragraph will be elaboration/examples of that idea (see the section on paragraphing in chapter 9). If you are familiar with the structure of a paragraph, you will see that the main point is usually quite simple though it may be shrouded in complex language.

Try to arrive at a conclusion about the passage with regard to your own research. What do you *think* about the writer's evidence, arguments and assumptions? Put your ideas about these things in your notes. How does this writer's work compare with the work of others? Make the *similarities* and *differences* clear in your notes.

Step 6: Read with a question in mind

You should be reading and taking notes with a **question** in mind. Never read *mindlessly* – be a **'brain-on' reader**. The question might be your own question or based on your reading. Questions might include:

- What is the writer's main point? (This is sometimes called the hypothesis or thesis statement.)
- What is *your* main point in response to reading the writer's work (*your* thesis statement)?
- What is the evidence raised to support the writer's main point?
- Who or what position does the writer *disagree* with and why?
- Who or what position does the writer *agree* with and why?
- What are the problems or inaccuracies with the writer's position?
- Is the evidence accurate?
- Is the argument coherent, logical and valid?

Read each article and see what evidence and arguments each writer raises to support or reject your **hypothesis** or **thesis statement**. Clearly distinguish between direct quotations, your paraphrases or summaries and your own ideas about the article. See the website for an example of how to read and take notes for a research essay.

Step 7: Modify your thesis statement and reread

Once you have read several articles, you may find that you need to modify your hypothesis, research question or thesis statement. If so, you may need to go back and re-read the earlier articles in the light of this modified statement. It is important to do this, because the difference between the original question and the modified one might be very subtle – and a writer might agree or disagree with one and not the other.

Step 8: Make a rough plan or map

When you have notes on a number of articles, you need to collate the findings in your literature review. Start by making a rough plan or **overview of the main points** that you have uncovered in your reading. Add the various views that **support** these points. Put in the **assumptions** that lie behind these supports, and the **evidence** given (see chapter 14).

Step 9: Work out the major and minor points related to the issue
It is important that your research essay is *issue-* or *problem-based.* If an article is fairly uncontroversial, and its claims are clear-cut (from the point of view of your research), your notes on that article should be brief. You should have more notes on controversial articles.

Reference to uncontroversial articles can be *subordinated* to more important articles that express a similar view. You might *mention* such texts, but should devote more time to the articles that agree and disagree with your view. There is no point reading a lot of articles that say the same thing, that say nothing very interesting or nothing very new. For example, if the article by Harry doesn't say much more than the article by Jones, you can write: Jones argues that ... (Jones, 1999, p. 72; see also Harry, 2000, p. 34). Move on to new articles that have a very different point of view.

Step 10: Read a lot but discard what you don't need
It is important to read correctly, but it is equally important to read the right things (see chapter 4 for coverage of peer-reviewed papers).

● 5 Summary

This chapter has covered the variety of reading skills needed to be a successful post-graduate. The main point to remember is that there are different reading skills needed for different reading purposes. To become very good at using these skills in English you must practise the suggested activities on a daily basis. Within two or three weeks of dedicated daily practice you will begin to see the difference in both your reading speed and your comprehension. Within a month your reading speed will have improved significantly.

This chapter also outlined ways to begin reading for an assignment or research essay. Postgraduates need to read widely and use sources that are not provided by lecturers. As much as possible, these sources should be recent and up-to-date. Postgraduates are also expected to be able to synthesise their reading, and to understand the main points clearly and with little or no assistance from academic staff. Postgraduates are expected to manage their own reading, record citation information accurately, and be able to distinguish quotations and paraphrases. They need to be able to summarise the ideas of others and see where trends are in the literature (the areas of agreement and disagreement). Above all else, postgraduates need to be able to *think for themselves* and arrive at their own well-supported views based on the research literature.

Part III

Perils and Pitfalls

5 Plagiarism and Paraphrasing

1 Introduction

This chapter teaches you how to quote and paraphrase correctly as a means to avoid plagiarism. These skills are critical for success in postgraduate education.

Paraphrasing is one of the most important skills one acquires while at university. Subject knowledge is important too, but that changes over time and is easily forgotten. The ability to paraphrase is a transferable skill necessary for all professional occupations. Once acquired it is rarely forgotten. However, it takes a lot of practice to do it well.

> ### Key terms
>
> - A *direct quotation* is putting the exact words of someone else into inverted commas ('...') and providing accurate publication details and page numbers.
> - A *paraphrase* is taking a passage written by another person, completely rewriting it in your own words, and providing accurate publication details and page numbers.
> - Direct quotations must appear in inverted commas ('...'). They end with a 'citation' (reference). No inverted commas are required for a paraphrase as you wrote it yourself, but the citation at the end is still necessary. Citations are discussed in chapter 6.

2 What is plagiarism?

Plagiarism can be defined as *the intentional use of the words or ideas written by someone else without acknowledgement*. Notice that this definition refers to words *and* ideas. Most people know that if you use someone else's words without **acknowledgement** it is plagiarism. But the definition of plagiarism adopted in universities is much stricter than this. If you use someone else's *ideas* (in your own words) without acknowledgement, it is also plagiarism. There are intentional and unintentional forms of plagiarism:

Intentional
- buying essays;
- not showing exactly where information is from;
- quoting without using quotation marks or inverted commas ['...'];

- changing only few words from another source;
- submitting an assignment produced by or with other people and pretending it's all your own work.

Unintentional

- not paraphrasing, summarising or quoting properly;
- not properly showing where the information is from.

Plagiarism is probably the worst academic sin you can commit. When academics plagiarise it is called 'academic misconduct' and there are university policies outlining what happens if it occurs. Repeat instances of plagiarism can result in students failing subjects, being asked to leave the university, and even having their degree revoked. It is *that* serious.

It is also important to consider the consequences on your learning, as ultimately, plagiarism cheats those who do it. Students who plagiarise lose opportunities to gain understanding, skills in research, writing and critical thinking, and valuable feedback. Committing plagiarism fundamentally goes against the spirit of what being at university is all about. In short, if you plagiarise you cheat yourself.

Sometimes it is hard to say exactly what plagiarism is. Consider the following example:

> The two most important legal systems in the Western World today are the English Common Law and the Roman Civil Law. Countries such as Australia and the United States have inherited the Common Law (Brennan and Marantelli, 1980, p. 175).*
>
> ———
>
> * J. J. Brennan and S. E. Marantelli (1980), *Commercial and Legal Studies*. 4th edn. Melbourne: Hargreen, p. 175.

The following text, if written by a student in an assignment, would be a clear example of plagiarism. If it was one of a number of such examples, it would be grounds for failure of the essay:

> The two most important legal systems in the western world today are English Common Law and Roman Civil Law. Countries such as Australia and the United States have inherited Common Law.

However, note that the following is *also* an example of plagiarism:

> The two most important legal systems in the western world today are English Common Law and Roman Civil Law. Countries such as Australia and the United States have inherited Common Law (Brennan & Marantelli, 1980, p. 175).

The student has cited the source of the quotation, and the full reference details (*)

would be found in the reference list at the end of the student's assignment. However, it is still plagiarism because the student has used the exact words without quotation marks: ('...'). To use these words correctly, and to avoid plagiarism, the student would have to write the passage as follows:

> 'The two most important legal systems in the western world today are English Common Law and Roman Civil Law. Countries such as Australia and the United States have inherited Common Law' (Brennan & Marantelli, 1980, p. 175).

What if the student has used just a *part* of the quotation? What if only a small part of the original text has been used without acknowledgement, like this:

> The two most important legal systems in the western world today are English Common Law and Roman Civil Law. The impact of these systems on a number of first-world countries around the world has been considerable. According to Brennan and Marantelli, 'countries such as Australia and the United States have inherited the Common Law' (Brennan & Marantelli, 1980, p. 175).

The student has used the second sentence of the passage as a quotation correctly. However, the first sentence has been used without acknowledgement, along with some of their own words. Is this an example of plagiarism?

On the one hand, Brennan and Marantelli's *exact* words have been used: 'The two most important legal systems in the western world today are English Common Law and Roman Civil Law.' The student has *intentionally* taken these words and has not made it clear where these words come from (the reference appears to be given for the second sentence, not the first sentence). On the other hand, this information about legal systems is true. Everyone who knows a little about the law knows this claim to be true, and – for law students at least – it is also obvious information that does not require justification. Therefore, what can be wrong with just taking the sentence from Brennan and Marantelli and using it?

The appropriate thing to do is *not* to take Brennan and Marantelli's exact words but to put the idea in your own words and provide a citation. This technique is known as *paraphrasing*. For example:

> In the western world today two legal systems predominate. These are known as English Common Law and Roman Civil Law. The impact of these systems on a number of first-world countries around the world has been considerable. According to Brennan and Marantelli, 'Countries such as Australia and the United States have inherited the Common Law' (Brennan & Marantelli, 1980, p. 175).

This would not be plagiarism because: (1) your own words have been used ('In the western world today two legal systems predominate. These are known as English Common Law and Roman Civil Law'). Note that you cannot easily paraphrase proper nouns so 'English Common Law' and 'Roman Civil Law' remain the same; (2) you have quoted the source of the information ('According to Brennan and Marantelli ...'); (3) You have identified where you obtained this information after the quotation (Brennan & Marantelli, 1980, p. 175). The reader can assume that the preceding facts are given by Brennan and Marantelli as well as the material you quoted, and they can consult that book if they want.

A *fully* paraphrased version (with no quotation) might look like this:

> In the western world today two legal systems predominate. These are known as English Common Law and Roman Civil Law. The impact of these systems on a number of first-world countries around the world has been considerable. Developed countries such as the USA and Australia gained the use of Common Law by inheriting it from earlier decisions of courts and similar tribunals (Brennan & Marantelli, 1980, p. 175).

This is better. You are putting all of Brennan and Marantelli's ideas and information into your own words. Note that the citation is still provided – even though no quotation is used – *because the information is from Brennan and Marantelli.*

But I had the same idea!

A natural and understandable reaction from students is that the view of plagiarism described is too strict. Surely, Brennan and Marantelli's information is not rocket science! It is common knowledge and obvious – obvious, that is, to anyone who has studied or knows something about western legal traditions. Western legal systems are known to have descended from these earlier traditions. There is nothing new or original here. Therefore, a student should not have to go to the trouble of citing and paraphrasing passages like this. A student should therefore be able to ignore Brennan and Marantelli completely and not provide a citation.

The fact is that you *have* read this information and it is *not* your information (even if it is may be obvious and you may agree with it). Not citing Brennan and Marantelli is *the intentional stealing* of the information of another scholar. Whether your intention has been to plagiarise, or you have done so 'accidentally', you will be viewed as having stolen the information. Plagiarism is not just the stealing of words, but also *ideas*.

Of course, if you did *not* read Brennan and Marantelli, and you *did* have the same idea, this is not plagiarism!

● 3 How to avoid plagiarism

In my experience, many international students simply don't understand plagiarism. Yet avoiding plagiarism is one of the biggest issues that international students face. The reasons for this are complex. In some countries, plagiarism is not treated very seriously; in some countries it is almost encouraged! This contrasts with western universities, where plagiarism is an extremely serious offence.

There are other reasons why students might plagiarise: a lack of time to write an essay before an assessment deadline (bad planning); belief that their English is not good enough (a wrong attitude); thinking that everyone else is plagiarising (an incorrect and dangerous attitude). They might even be too lazy to paraphrase properly. The important thing is: whatever your motivation, plagiarism is against university rules and you will one day be caught and fail.

> **Note:**
> - The shift in writing style makes plagiarism easy to spot. This is especially true of work by international students for whom English is a second language.
> - Lecturers can identify plagiarised passages easily (even down to the page number!). This is because they know the written material in their academic area very well.
> - If found guilty of repeated instances of plagiarism, students can be required to leave the university. Degrees can be withheld or withdrawn.
>
> Tertiary institutions are making increasing use of **plagiarism-detection tools** such as *Turnitin*. Lecturers often require that electronic copies of papers are submitted to these tools **before** they mark them (see chapter 6). These software tools do not determine whether or not plagiarism has occurred. Rather they scan the student's assignment in relation to a database of previous student papers and the internet and alert the academic if there may be an instance of plagiarism. The lecturer then decides whether or not the student has plagiarised.

In the passage below the italicised section has been plagiarised. The other parts have been written by an international student for whom English is a second language (grammatical mistakes have been underlined). There is an obvious dissonance between the well-written English and the badly written English. A lecturer can tell instantly if an international student has plagiarised by the difference in English competence.

Benchmarking keeps the organisation <u>with functioning well</u> by using an in-depth, ongoing study <u>on</u> the best-performance entity in the market. *The way benchmarking worked in quality improvement is not aiming to achieve the superiority, or the best in the market, but to make necessary improvements for the organisation and sustain the organisation in the competitive environment.* It encourages <u>the entity</u> to identify the customers' changeable needs <u>and meet</u> their satisfaction<u>s</u>, to solve the business problems as quickly as possible, <u>to adapt to the new competition environment in time and to maintain the motivation of the employ-</u>

ees, etc. Through <u>the</u> continuous learning and comparison with the best-in-class performers in the market, the organisation grows gradually and always keeps clear business goals in mind, <u>which keep it has a stable position in the competition.</u>

For further practice in identifying plagiarism, see the activity on the website.

● 4 Summarising and paraphrasing

Summarising and **paraphrasing** are often thought to mean the same thing. This is not correct. The former involves shortening and giving only the main points. The latter may increase the length of the original text and gives all the salient (important) details. Also, summarising involves no *interpretation*, while good paraphrasing often does. By paraphrasing and summarising, you show your lecturers that you understand and can interpret texts for your own research purposes.

Summarising is a useful skill for:

- taking notes from textbooks and articles when reading;
- taking notes from lectures;
- preparing for exams;
- writing a summary for a **critical review**;
- writing an **annotated bibliography** (short summaries of a variety of books or articles);
- adding information from reading and class discussions into reflective journals;
- gathering information to be used when speaking in seminars and tutorials.

When you summarise you present the main ideas of what you read. You don't need to present all the details, only the **main points**.

Paraphrasing is a useful skill for:

- taking notes from reading;
- taking notes from lectures;
- integrating evidence or sources in essays, research reports or other assignments;
- explaining information visually in tables, charts and diagrams;
- developing your own ideas from the ideas of others.

When you paraphrase you show what someone else thinks in order to develop those ideas or in order to agree or disagree with them. It is important to be faithful to the original ideas. Therefore you must include *all relevant details,* not just the main points.

To see the difference between a **summary** and a **paraphrase** let's look at the following example.

> The debate about Whorf's ideas has, until now, been mostly conducted in the context of the psycholinguistic empirical research tradition which grew out of anthropological inquiry into the relationships between language and other aspects of culture in the 1940s and 1950s.*
>
> _____
>
> * Penny Lee, *The Whorf Theory Complex*, Amsterdam: John Benjamins, 1999, p. 27.

This is a paraphrase:

> Our understanding of Whorf's work developed mainly from studies in other areas. Some of these studies were about the connection between language and culture. These studies were done by anthropologists between 1940 and 1960. Whorf's ideas have been looked at in terms of the scientific work done in psycholinguistics since then (Lee, 1999, p. 27).

Nothing has been excluded from the original passage. However, this is a summary:

> Lee (1999, p. 27) claims that Whorf's work derived from research in language and culture in the 1940s and 1950s.

Notice how only the main point is presented and how it is greatly compressed. The citation is still added as the idea is not your own.

1 Paraphrasing techniques

There are a number of techniques to use when writing the same information in your own words. Here are some tips when using the techniques:

- use as many strategies as you can *simultaneously* (one or two of the strategies are insufficient on their own);
- vary the strategies (don't use the same ones all the time);
- practise the techniques often and regularly. It is not easy to paraphrase. The ability to paraphrase well is the mark of a good writer, so you should take it seriously;
- only begin to paraphrase when you have a complete understanding of the source text.

There are five main ways to paraphrase:

1   use synonyms;
2   vary the sentence patterns and use different parts of speech;
3   change or reverse the order of ideas;
4   break long sentences into short sentences or change the sentence type;
5   make abstract ideas concrete (simplify);
6   change from the active voice to passive voice and vice-versa.

1 Use synonyms
- 'big in size' instead of 'very large';
- 'tertiary institutions' instead of 'universities';
- 'professional' instead of 'high-standard';
- 'assignment' instead of 'submitted work';
- 'expect' instead of 'anticipate';
- 'independent' instead of 'self-reliant';
- 'approximately five hundred' instead of 'it is estimated that no fewer than five hundred', and so on.

Use a good thesaurus or dictionary, but pay attention to usage. Not all words that are synonyms are used in practice. For example, the word 'beget' is old-fashioned and no longer used. One student used the word 'proclaim' as a synonym for 'state', but the *use* of these words is very different.

2 Vary the sentence patterns and use different parts of speech
Original:
   Darwin's ideas have had an impact on almost all academic disciplines.
Change to:
   Darwinian ideas have impacted on nearly all academic disciplines.
Better:
   The influence of Darwinian theory has been widespread and significant. Few academic disciplines have been left unaffected.

3 Change or reverse the order of ideas
One of the simplest paraphrasing techniques is to reverse the order of ideas in a sentence. By itself, this is not enough to avoid plagiarism, but in combination with synonyms it is a useful technique.

- The information technology revolution has changed the way we do business.
- The way we do business has been changed by the information technology revolution (*plagiarism – too close to the original*).
- Computers and digital communication have had a dramatic impact on how people do business (*paraphrasing*).

4 Break long sentences into short ones or change the sentence type
Sentences can be viewed as belonging to one of four categories:

1   Simple sentences (one independent clause)
    Product awareness is strong.
2   Compound sentences (more than one independent clause)
    Product awareness is strong, but sales are lower than expected.
3   Complex sentences (a combination of an independent clause and one or more dependent clauses)
    Although product awareness is strong, sales are lower than expected.
4   Combination sentences (a combination of compound and complex sentences)
    While product awareness is strong, sales are lower than expected, and investors are worried.

One helpful strategy is to break long sentences into short ones. By itself, this does not avoid plagiarism; however, it can be a good first step to make paraphrasing easier.

Think about the process as a series of stages. If you also use synonyms as well as shortened sentences you begin to avoid plagiarism (assuming a citation is provided and a reference is given). Add to this reversing the order of the sentences (putting the first sentence at the end and bringing the last sentence to the start), then you *are* avoiding plagiarism. In general, the aim of good paraphrasing is to create a new passage that is *as far away from the original as possible* but which still *means the same thing.* Your job as a graduate student is to show how clever you are in using your own words and phrases to explain other people's ideas but *keeping the meaning the same.*

Take the following example (the noun phrases have been underlined).

Original
This model provides a microeconomic theoretic rationale for why researchers have failed to find consistent evidence of the superiority of one teaching technique over another in the production of learning in economics. (Becker, 1997, p. 9).

Shortened version:
This model provides a microeconomic theoretic rationale. It explains why researchers have failed to find consistent evidence. They have not found the superiority of one teaching technique over another. These techniques have not led to better production of learning in economics (Becker, 1997, p. 9). (*plagiarised*)

Paraphrased version using synonyms:
This framework has a clear basis in microeconomic theory. The explanation accounts for why people working in the area have not proven their initial assumption. Their assumption was that one pedagogical technique has clear advantages over the others. However, the evidence was not conclusive. It did not show that one pedagogical style led to a better understanding of economics (Becker, 1997, p. 9). (*better*)

Paraphrased version using synonyms with order of sentences reversed:
The evidence did not show that one pedagogical style led to a better understanding of economics. The initial assumption was that one pedagogical technique has clear advantages over the others. However, the evidence was not conclusive. People working in the area have not proven their initial assumption. This framework has a clear basis in microeconomic theory (Becker, 1997, p. 9). (*even better*)

Note once again that while the aim of paraphrasing is to make someone else's idea or evidence your own (by rewriting it in your own words), you must always respect the fact that it is someone else's *idea*. You must, therefore, always provide a citation to the original source. Remember, pretending someone else's idea is your own is plagiarism.

5 Make abstract ideas more concrete
The next method of paraphrasing is probably the best method of all. It involves making complex ideas simple or more concrete. To return to the original example:

Original
This <u>model</u> provides a <u>microeconomic theoretic rationale</u> for why <u>researchers</u> have failed to find <u>consistent evidence</u> of the <u>superiority</u> of one <u>teaching technique</u> over another in the <u>production of learning</u> in <u>economics</u> (Becker, 1997, p. 9).

Simplified version:
This accounts for why theorists working in the area found the following: a student that is taught with Method A is no better prepared than if he is taught with Method B. The evidence does not show that either A or B is better in terms of learning outcomes (Becker, 1997, p. 9).

Once again, a citation is given because the *idea* is not your own!

6 Change the active voice to the passive voice or vice versa
In some cases, you may be able to change sentences written in the active voice into those in the passive voice, and vice versa.

- She presented the report. → The report was presented by her.
- McDonald's is implementing a diversification strategy. → A diversification strategy is being implemented by McDonald's.
- An audit needs to be undertaken. → (Someone) needs to undertake an audit.

Accuracy and care
- Check and *double check* the citation source for accuracy.
- Ensure paraphrased information *is true to the original*. You cannot paraphrase the information incorrectly – you must give the meaning the writer intended.

- If **ellipses** (...) are used to shorten source material, ensure that the shortened paraphrase is true to the original and that you have not left out something important or changed the intended meaning.
- Ensure that you *integrate quoted information into your text* by using critical review language (see chapter 10) and a mixture of author-prominent, weak-author, and information-prominent citation methods (see 'Quoting success-fully', below).

Recommended reading

Remember that paraphrasing is a vital skill and success depends on it. Poor paraphrasing at postgraduate level constitutes grounds for failure. Plagiarism is, in serious cases, grounds for dismissal at university. The following resources contain further advice and practice exercises for summarising and paraphrasing, as well as English grammar: Arnaudet and Barrett (1984), Currie and Gray (1987) and McEvedy and Wyatt (1990).

5 Quoting successfully

There will be times when instead of paraphrasing somebody else's words you want to provide a direct quotation. There is nothing wrong with quoting other people's work. Every professor and lecturer does it. However, you must not over-quote, and you must do it correctly. You may quote using three main methods, which help to show variety in your writing:

- author-prominent citation;
- weak-author citation;
- information-prominent citation.

(Adapted from Weissberg & Buker, 1990)

These techniques are used alongside paraphrasing and summarising. They are especially important when quoting to avoid the 'he said, she said' style of quoting, which can sound very dull and boring.

1 Author-prominent citation (direct author)

In author-prominent citation the name of the author appears prominently in your work before the quotation. For example:

- Theorists have held different views on production costs. Jones (1996, p. 7), for example, argues that 'the cost of production is not the same as the cost of ...'.
- More developments in this field are likely in future. According to Smith (2000, p. 83), there has been 'a remarkable increase in the growth of internet technologies ...'.
- Overhead costs are at an all-time low and airline companies are competing

for customers. Jackson (2008, pp. 109–110) argues that 'there has not been a better time to travel overseas'.

Note:
- Quotations should not suddenly appear. They should be integrated into the flow of the general argument. You should always explain the relevance of the quotation for your argument, using *your own words*.
- In author-prominent citations the name of the author sits outside the brackets.
- Quotation marks should be inserted in a way that makes reading both comfortable and natural, unlike the following, which is not elegant at all: Jackson (2008, pp. 109–110) 'There has not been a better time to travel overseas ...'

The following is also wrong because it is not author-prominent and the name is not integrated into the text:

- 'There has not been a better time to travel overseas.' Jackson (2008, pp. 109–110).

In these two examples, there are no connecting phrases to lead the reader into the quotation and to guide the reader from what the writer (you) was arguing to the support you are providing by citing the work of others. You must not simply insert a quotation and expect the reader to make sense of it. Instead, you must ensure it is connected well with your essay, report or assignment.

2 Weak author-prominent citation
Using author-prominent citation all the time will make your essay look a bit like a shopping list: 'Smith says ... Jones argues ... Harrison claims ...', and so on. This can make it boring to read!

Weak author-prominent citation is a variation of the first technique and is used in most disciplines where qualitative research is reported. In this method, the reference appears at the end of the quotation and *the present perfect tense* may be used:

- Theorists have held different views on production costs. For example, *some have claimed* that 'the cost of production is not the same as the cost of ...' (Jones, 1996, p. 7).
- More developments in this field are likely in future. Indeed, writers *have argued* there *has been* 'a remarkable increase in the growth of internet technologies ...' (Smith, 1998, p. 83).
- Overhead costs are at an all-time low and airline companies are competing for customers. Many analysts in the tourism industry *have suggested* that 'there has not been a better time to travel overseas ...' (Jackson, 2006, pp. 109–110).

> **Note:**
> - In weak author-prominent citation the author's name occurs inside the brackets.
> - The quoted material is still part of the flow of the argument of the essay – it does not stand on its own.
> - The references are not presented as facts but as the work or arguments of the writers mentioned.

3 Information-prominent citation

There is a variation to weak author- prominent citation, called information-prominent citation, which is used for reporting facts. It is especially useful in scientific writing. The *present tense* is used for describing facts. For example:

- 'These two aspects of language are captured in the distinction between the propositional and illocutionary (or functional) levels of language' (Nunan, 1989, p. 25).
- 'The facts that control the concentration of aluminium in seawater *are* poorly known' (Jones, 1988, p. 10).

> **Note:** You can use all methods of citation, but the first and second methods are the most common. You should try to mix them and use at least the first two.
>
> You should generally avoid using the information-prominent method when an opinion is provided on an issue. Use it mainly in the case of statements of fact (Weissberg & Buker, 1990).

The differences between these citation methods can be summed up in the following table:

Information-prominent	Information This aspect of the tax		Reference (Larson, 1971)
		system is/was ...	
Author-prominent	Last name of author Larson	Reference (1971) suggests/suggested that ...	Information this aspect of the tax system was ...
Weak author-prominent	Authors	Topic	Reference
	Many researchers have shown that	this aspect of the taxation system is/was ...	(Larson, 1971; Higgins, 1990)

3 How much can I quote?

Many international students over-quote and get bad marks for doing so. How much can a student quote? In short: only as much as is absolutely necessary. For average university essays (i.e. between 2000 and 3000 words) this should usually not be more than three lines of text. Relying on large pieces of what other people say may mark a poor writer and student, so you should paraphrase where possible. There is no restriction for longer documents such as Master's or PhD theses, but it would be unusual to quote more than a paragraph or two.

4 When should I quote?

There are three main reasons for using quotations:
1 when agreeing with someone's ideas;
2 when disagreeing with someone's ideas;
3 when an expression is perfectly suited to your aims and paraphrasing would diminish the value of the ideas being expressed.

1 When agreeing with someone's ideas
Quoting someone's exact words is useful when you need to demonstrate that a writer did, in fact, make a specific claim of some kind. Using a quotation in this way helps to support your own argument. If you can find others that have the same view as yourself, this shows that you are not alone and that your opinion is well-founded. Typically a *paraphrase* of the writer's idea would be sufficient for this purpose. However, sometimes it is important to *prove* that a writer made a specific claim. This is a good reason to quote.

Note: In such cases it is not adequate just to quote someone's words. You must also *explain what the point is* and consider it in the context of your own argument. For example:

Abel claims that 'there is no such thing as the structure of the world' (Abel, 1976, p. 6). However, what evidence does he give for this, and what exactly does he mean? It can be argued that Abel means that ... For example, he shows that ... On the other hand, he might hold the view that ... [here you are explaining the meaning of the quotation given in your own words before going on to agree or disagree with it].

Don't just include the quotation and expect the reader to make the connections! (See the 'Writing for a selfish reader' principle in chapter 9.)

2 When disagreeing with someone's ideas
In this case, you quote someone to prove their exact stated views before you go on to criticise those views. Again, this use is rare and usually a paraphrase would be sufficient. If you need to quote for this purpose, always make the point in your own words in the context of your argument.

3 When an expression is perfectly suited to your aims
Usually, a paraphrase can be made of a writer's views. However, on rare occasions the

exact words used by the writer are so succinctly expressed, use a specific technical terminology or are so well-known and famous that a paraphrase would diminish the use of the writer's ideas.

Example

- Sartre once said that 'Man is a useless passion' (1943, p. 636). By this he meant ...
- Kant claims that 'Intuitions without concepts are blind' (1781/87). Kant's notion of 'Intuition' refers to ...
- Chief Seattle once said that 'Man does not weave the web of life, he is part of it. And what he does to the web he does to himself.'

Note: Single and double quotation marks can both be used for quoting information. American English uses double quotation marks more often than single quotation marks for this purpose. But whether you use single or double quotation marks, use them consistently. Single and double quotation marks can also have a different use: if the single ('...') shows a quotation, the double ("...") shows emphasis on a word. Double quotation marks can also be used for quotations *within* quotations.

Epigraphs are another type of quotation; however, this usage is not common for students. An epigraph is a short, powerful and appropriate passage given at the start of a chapter, section or book to sum up the main point of the text that follows. This draws the attention of the reader and conveys excitement or anticipation of the next passage.

Note: Quotations should be used only when necessary. It is always better to paraphrase. At university, students are assessed on how well they write, not on how much they can quote or copy. It is expected that students will make extensive use of the *ideas* of published work by academics. However, it is expected that students can summarise and paraphrase those views in their own words. Over-quoting is a common reason why students do not do well in assignments.

5 Integrating quotations

Quotations should be integrated into a student's writing and clearly explained. In rare cases when it is necessary to quote a passage of three lines or more, the convention is to *indent* the quoted material separately into the essay, as follows. Consider the following example:

> *Your text Your text.* There is another view regarding the alleged universality of English. According to Bretag, Crossman & Bordia (2007, p. xxii):
>
> > There is no one, 'correct', or universal dialect of English. There is no such thing as a 'native speaker' in the sense of a person being able to claim an inherent hold on the full extent of the language. *However,* in practice, there is the perception that some people speak 'better' English than others.
>
> This view is acknowledged by other theorists such as Paikeday (1985). Many of the *... Your text. Your text. Your text. Your text. Your text. Your text. Your text. Your text. Your text. Your text. Your text. Your text. Your text. Your text. Your text.*

Note:
- the quotation is indented at least 1 cm in from the left margin of the main text;
- inverted commas ('...') are not used for *indented* quotations;
- indented quotations are three lines of text or longer.

The citation can be either placed before the quotation (author-prominent citation; as shown above), or after the quotation (weak-author). For example:

> *Your text Your text.* There is another view regarding the alleged universality of English. According to some academics:
>
> > There is no one, 'correct', or universal dialect of English. There is no such thing as a 'native speaker' in the sense of a person being able to claim and inherent hold on the full extent of the language. *However,* in practice, there is the perception that some people speak 'better' English than others. (Bretag, Crossman & Bordia, 2007, p. xxii)
>
> This view is acknowledged by other theorists such as Paikeday (1985). Many of the *... Your text. Your text. Your text. Your text. Your text. Your text. Your text. Your text. Your text. Your text. Your text. Your text. Your text. Your text.*

In this case, the reference comes after the quotation at the end of the indented passage.

6 Omitting parts of the quotation

Sometimes you will want to quote part of a passage, but not all of it. What do you do?

Ellipses are a series of three dots (...) placed in the middle of a quoted passage to indicate that words have been deliberately omitted. The ellipses tell the reader that information has been excluded.

For example, suppose I only wished to use only *some* of the quotation from the earlier quote by Bretag, Crossman and Bordia. If I omitted the middle part, I would insert ellipses in the following way:

> There is no one, 'correct', or universal dialect of English. ... *However,* in practice, there is the perception that some people speak 'better' English than others (Bretag, Crossman & Bordia, 2007, p. xxii).

Ellipses must be used with great care. It is easy to change the meaning the author intended, and it is essential that you avoid doing this.

For example, in leaving out the middle part of Bretag, Crossman and Bordia as I have done above, the important definition of a 'native speaker' as 'a person being able to claim an inherent hold on the full extent of the language' would not be known to the reader. However, this might be important, as the claim that 'There is no one, 'correct', or universal dialect of English' would be more questionable without the definition.

If you use ellipses carelessly, then a lecturer who knew Bretag, Crossman and Bordia's work might penalise you for being selective in using their remarks. Even worse, ellipses can lead to *misinterpretations* of quotations. Misusing quotations makes for very poor scholarship and is dishonest. When quoting, you are obliged to be true to the original text. You must not change the meaning to suit your own purposes by leaving important information out.

6 Misusing quotations

A well-chosen quotation, used *very* sparingly, is very useful. However, using too much of a good thing is not effective at all. Assignments are set so that a lecturer can see how well *you* can write – not how well you can quote others. Anyone can copy words and put them in inverted commas – that's easy! It is much harder to write someone else's ideas in your own words (paraphrase). A lecturer will fail any assignment mostly comprised of direct quotations with only a small proportion in your own words. It gives the message to the lecturer that you cannot write well yourself. Sometimes this arises from a cultural misunderstanding. Students from many Asian countries are encouraged to copy many words. This shows deference to the author. In western culture it shows an inability to write oneself, and (sometimes) a disregard for the rules associated with academic honesty (i.e. plagiarism). Always paraphrase by preference. Quote when absolutely necessary. As a *very* rough guide, 98 per cent of an assignment should be in your own words. These words may express *ideas* from other writers as long as citations are provided. One three-line quotation for each 3,000-word assignment is acceptable, but seldom more than this.

● 7 Summary

This chapter has outlined plagiarism as a concept and given advice on how to avoid it. To avoid plagiarism you must provide citation of others in your work. Citations are needed to show: (1) where ideas originated; and (2) where the exact words of others are used. Paraphrasing is a critically important skill to avoid plagiarism. It is one of the most important skills one acquires as a postgraduate student. To become good at paraphrasing you need to practise it, preferably on a daily basis.

6 Referencing: The Importance of Acknowledgement

● 1 Introduction

Referencing is a crucial skill for all postgraduate students. The rules of referencing seem complicated at first – a little like the rules of the road when you first learn to drive. Once learnt, the rules of referencing seem intuitive, clear and very natural. This chapter covers the basics; consult a specialist book on referencing, such as Pears and Shields (2010) for more information.

Specifically, referencing:

- helps to avoids accusations of plagiarism, failure in assignments and potential legal action. This is because, by referencing, you are showing readers exactly where you have sourced your information;
- demonstrates that you have read and understood published literature in your area of study (this is important for lecturers when assessing your assignments);
- helps the reader see that the claims being made are well-founded on evidence and based on published literature;
- allows readers to source the material you have used for themselves.

● 2 The different kinds of referencing systems

You should always use the referencing system that your lecturers stipulate. Most Faculties and departments have a **style manual** that includes information and examples of the referencing system you are expected to use. At the very least, there should be a photocopied handout explaining the required referencing conventions. It is important that you become familiar with and consistently apply the referencing system that is used in your subject area.

If no advice is provided you should ask your lecturer directly which style they prefer, and if no style is preferred you should consult one of the better journals in your subject area, e.g. the *Journal of Marketing* (if you are studying Marketing), the *Journal of Information Sciences* (if you are studying IT), the *Journal of Philosophy* (if you are studying Philosophy), etc. Follow the referencing system used there and you cannot go far wrong.

This chapter provides a brief introduction to the different referencing systems so you can understand how they operate. Always defer to your lecturers if there is a discrepancy between the information presented here and that given to you in your course.

The three main referencing systems in common use are **the Harvard system** (and variations on it), **the footnote system** and **the endnote system**. The footnote and endnote systems have only small differences between them.

> Many postgraduate students use a variant of the Harvard system. However, you are still required to *understand* the use of the footnote system because it is used in many books. Likewise, if you are using the footnote system, you should understand how the Harvard system works.

Arts subjects (History, Philosophy, Literature), some Social Science subjects and Law use the **footnote system**. The MLA system (based on Harvard) is also commonly used in Arts at postgraduate level. There are also numeric systems, such as the Chicago (or Turabian) system and the Vancouver system (which is commonly used in Medicine and the physical sciences).

'Hard' science subjects (Physics, Geology, Biology) and some Social Science subjects (Commerce, Management, Economics) use the **Harvard** or **APA system**. The Harvard/APA systems (there are few differences between them) are sometimes jointly known as the 'Author–Date' system, though this is not technically correct.

● 3 What is a reference and why do we use them?

There are two *types* of reference: an **in-text** reference, and a **bibliographic** reference (they are both sometimes called **citations**). **In-text citations**, as the name suggests, can occur *in the text* of an article. They can also occur at the end of an article (as endnotes) or at the bottom of a page (as footnotes). 'In-text' citations are different from **bibliographic citations**, which appear at the end of your assignments in the form of a list. Both are necessary.

1 In-text citations using the Harvard system
An in-text citation in the Harvard system uses minimal detail:

- the author's family name;
- the year of publication;
- sometimes page numbers.

The citation is placed **in the text** of the essay or article. All of the following examples – author-prominent, information-prominent, or weak-author – are acceptable in the Harvard system.

Author-prominent:
According to Paikeday (1985, cited in Willinsky, 1998, p. 194), 'There is no one, "correct", or universal dialect of English. There is no such thing as a "native speaker" in the sense of a person being able to claim an inherent hold on the full extent of the language.'

Information-prominent:
'There is no one, "correct", or universal dialect of English. There is 'no such thing as a "native speaker" in the sense of a person being able to claim an inherent hold on the full extent of the language' (Paikeday, 1985 cited in Willinsky, 1998, p. 194).

Weak-author:
Some claim that there is a 'correct' version of English. However, others argue that 'There is no one, "correct", or universal dialect of English. There is no such thing as a "native speaker" in the sense of a person being able to claim an inherent hold on the full extent of the language' (Paikeday, 1985, cited in Willinsky, 1998, p. 194).

For further information on the difference between author-prominent, information-prominent and weak-author citations refer to the section on quoting in chapter 5.

Locate the three *in-text references* in the following example.

'There is no one, "correct", or universal dialect of English. There is no such thing as a "native speaker" in the sense of a person being able to claim an inherent hold on the full extent of the language' (Paikeday, 1985; cited in Willinsky, 1998, p. 194). 'However, in practice, there is the perception that some people speak "better" English than others' (Bretag, Crossman & Bordia, 2007, p. xxii).

The in-text references are (Paikeday, 1985), (Willinsky, 1998) and (Bretag, Crossman & Bordia, 2007). (Paikeday, 1985) is a so-called **primary source** reference (where the idea was first published) and it was found in the publication by (Willinsky, 1998). This is a **secondary source** reference where Paikeday's idea was cited and used. (Bretag, Crossman & Bordia, 2007) is the source that you are reading in the example which mentions both the primary and secondary source.

Each of the references shows the surname name of the author(s) being referred to and the date of the author's(s') publications: in this case, 1985, 1998 and 2007, respectively.

Locating the date of publication

To locate the date of publication of a **book** you need to look within the first few pages for the left-hand side of the page known as the **imprint page** (note that it will never be titled this in the book itself). You are trying to locate when it was published. **Note:** it does not matter if it has been **reprinted** since its original date of publication. However, if the book was reprinted several times it is important that you write down the date that your edition was published. For example, in the imprint page of the book: *Authoring a PhD: How to Plan, Draft, Write and Finish a Doctoral Thesis or Dissertation,* by Patrick Dunleavy, you can find the following (along with lots of other information):

Information provided on imprint page	Explanation
© Patrick Dunleavy 2003	This is the author's name and notice of copyright
All rights reserved. No reproduction, copy or transmission of this publication may be made without written permission.	These are the copyright terms and conditions
First published 2003 by Palgrave Macmillan	This is when the book was first published and the name of the publisher
Houndmills, Basingstoke, Hampshire RG21 6XS and 175 Fifth Avenue, New York, NY 10010 Companies and representatives throughout the world.	This is the place and address of the publisher in the UK, along with its American representative which also belongs to the same company.

If a book is reprinted, it will read: 'First edition, 2003', 'Second edition, 2005', and so on. If this appears, note the most recent edition, which is the one that you are holding.

Locating the date of publication of a **journal article** is easy. Usually, journal articles print the volume, issue and year on the first page of the article itself. It is also given on the cover or spine of the issue of each journal as well as on the inside cover.

In the earlier examples a page number was not given for (Paikeday, 1985), but a page number was given for (Willinsky, 1998) and (Bretag, Crossman & Bordia, 2007). This raises the question: when do I add page numbers? The purpose of referencing is partly so that your reader can find the work you use – to 'chase up' your facts and evidence. Therefore, if you take a specific idea from a specific page, it is a courtesy to your reader to provide the exact page number(s).

On the other hand, if you take an idea which forms the main point of an entire article or book (i.e. it occurs throughout the article or book and can be found on many pages), then you do not need to provide page numbers. In older books and articles, one often sees the use of the Latin abbreviation *passim* (meaning 'throughout'). This means the idea being cited is not given on a particular page in the original source.

2 Additional rules for in-text citations in the Harvard system

There are a number of additional rules for in-text citations, which are set out in the *Australian Government Publishing Service's Style Manual (AGPS, 2002)*. These are as follows:

Rule 1: Use a comma between the year and page

   e.g. (Cashin, 1999, p. 56)

Rule 2: Use a semi-colon between multiple citations

   e.g. (Cashin, 1999, p. 56; Boex, 2000, p. 212)

> **Note:** Multiple citations are always listed chronologically, from earliest to latest.

Rule 3: When authors' names are incorporated in the text as an author-prominent citation, parentheses (...) are placed around the year.

   e.g. Cashin (1999) suggests that ...

Rule 4: In the case of a work that has more than three authors, *list all authors in the first
citation*, then use only the surname of the first-listed author followed by et al. ('and
others') in subsequent references.

   e.g. Abrami et al. (1980) have found ...

Rule 5: When reference is made to more than one work by the same author, arrange
the works in chronological order from least recent to most recent and separate them
with commas or semi-colons as per rule 2.

   e.g. Cashin (1990, 1990, 1992) was unable to explain ...
   Cashin and Fix were unable to explain ... (Cashin, 1990; Fix, 2000).

Rule 6: Reference to a number of works published by the same author in the same year
should be distinguished by using lower-case letters attached to the date.

   e.g. Feldman (1989a, p. 584; 1989b, p. 644) suggested ...

Rule 7: In the case of two authors with the same surname, use the first given initial to
distinguish them.

   e.g. (A. Smith, 1999)
   (B. Smith, 2001)
   If the first given initial is the same, use the second initial as well.

Rule 8: In general, where no author's name is given, use the name of the organisation
that has produced the work, or failing this, the title of the item to be referenced.

   e.g. UNESCO (2007) in its recent report ... or ... (*Bringing up Parents*, 1993)

Citing unpublished materials

Information resulting from telephone calls, interviews, lectures and correspondence must be cited when used. Follow the rules given above in creating the citation in the text of your paper if that information is publicly available (e.g. as lecture notes, or tape recordings available in the library). Note that the year is still necessary and the precise date of the telephone call, interview, lecture, or correspondence should be included.

If a student cited information from a lecture given by Dr John Smith on 18 July 2009, and this information is available as a recorded lecture for public use, it would appear in the text as:

(Smith, 18/7/2009)

The other details (where the recording is available, the library CALL number of the item) would be in the bibliographic reference (see later in this chapter).

If this information is not publicly available, one needs to use the abbreviation 'pers. comm.' (personal communication) in the citation. You also need to **introduce the person clearly** and add their position or title. However, unless personal communication can be physically located, it is not necessary to add these sources to the bibliographic reference at the end of your assignment. The in-text citation for personal communication would be presented something like this:

> Example
>
> According to Professor A. K. Jones, Head of the Department of Computing, 'there have been exponential advances in software development in the past decade' (Jones, *pers. comm.* 13/7/01).

> **IMPORTANT:** Never overuse personal communication sources. They are not published or publicly available for checking by your reader. For this reason, they are not considered reliable sources (even if they may sometimes be unavoidable). Always use **published sources** in preference.

Citing online resources

The normal Harvard System practice applies for these sources. For example, if the website is clearly identified as being written by Bob Jones, the in-text reference should be:

(Jones, 2004)

If there is no author, then **Rule 8** applies, in that the organisation's name is used, or if this is also not available, then the title of the page is used. Note that the title given is not normally the 'index' or main page of a website. It is usually the *exact site from where the information used came* (which may be several links from the index page). If there is no author you must give the *exact site information* in the title for the in-text reference. For example, if you obtained information from the website of the Department of Management, which is a department of the Faculty of Business and Economics, you identify *the title of the page you are citing*:

> i.e. (Department of Management, 2001) not (Faculty of Business and Economics, 2001)

even though the former is part of the latter. The fact is that your information came from the linked page(s), not the index page. The following diagram makes this clear.

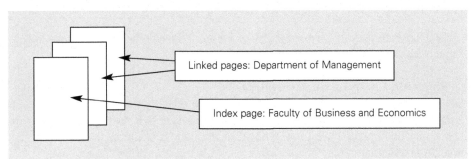

> **Note**: It is a good idea to avoid placing URLs in the text. They clutter and distract from your assignment's ideas and presentation. Only provide the title of the page used and the year of publication. See 'Citing Online Sources' later in this chapter.

3 In-text citations using the footnote system
Two types of footnotes can be used in assignments. The first is the **explanatory footnote**, which used to include additional information or an explanation that is not included in the text itself because it is not directly relevant to the main argument. The **reference footnote** or an in-text citation using the footnote system of referencing is used to:

- acknowledge a direct or indirect quotation;
- provide readers with additional references relating to the particular point;
- validate an argument or point being made using references.

> Reference footnotes must include the following information in the following order:
> - author's initials and surname
> - title of the source (e.g. title of article, title of book)
> - place of publication and publisher
> - year of publication
> - exact page(s) of the source.

Footnotes, whatever their type, are placed at the bottom of the page. More information is provided in the text using the footnote system than in the Harvard system, but none of it is in the text itself (despite this, it is still called an 'in-text' citation). Instead, all the information is given at the 'foot' or bottom of the page. In contrast, the information given using the Harvard system is not very extensive; in fact, you include the *least* amount of information possible.

The small 'superscript' number identifies where to find the reference at the foot of the page. The footnote number is placed at the end of the sentence and outside the full stop. Another significant difference is that the surnames are not given in alphabetical order in the in-text citation footnote and endnote systems. They are given in order of *use*.

The footnote system uses a system of Latin abbreviations to avoid repeating the same references (outlined below).

4 Rules used in the footnote system

Like the Harvard system, however, there are some rules that are worth noting as you attempt to familiarise yourself with the different systems. Note that in the example below you do actually have to look down to the bottom of the page to find the foot-note/in-text citation.

Endnote citations

The rules for endnotes are largely the same as for footnotes, including in the use of Latin abbreviations. One difference is that you should use **consecutive numbers** throughout your document for each section, or (in the case of a book), each chapter. There are no notes at the foot of the page, but rather a list of 'Endnotes' at the end of the chapter or section which can contain abbreviations. In some books this method is preferred. But it has the great disadvantage that a reader has to move back and forward from the body of the text to see references.

Rule 1: Place a superscript number one space at the end of a quotation or sentence and after the full stop

Example:

- Correct referencing ensures that the reader can 'trace the source of your material easily and accurately'. [1]
- Separate the footnotes from the text by placing them at the (foot) bottom of the page. Use a new line for each footnote. [2]

---

1 Footnote goes here. It is usually in smaller print than the main text and single-spaced. Notice also that the super-script number goes outside the punctuation mark. [sample reference only].

Rule 2: Use consecutive numbers on the same page
- Footnotes begin on each page with '1' and follow consecutively, i.e. '2, 3, etc.', throughout the document. [3]

Rule 3: Consecutively number references

- It is preferable to number footnotes consecutively from one page to the next. It is possible, but much less common to start with '1' on each page. The most important thing to remember is that the footnote must appear at the bottom of each page. *Note that we used footnote number 1 on the previous page.* [4]

Rule 4: The first time you mention a reference, you must provide all details

Example:
J. Anderson and M. Poole, *Thesis and Assignment Writing*, Brisbane, Australia: John Wiley, 1994, pp. 101–108.

Rule 5: Shorten subsequent references

- When mentioning previous references, there are two methods of shortening the reference.

(a) Use authors' surnames and page number(s)

- J. Clanchy and B. Ballard, pp. 102–105.

(b) Use Latin abbreviations

- Latin abbreviations are complicated to use. Because of this, they have fallen out of favour in preference to Harvard-style referencing. However, they are still used in some subjects (e.g. Law) and can be found in some older books. There are three abbreviations: *ibid., op. cit.,* and *loc. cit.* (For other common abbreviations used in referencing, see the list of abbreviations on the website.)

---

2 J. Clanchy & B. Ballard, *Essay Writing for Students*, Melbourne, Australia: Longman Cheshire, 1991, p. 122 [sample reference only].

3 J. Anderson & M. Poole, *Thesis and Assignment Writing*, Brisbane, Australia: John Wiley, 1994, pp. 101-108 [sample reference only].

4 When using consecutively numbered footnotes, the numbers are incremented on each page, and start at '1' again in the next chapter. [sample reference only].

- Meaning 'in the same place', *ibid.* is used when you are using the same author and the same page as a previous reference *immediately* above in a reference list. It can also be used when a new reference is from a new page from the same author as immediately given above.
- *Op. cit.*, meaning 'in the work cited', is used when a reference to a different author precedes it earlier in the current list of footnotes (but not immediately above).
- Use *loc cit.* ('in the location cited') to refer to exactly the same page of the previous citation of this author.

Look at the following example of a sample list of footnotes with Latin abbreviations. Explanations to help you are given in square brackets.

1. M. McEvedy & M. Jordan, *Succeeding at University and College,* Melbourne: Thomas Nelson Australia, 1990, p. 27.

2. *ibid.*, p. 90. **[this is the same reference above at a different page]**

3. *ibid.*, p. 7. **[this is the same reference above at a different page]**

4. **Clanchy & Ballard, *Essay Writing for Students,* Melbourne, Australia: Longman Cheshire, 1991, p. 75. [this is a new reference]**

5. J. Anderson & M. Poole, *Thesis and Assignment Writing,* (2nd edn), Brisbane, Australia: John Wiley, 1994, p. 75. **[this is a new reference]**

6. Clanchy & Ballard, *loc. cit.* **[this is the same reference as [4] and exactly the same page]**

7. J. Gibaldi & W. Achtert, *MLA Handbook for Writers of Research Papers* (7th edn), New York: Modern Language Association of America, 2009, p. 75. **[this is a new reference]**

8. Clanchy & Ballard, *op. cit.*, p. 92. **[this is the same reference as [4] and a different page]**

9. Gibaldi & Achtert, *op. cit.*, p. 180. **[this is the same reference as [7] and a different page]**

Note that in footnote in-text citations:

- authors' initials appear *before* the surname in footnotes and dates at the end in the first instance (and not when the references are repeated);
- surnames of authors, and only the surnames, *must* be used with *op. cit.* and *loc. cit.*;
- numbers are used for footnotes or endnotes but they are not used in the bibliography, which is in alphabetical order by surname or title;
- Latin abbreviations such as *ibid., op. cit.* and *loc. cit.* should be italicised (though this may vary in some texts).

Note:
- You cannot 'mix' the referencing systems. You should consistently use one or the other. Of course, you may use explanatory footnotes with the Harvard system of referencing, but you should not use referencing footnotes with any other citation method than the footnote system itself.
- Take care with the style and punctuation used. Using the wrong punctuation will probably cost you marks in an assignment.

4 Bibliographic citations

In-text references alone are not enough. Accurate and complete referencing also requires **bibliographic references** (otherwise known as reference list citations) to give the reader an overview of all of the resources used, with details about those resources. Bibliographic references provide a complete list of references at the end of an article, essay or book.

The footnote and endnote systems still require bibliographic references, despite complete information appearing in the footnotes. Bibliographic references appear in alphabetical order. In the Harvard system, bibliographic citations are the only place where all of the publication information is given. Using the Harvard or note systems without a bibliography is incomplete and therefore wrong.

What information is included in a bibliography? It depends on what items are used. These can be books, printed journal articles, internet sources, conference papers, audio/visual sources, or any number of other things. Most students use books and journal articles, so we will look at these first before briefly considering some other resources.

1 Bibliographical citation for a book
A bibliographic reference for a book, regardless of what system you are using, contains the same details. In the Harvard system these details appear in the following order:

- **the name** of the author (usually only the *initials* of his or her given name/s), in *alphabetical order*, with **surname** first, followed by their given-name initials;
- **the year of publication** (in brackets);
- **the title** (underlined or in *italics*);
- **the editor's name and/or edition number** (when relevant);
- **the place of publication**
- **the publisher** [the place of publication and publisher are sometimes given in reverse order]

For example:
Dunleavy, P. (2003), *Authoring a PhD: How to Plan, Draft, Write and Finish a Doctoral Thesis or Dissertation*, Basingstoke, UK: Palgrave

> **Note:**
> - 'Basingstoke' is the city of publication and 'UK' is the country. Sometimes the city is abbreviated, e.g. 'NY' is 'New York'; also, in the US, the state, e.g. 'NJ' stands for 'New Jersey'. You must identify the city of publication, not the country.
> - Sometimes the name of the publisher is also abbreviated: for example, 'HUP' is 'Harvard University Press', 'OUP' is 'Oxford University Press' and 'MUP' is Melbourne University Press.

> Note: You can't make up your own abbreviations; they must be those given on the **imprint page** (that is, the reverse side of the title page of the book).

Sometimes you may need to refer to a particular **chapter** or section within a book, and not the entire book. In this case, it is acceptable to refer only to a chapter within a book in the reference list. For example:

In this example only a chapter or section was used. The chapter was written by Peter Slezak; it is called 'Cognitive Science', and it appears in a book edited by Graham Oppy and Nick Trakakis, called *A Companion to Philosophy in Australia and New Zealand*. The book was published in 2010. It was published in the city of Clayton, in the country of Australia by Monash University Publishing.

Slezak, P., (2010). 'Cognitive Science'. In Oppy, G. and Trakakis, N. (eds), *A Companion to Philosophy in Australia and New Zealand* (pp. 117–120), Clayton, Australia: Monash University Publishing.

An **editor** is someone who compiles a book from a number of sources. The editor might write a preface or introduction, and make small changes to other authors' contributions, but most of the book is written by other people. An editor is identified by means of (ed.) or (eds.): e.g. Oppy, G. and Trakakis, N., (eds.) (Note that 'ed.' is singular)

A **monograph** is a specialised book on a narrow topic area. This is different from a textbook, which is written for students. A monograph is sometimes used generally to mean 'book'. Sometimes it is used to mean a more technical type of book that occurs as part of a series of similar books on highly specialised technical topics.

In the APA system (a different, but similar in-text citation style from the Harvard system) the order in which the information is presented differs: the place of publication comes before the publisher. The remaining order follows the Harvard system.

In the footnote and endnote systems, the order of the publisher and place of publishing are the same as in the Harvard system, but the date is placed at the very end of the citation.

Punctuation of citations differs between referencing systems. Even tutors and lecturers are sometimes inconsistent in what they believe the punctuation conventions to be. For this reason, it is probably wise at the start of your course to ask the person correcting your work to check a draft of your bibliography before you submit the final draft. Also check the referencing system as it is used in a professional journal in your subject area.

A comparison of punctuation used in the Harvard and APA systems is available on the website.

2 Biographical citation for a journal article

A bibliographic reference for a printed journal article contains the following details, which must be placed in this order in all author–date style referencing systems:

- **name of the author** in alphabetical order with the surname first, followed by the given-name initials;
- **date of publication** (in parentheses);
- **title of the journal article** (in *single* inverted commas);
- **journal name** (underlined or in *italics*);
- **journal volume number**;
- **journal issue number (if applicable)**;
- **inclusive page numbers** (i.e. the page numbers from the start to the finish of the article, not the pages you have referred to in your essay – these are provided in the in-text citation).

Here is an example:

McClure, J. W. (2005), 'Preparing a laboratory-based thesis: Chinese international research students' experiences of supervision', *Teaching in Higher Education,* Vol. 10(1): pp. 3–16.

In this case the article is published in the **first issue of the tenth volume** of the journal titled *Teaching in Higher Education* (see chapter 3 for the difference between 'volumes' and 'issues').

Note:
- The title of the journal name is given in *italics*.
- The first letter of each word of the title of the journal is in upper-case (i.e. capital) letters.
- The volume and issue numbers are often written differently depending on different journal conventions. For example, the above citation could also be written X (1). Some American journals use seasons (Fall, Winter, Summer, Spring) instead of volume numbers (see chapter 3).
- Depending on the referencing system used, volume numbers can be sometimes given in parentheses, e.g. (7), and sometimes followed by an issue number written like this: No. 2. A journal might publish six issues in one volume. If the issue you were citing was Issue 6 of Volume 6, the reference could appear as Vol. 6, No. 6, or Vol. VI (or even (6), No. 6). All these forms are acceptable, but ensure you are consistent in how these are shown in the bibliography.
- Inclusive numbers are given to show the starting page and the ending page of the article ('pp.' is the plural abbreviation for 'pages').

3 Additional rules governing entries in the bibliography (the Harvard system)

The reference list or bibliography is also subject to some other rules in the Harvard System.

Rule 1: Arrange entries in alphabetical order by the surname of the first author, alphabetise letter by letter, and alphabetise the prefixes, i.e. M. comes before Mc, and Mac comes before Mc

> 'Anderson' is before 'Antigone' in an alphabetical list (both begin 'An' but 't' is after 'd', etc).

> **Note:**
> Abrami, P. C., d'Appollonia, S. & Rosenfield, S.
>
> comes before:
>
> Abrami, P. C., Dickens, W. J., Leventhal, L. & Perry, R. P.
>
> This is because 'd'A' is alphabetically prior to 'Di'.

Rule 2: Single-author entries precede multiple-author entries that begin with the same surname

> Kaufman, J. R. 1978, ...
> Kaufman, J.R. & Wong, D.F. 1978, ...

Rule 3: References with the same authors in the same order are arranged by year of publication, the earliest first

> Kaufman, J.R. & Jones, K. 1977, ...
> Kaufman, J.R. & Jones, K. 1980, ...

Rule 4: Several works by different authors with the same family name are arranged alphabetically by first initial

> Eliot, A.L., 1983, ...
> Eliot, G.E., 1980, ...

Rule 5: Specify which edition the book is, if it is a multiple-edition book

> Yura, H. & Walsh, M. B. (1983), *The Nursing Process, Assessing, Planning, Implementing, Evaluation* (4th edn), Norwalk, CT: Appleton-Century-Crofts.

Note: In a bibliography, you format the reference using a 'hanging indentation', which means the second and subsequent lines of the reference are indented about 1 cm in from the first line. The reason for this is to show the alphabetical order clearly. It is important you do this as it looks more professional.

Bibliographic online citations using the Harvard system

There is no standard means of showing the reference details for online sources in the bibliography. The rules are ambiguous and often not followed precisely.

As a general rule, you identify these bibliographic references by surname of author (if available) as usual. If there is no author mentioned, the following conventions apply:

- name of article/page (this is the page you are citing from, not necessarily the 'index' or main page)
- year in round brackets (parentheses) (...)
- *name of journal/main website page* (in italics)
- URL: http://etc. – in round brackets (...)
- the date the site was created, e.g. 14/5/2001

PLUS:

- when the page was accessed: **the date you used the page** (i.e. when you downloaded it) in square brackets [...].

The date on which you access the page is usually different from the date when the page was last updated, and it is therefore important for accuracy to give both dates, given that pages are continually updated, e.g.

'The Department of Management' (2001) *Faculty of Business and Economics* (URL: http:// etc. ...) 14/3/01 [Accessed: 30/4/01].

Note: URL stands for Uniform Resource Locator, which identifies the source of the material. This begins with a code for the type of access involved ('http://', 'ftp://', 'gopher://', etc). To cite the document that I referred to for my information about online citations, it would be:

Quinion, M., (1999) *Citing Online Sources* (URL: http://www.worldwidewords.org/articles/citation.htm) [Accessed: 10/3/2011].

Make sure you break the lines in a sensible place, and never introduce hyphens.
(Quinion, 1998)

Personal communication

As noted earlier, personal communication may include letters, memos, telephone conversations, interviews, and other forms of communication that are unpublished and generally not retrievable (you cannot find them again). These references are cited in the body of the essay and should appear in the bibliography as well, if they can be found

> **For example:**
> *In-text:* According to J.O. Reiss, Lecturer in Accounting, 'There has never been a better time to study accounting' (Reiss, *pers. comm.,* April 28, 2003).
>
> This would appear in the bibliography as:
>
> Reiss, J. O. (2003), *Subject Handbook for Lectures in Accounting,* University of Western Australia, 28/4/2003.

(i.e. if they are publicly available). If they **cannot** be found, they should not be listed in the bibliography but they **must** appear in the in-text citation.

Material used by lecturers is often accessed from subject texts or weekly specified reading. These should be referenced in preference to the lecture notes.

Other resources

There are times when you will use resources other than books, journals and online texts. These sometimes have no author, e.g. newspaper articles, or in the case of films, they have a writer, producer and director. How to reference them can be problematic. The general rule is that if there is no author, then you identify it according to its title. Such a citation should also be included alphabetically in the list of references under the **first letter of the title**. (If a title begins with an article 'The' or 'A' it is customary to ignore this and alphabetise from the first letter of the second word.)

> **For example:**
> Brandis, G. (1987), 'The Liberals: Just who is forgetting whom?', *Weekend Australian,* 24–25 Jan., p. 19.
>
> 'Killing bin Laden won't end the terror' (2001), *The Age,* 19/10/01, p. 26.
>
> Legge, K. (1987), 'Labor to cost the 'Keating Factor', *Times on Sunday,* 1 Feb, p. 2. *Financial Review* (1987) 23 Jan, editorial.

If you are unaware of the author, ask yourself: 'Should I really use the reference? Is the source sufficiently reliable?' This is particularly important when you encounter internet articles with no clear author. Be discriminating in your use of references. There are many poor-quality sources available.

When you come across a resource that you do not know how to reference, look at how it was referenced in the library catalogue. If it was referenced using a different referencing system, change the order accordingly. Also, do not be afraid to ask your tutor or a librarian. Everybody had to learn to reference at some point and there are not many people who would know how to reference every type of resource in the library without consulting a written guide or online website. There are literally hundreds of useful online guides to referencing, including at your own university.

5 Final tips

Make sure that when you are learning referencing you are *consistent* in punctuation and formatting style. Take particular care with the brackets, italics, commas, semicolons, full stops and hanging indentations. Formatting and punctuation can be simplified by using a specific computer program designed for the purpose, such as EndNote (see www.endnote.com) or RefWorks (see http://www.refworks.com). Your university may have a site licence for these or similar software. If you don't have the time or inclination to learn how to use EndNote or similar programs you need to take considerable care with the formatting and presentation order of references.

6 Summary

This chapter has covered the basic skills of referencing. It has outlined different citation methods, including the Harvard and footnote/endnote systems. Correct referencing might seem complicated and frustrating; however, it is critical, and separates serious academic students from weak students. Referencing systems are the 'road rules' of being an academic. You can lose marks needlessly on assignments due to poor referencing, so you must master these skills to succeed at higher education.

Part IV

Standing on the Shoulders of Others: Doing Research

7 The Research Process

● **1 Introduction**

This chapter will provide a very brief introduction to research methods. More detailed information is provided elsewhere, including in this study skills series (see Grix, 2010). If your postgraduate course includes a research component, then you will normally also study a research methodology unit as part of your course. If this is not the case, make sure that you borrow or buy a book about research before you begin. The information in this chapter is adapted mainly from Grix (2010), Sekaran (1992) and Yin (1994). There are many excellent books on research available and you should consider reading them before beginning your postgraduate course of study.

Research can be understood in different ways in different disciplines, and it is important to understand what is expected of you by the university before you start. This chapter only outlines the 'empirical' method of research, which is very common, to give you an overview of some of the common concepts associated with research in a university.

● **2 What is research?**

Research is defined by Nunan (1992, p. 232) as 'a systematic process of inquiry consisting of three elements or components: (1) a question, problem or hypothesis, (2) data, and (3) analysis and interpretation of data'.

Research follows a series of steps, and is normally initiated by a desire to test out a theory, resolve or come to a better understanding about an issue, or answer a question. To do this, you must collect information related to the theory, issue or question. This is not as easy as it sounds. If a question is too broad then it may not be possible to compile the necessary information to answer it. Likewise if a problem is too complex, you may be able to compile information, but be incapable of assessing its impact on the problem in relationship to the other factors. How you go about collecting your data also depends on what you are studying. Collecting data when researching the impact of alcohol on driving ability, for example, is going to be different to researching the impact of a government's tax incentives for women choosing to have a third child. The first study could be carried out over a short period of time with a random group of people in a controlled environment, using a driving simulator. The second study would probably involve data being collected via statistics, interviews or questionnaires.

For this reason, research often is divided into types. It is important to be aware of these types, but also to understand that research varies enormously and may not neatly conform to the descriptions given below. The following outline is intended to give a very general introduction to two major kinds of research.

1 Quantitative and qualitative research

Quantitative research and **qualitative research** are often referred to in research books. Generally, quantitative research is associated with scientific research and the concept that facts and truths can objectively be discovered via research. Qualitative research, on the other hand, is generally associated with the social sciences. These areas often reject the idea of an objective observer examining a fixed reality. This can then result in a researcher engaging in subjective data-collection methods, such as interviews. These types of research can be expressed schematically as follows.

Quantitative (deductive/linear)
Quantitative research typically follows a linear path: one starts with a testable hypothesis, collects data, analyses the data and then accepts or rejects the hypothesis.

Hypothesis → Data collection → Analysis of results → Accept/reject hypothesis (theory)

(e.g. The more the interest rates rise, the greater the impact on household spending)
(Hurworth, 2003)

Qualitative (spiral/inductive)
In the case of **qualitative research**, the researcher starts with a tentative idea or question, e.g. 'What is it like working for a major software company in the current economic climate?' One then observes and asks questions, and analyses what one has found. This guides more specific questioning. Further investigation reveals themes and patterns in the research, which leads the research to appropriate theoretical study. Finally, one ends with tentative conclusions based on the theoretical insight that one has acquired during the research.

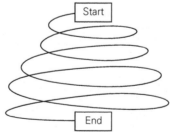

(Hurworth, 2003)

In general, *quantitative* research *starts* with a theoretical statement or position (the hypothesis) and tests this for accuracy. This is, therefore, **deductive** research (moving *from* theory to results). In *qualitative* research, one starts with observation and ends with a theoretical position or stance. This is, therefore, **inductive** research (moving *to* theory from speculations).

Of course, these research methods are not exclusive. Qualitative research may end in a hypothesis that can be quantitatively tested later. Quantitative research may involve qualitative research elements. You might like to think of research as a *continuum*, with quantitative and qualitative at either end, and most research falling somewhere in between.

Be aware of this as you look at the differences between these kinds of research methods summarised in the following table:

	Quantitative	Qualitative
Purpose	To determine cause and effect relationships.	To describe ongoing processes/phenomena in the real world.
Hypotheses	These are stated before the study and tested during the study.	These are usually developed and refined during the investigation. Questions raised determine where the study goes.
Theories	These deductively determine the study.	These are developed at the end of the study by inductive reasoning.
Variables	These are controlled and manipulated to shed light on the hypothesis.	No explicit variables. The focus of qualitative research is to study naturally occurring phenomena to discover important variables.
Data collection	It is important that data are collected objectively.	Data can involve subjectivity (e.g. interaction with participants and the aim is to build rapport (i.e. through interaction with participants).
Design of study	This is stated at the outset and does not change.	This can change as the study develops. The design is flexible.
Presentation of Data	This is usually numerical (e.g. statistical).	This is usually done in the form of analysis using language (narrative form) or pictorally (e.g. through the use of video, photographs, drawings, etc.).
Validity and reliability	This is ensured by means of statistical tests.	This is ensured by means of triangulated (multiple sources) of data/evidence.
Data samples	These are carefully chosen to represent larger populations.	Individual cases are studied to shed light on other groups/cases.
Threats to validity	Avoided by means of statistical methods.	Avoided by means of logical analysis to rule out alterative explanations.
Subject of analysis	Simplified and reduced as much as possible.	Studied as a whole, as phenomena occur within reality as a complex system.
Conclusions	These are stated with statistical measures of confidence (e.g. alpha levels).	These are suggestive and always tentative and subsequent studies can cast doubt on them.

(Source: Clarke, 2003)

2 When is qualitative research needed?

The role of quantitative research is generally well known, but it may be useful to outline when qualitative research is needed. Qualitative research is more appropriate in the following situations:

- when the research is looking at an area that is not well studied or understood;
- when a subject needs to be studied in a great deal of depth;
- when a holistic perspective is needed;
- when attitudes or behaviours of people need to be studied;
- when measurement techniques like questionnaires are not considered suitable;
- when you are more interested in the process of something (how it works), not the product (the outcome);
- when you want to put 'content' on statistical results to make the results meaningful;
- when observation of people is considered to be important.

(Adapted from Hurworth, 2003)

Case study method (discussed later in this chapter) uses elements of both qualitative and quantitative research methods.

● 3 Research questions

Research, regardless of its type, is always carried out with a research question, problem or hypothesis in mind. In chapter 4 we discussed reading with a question or statement in mind. It is also important to be sure that the concepts within the question – sometimes referred to as 'constructs' – can be researched successfully. It's not much good having a construct that is so vague or imprecise that it cannot be researched.

1 What is a construct?

A *construct* is a concept used in research. For example, 'job satisfaction' or 'customer satisfaction' are constructs, as is 'short-term pressure on interest rates'. You must be clear how the constructs in your proposed study can be objectively tested, i.e. made **operational**. You need to ask yourself questions such as these:

- How do I decide what 'job satisfaction' means?
- How can 'job satisfaction' be measured?
- What counts as an example of 'job satisfaction'?

Similarly, constructs like: 'intelligence', 'company performance' and 'interest' need to be made operational before you can commence your research project.

2 What is a hypothesis?

A **hypothesis** is a statement that relates two or more **constructs**. For example: *The greater the stress experienced in the job, the lower the job satisfaction of employees.* Here you need a clear operational definition of the constructs 'stress' and 'job satisfaction'. Clearly, the terms you use in questions and problems also need to be defined, or *operationalised,* before you can research them. The hypothesis, associated with quantitative research, is **tested** by the research that you propose to do. In research you *define* or **operationalise** constructs and you *test* hypotheses.

4 Data collection

How you go about collecting your data will depend on your question, hypothesis or problem. You may choose to use a questionnaire, to do interviews, observe interactions, collect statistics or collect a series of written texts or drawings, or to do something completely different. Whichever method you choose, it should possess **validity** and **reliability**.

1 Validity

Validity refers to the 'extent to which the design of the study, the instrument used to collect the data (e.g. questionnaire) and the results investigate the research questions they were intended to investigate' (Clarke, 2003). It also looks at whether the results can be applied *beyond* the thing or people being researched to other contexts. In other words, validity is a measure of whether what you are testing is what you *say* you are testing (as opposed to something else); it is also a measure of whether your results can be **generalised** to other similar situations.

2 Reliability

Reliability refers to 'the extent to which an investigation produces consistent results' (Clarke, 2003). This means that somebody else could look at your research and reach similar conclusions or could *repeat* your research and get results that were similar. This goes further than just data collection, also referring to the *interpretation* and *analysis* of data.

5 The hallmarks of scientific research

The following 'hallmarks of scientific research' are appropriate to research in all scientific and social science disciplines, though they are generally more appropriate for quantitative research. Read them and then consider your own proposed postgraduate research project(s).

1 Purposiveness

The research must have an *aim;* i.e. it should be problem-based, unified and directed, not pointless and random.

A testable hypothesis is normally needed in scientific writing to consolidate the **purpose** of the study. This also 'narrows down' the project or topic to a manageable size. (This 'narrowing' is also essential in order to complete the project in a limited time.)

> **Example:**
> Consider the following topics:
>
> (a) The environment and the US economy.
> (b) The problem of pollution in the environment and its impact on the US economy.
> (c) The problem of ocean spills and their economic impact on the US economy.
> (d) The problem of oil spills and their economic impact on the US economy.
> (e) The 1989 Alaskan Oil Spill and its impact on the US economy.
> (f) The consequences of the 1989 Alaskan Oil Spill on the Alaskan economy from 1989 to 2002.
>
> (f) is more narrow and has a much clearer purpose than (a)–(d).
>
> For examples of clear business research topics, see Sekaran (1992, pp. 43–44).

2 Rigour

The project should have sound methodological design. It should be 'scientific' and 'logical': conclusions must follow from accepted premises defended and tested in the course of the research. You can't, for example, base conclusions on just a few interviews with company employees in the lunch room. You need a good sample size of a range of employees. They need to be male and female, young and old, full-time and part-time, long-term and short-term employees, and so on.

In the above example, (f) lends to a **rigorous** approach *only if* a number of features of the Alaskan economy are considered and tested under a range of different conditions and if 'consequences' are measured using a number of independent economic models.

> **Consider:**
> - the phrasing of research questions;
> - the phrasing of survey questions;
> - the sample size (how many are needed?);
> - the cause and effect (which is which?);
> - the choice of relevant variables.

Rigour is also ensured by an appropriately wide search and **discussion of the literature** in the area. This not only helps in making the study rigorous by avoiding problems in these areas that others might have made, but it ensures that the study is unique (see chapter 14).

3 Isolating variables

Getting clear about your variables is critical: you must distinguish your **dependent** variable(s) (DV) (the things you are looking at) from the **independent** variable(s) (IV) (things that influence the dependent variable) and the **moderating** variable(s) (MV) (things that modify the relationship between the DV and the IV) and the **intervening** variable(s) (InV) (things that may turn up after the moderating variable(s) have had their effect(s), but do not change that relationship).

> For example, in the previous case:
>
> - the Alaskan economy is the *dependent* variable;
> - the 1989 Alaskan oil spill is the *independent* variable;
> - the general influences on the Alaskan economy are *moderating* variables (e.g. the state of the world economy, trade with other countries, etc.);
> - other factors which may normally have an impact on an economy (consumer sentiment, terrorism, etc.) but need not change the relationship between the DV and the IV might be *intervening* variables (InV).

4 The hypothesis

A clear **hypothesis** (*even if not explicitly stated in the research project*) will ensure that your research has a focus, purpose and direction. It also ensures that you answer a research question of some kind, rather than ramble from one topic to another. The hypothesis is the *connecting membrane* that holds the research together. If any of the data conflicts with the hypothesis, the hypothesis is said to be *falsified*. This is called the **negative case-analysis method**. A single falsification of the hypothesis requires that it be revised.

5 Testability

Quantitative research at least must be testable. It is no good having a clear research purpose if the project aim isn't testable.

For example, the hypothesis *that oil spills have an impact on where consumers go shopping* is not testable (even though it may be true). How would one test this claim? How would one *know* that the independent variable was the *only* factor influencing shoppers' choices?

6 Replicability

Your research must, *in principle,* be able to be repeated by others. This requires:

(a)   that the experimental/case aims and procedures are sound;
(b)   that the report is written in a clear and comprehensible manner, so others can follow it (to this end, a **methodology** or **methods** section is usually included in the text using any scientific research method).

A project that both 'stands alone' as a sound piece of research and can also be repeated by others in other situations is obviously better than one that can't be repeated.

7 Precision and confidence

'The more precision and confidence we aim for in our research, the more scientific the investigation, and the more useful the results' (Sekaran, 1992, p. 12).

This simply means that the results must be as close as possible (accurate) to the actual state of affairs that you are studying and that others can rely on those results to a high degree.

These requirements are obviously not static: that's why research needs to be done constantly to improve our knowledge and experimental accuracy in a changing world. For example, the exact reason why people buy trouser braces is somewhat different now to the reasons people bought them three centuries ago (then they were needed to hold trousers up, now they can be just a fashion statement).

You may use statistics (e.g. alpha levels) as a **measure** of significance (confidence) but the precision of your data, prior to submitting it to statistical analysis, must be constantly reassessed.

8 Objectivity

Conclusions should not be based on subjective/emotional values but on the **facts** resulting from the data analysis: 'The data should be stripped of personal values and biases' (Sekaran, 1992, p. 13).

There is no point in doing a serious experiment or case study if the conclusions you make are not based on data, but rather on your pre-judged opinion of what should have happened. (This would be circular and self-justifying.)

What happens if you do not support your hypothesis as expected? Providing you have adequately set up experimental conditions and used a number of data sources, and interpreted the data correctly, the project is not a failure.

From the point of view of good research design, it is as important to find out, for example, that aerobic activities do not increase cognitive speed in older adults, as to find out that they do. Other researchers can then forget this variable and look at something else. A salutary lesson about research is this: 'The [researcher] is a mere private in an army pursuing truth' (Perry, 1994, pp. 7–8).

9 Generalisability

The more that a given research project can be generalised to other situations, the better. 'If a researcher's findings that participation in decision making enhances organisational commitment is found to be true in a variety of managerial, industrial and service organ-isations and not merely in the one organisation studied by the researcher, then the generalisability of the findings to other organisational settings is widened' (Sekaran, 1992, p. 13).

There is a tension here, of course, with other aims: to aim to complete a project that is both **generalisable** and also manageably narrow in focus is difficult. The aim of generalisability is a regulative ideal, rather than being essential. If your research project is generalisable *as well as* narrowly focused, it is an added bonus.

10 Parsimony

Economy of explanation is preferred in research work that you are undertaking. Aim to uncover a **small but meaningful result** in your work, not something vast and complex. Making a small, simple but significant point forcefully (using a number of independent tests) is better than trying to do too much and over-extending yourself. In research, 'don't be miles wide but inches deep'.

6 The research process

The research process for **quantitative** research is often taken for granted as something that research students should know and is not made explicit. The research process involves several stages:

- observation
- preliminary data-gathering
- theory formulation
- hypothesis formulation
- further data-gathering
- data analysis
- deduction(s)

Because this process moves from observation to theory and then deductions are made about the data in light of the theory, this is sometimes known as the **hypo-thetico-deductive method**. Of course, a student's own research may not follow all these stages sequentially. There are also many different kinds of research project, such as case studies and 'pure' or 'applied' research. However, most research projects have at least some of the stages listed above.

It may turn out that the research you are required to *produce* (in terms of written work) in your department is strictly quantitative or qualitative. However, in practice, your research will progress through many of the stages given above. (For tips on how to produce formal reports, based on a research design like this, see chapter 11.)

7 Case-study research

The term 'case study' can refer to different tasks. Typically, it refers to social science research, and/or research in particular business situations. As a student you may be asked to conduct a case study of a business or social situation that involves use of research methods. For example, you may be asked to investigate the performance of a small business in a particular industry that interests you. This is an entirely different task from that of analysing a case that is presented to you by your lecturer for analysis with reference to your course book and wider texts. So *writing a case study* is quite different from *analysing a case study*. This section is designed as a brief introduction to case studies, with an emphasis on writing a case study. More detailed texts are available that offer specialist advice, e.g. Yin (1994).

● 8 What is a case study?

There are three main kinds of research methodology used in most universities:

- projects involving forms of conventional **empirical or experimental** research (surveys, statistics, questionnaires, fieldwork);
- **theoretical** projects looking mainly at conceptual issues;
- **case method**: an analysis of a real-world problem which students have experienced or been able to observe.

All of these forms of investigation have advantages and disadvantages. For example, empirical work requires enormous effort in terms of question design and in carrying out fieldwork. The results of empirical work may be inconclusive, so retesting is sometimes required. However, empirical work is useful because it is 'real-life' data that can be measured. Most empirical studies are 'large-n' studies (involving many participants), so the results can be shown to be statistically significant.

Theoretical or conceptual research, on the other hand, can often be a solitary and isolating experience that has little immediate real-world application. However, it has the advantage of being easier to carry out, as there is no need to plan and set up empirical tests – only articles and books are needed, as well as time to think.

Case method has the advantages and disadvantages of both forms of inquiry. Below are some useful definitions of the term 'case study' from two dictionaries:

- A detailed analysis of a person or group, especially as a model of medical, psychiatric, psychological, or social phenomena.
- A) A detailed intensive study of a unit, such as a corporation or a corporate division that stresses factors contributing to its success or failure. B) An exemplary or cautionary model; an instructive example (*The American Heritage Dictionary of the English Language,* 2000, as cited in *The Free Dictionary,* 2008).
- An analysis of a group or person in order to make generalisations about a larger group or society as a whole (*Collins Essential English Dictionary*, 2006, as cited in *The Free Dictionary,* 2008)

Robert K. Yin defines the case study research method as:

'... an empirical inquiry that investigates a contemporary phenomenon within its real-life context; when the boundaries between phenomenon and context are not clearly evident; and in which multiple sources of evidence are used' (Yin, 1994, p. 23).

There are real strengths to the case-study method, if it is done correctly:

- it involves detailed, holistic investigation (e.g. all aspects of a particular company);
- data can be collected over a period of time;
- data is contextual (relative to a certain industry);
- a range of different measurement techniques can be applied (the researcher is not limited to any one methodological tool);
- the histories and stories that can be told about the company can be assessed and documented – not just empirical data. For example, stories and anecdotes about how the company interacts with the marketplace.

The virtue of the case study is, therefore, in its degree of variability in data-collection techniques, and comparative flexibility as a methodological tool. In establishing your conclusions and collecting your data, there are no limits as to what you can study and use, and no restrictions on the analytical instruments you can apply.

9 Strengths and weaknesses of the case-study method

The case-study method has the strengths and weaknesses of both empirical and conceptual forms of inquiry.

Weaknesses

Case studies involve analysis of small data sets, such as one or two companies, that may lead the researcher to gain some general insights into trends in relevant industries. For example, a case study about the Ford Motor Company might be used to generalise about similar companies in the automobile industry. The data is 'real-life' in the sense that a company or companies have been chosen as the source of the data. However, the studies involve 'small-n' data and therefore conventional empirical techniques cannot be used, or where they are used, they may have limited application as there may not be enough data to meet requirements for statistical significance.

Strengths

The case-study method involves detailed, holistic investigation (e.g. all aspects of a company) and can utilise a range of different measurement techniques (the case-study researcher is not limited to any one methodological tool). Data can be collected over a period of time, and they are contextual (relative to a certain industry). The histories and stories that can be told about the company are also something that can be assessed and documented – not just empirical data.

● 10 What is case-study analysis?

Case-study analysis is also typically an assessment task used in the social sciences. The aim in case-study analysis is usually to pretend that you are a consultant (or manager) with a particular business problem that you need to solve. In analysing a case study, your lecturer will give you an article about a company or companies, and you will have to produce a report or essay-style response to it. (See chapters 11, 12 and 13.)

> 'A case study [analysis] presents an account of what happened to a business or industry over a number of years. It chronicles the events that managers had to deal with, such as changes in the competitive environment, and charts the managers' response, which usually involved changing the business- or corporate-level strategy' (Seperich, Woolverton, Berierlein & Hahn, 1996).

Case-study analysis is a response by you (as the manager or consultant) to the situation in a company or companies and your recommendations for overcoming the problems.

There are good reasons for learning the skills of case-study analysis:

- they provide organisational problems that you probably have not experienced but may need to solve when you begin working in a real company;
- they provide a situation in which you can identify and solve problems by applying the knowledge gained during the course (i.e. the theories and concepts);
- they are a good focus for discussing ideas in class. You may have to present your solutions to the case in class and argue for them. Debating is a useful skill;
- debate and discussion about real cases simulates what happens in the business environment, so it is very appropriate for intending managers and future CEOs;
- most corporate decisions are made by groups and, therefore, most case-study analyses are done as groupwork. Putting together a final report from parts written by different members of a group, keeping others motivated, etc., is not easy – but this is exactly what you have to do as a manager.

● 11 Writing a case study

Seven steps should be followed in writing a case study:

Step 1: Establish the broad case to investigate
When choosing a suitable case to study, you must be practical. Consider carefully:

- If you can gain access to the company. Is it local or offshore? Is the data available or subject to commercial confidence?
- If there will be enough published information on the company.
- If there is too much information already available.
- If you will be able to conduct your study in the time you have available.

You want to choose a **lukewarm** area to investigate, not something that is **cold** (there is no information available) or **hot** (there is too much information already).

Step 2: Establish the research question(s)
After you establish the broad 'case' you want to investigate, you need a question(s) that you are going to answer. Most research questions begin with: 'how', 'why' 'what' or 'can'. They are clearly formulated, narrow and researchable (they must be testable). An example of a testable research statement is: 'There is a difference between the work ethic values of Australian and Asian employees working in the Ford Motor Company in Melbourne and the USA.' Your case study ascertains what this difference is. If you find no differences even this might be of interest.

Once a hypothesis or research question or statement is devised, you need to do an extensive **literature review** to find what others have done in this area (see chapter 14).

Step 3: Select the precise case(s) to be used
You then need to choose the exact case or cases you are going to study. A single case might be, e.g. the operation of a certain private hospital; a multiple case might involve looking at several different companies operating in the wine industry.

When using multiple cases, you need to treat each 'case' as a *single* case. You would best devote a chapter or section of your study to each case. The conclusions from each part can then be used as information contributing to the whole study, but each case should remain separate in your treatment.

It is useful to select cases that:

- represent a variety of geographical regions;
- represent a variety of size parameters (i.e. big and small companies with a large/small client base);
- represent different market segments;
- use different raw materials, etc.

In other words, choose cases that are distinctive in different ways.

Step 4: Determine data-gathering and analysis techniques

Good case studies use a number of the different research tools available in order to increase the validity of the study. For example, you can use both **qualitative** and **quantitative** approaches, different data-collection instruments (surveys, interviews, documentation reviews, artefact collection), and so on. You should aim to **triangulate** your research instruments and techniques so that they provide different views of the case (this avoids the problem of 'observer bias' – i.e. your choice of instrument measuring what you want to see rather than what is really there).

It is best to use multiple cases in your study, as this provides more evidence. If, however, you are analysing a single case study, make sure that you look at different levels of analysis, such as a firm that is part of an industry and the industry itself (e.g. Mitsubishi in Australia and the car industry at large). This type of case study increases the complexity and amount of data that can be evaluated. The aim in a case study is to *collect data from many different sources, so that light will be shed on your research question from many angles.*

Construct, internal and external validity and reliability

You must conduct your research well. In particular, you must ensure *construct validity, internal validity, external validity,* and *reliability.*

- *Construct validity* means selecting the most appropriate measurement tool for the concepts being studied. *Does your tool really measure what you want to assess?*
- *Internal validity* is another term for using different methodological tools to triangulate the data. *What other methods can you use to check for the same phenomenon?*
- *External validity* refers to how well the data can be applied beyond the circumstances of the case to more general situations. *Can you apply your data across the industry and to others as well?*
- *Reliability* means the extent to which the results can be repeated and yield the same results. That is, the accuracy and stability of the results. *Are you confident that your study can be repeated by others and the results will be the same?*

Step 5: Collecting the data

You need a method of coding, categorising and sorting your data. Case studies can generate many different kinds of data, so some methods for keeping everything in order are needed.

It is no good conducting your study and then finding that all the good data was not recorded properly or that you missed opportunities. You might consider establishing any or all of the following:

- databases designed to codify data;
- protocols for interviews and surveys;

- pilot studies that capture the concepts and data needed;
- formats for narrative reporting;
- field notes;
- procedures for tape or video recordings.

When carrying out the study, investigators need to be very flexible in real-life situations. They need to have well-worked-out contingency plans, if something goes wrong. They should:

- anticipate key events and problems;
- have a plan when there are unexpected changes, delayed appointments, a lack of office space, unavailability of staff, etc.;
- be open to contrary findings and unexpected events or responses to interview questions;
- delicately approach people who may be threatened or unsure of what the case study will bring;
- be prepared to revise the research design.

Step 6: Collect data in the field
Several points need to be kept in mind when collecting data in the field:

- Evidence must be collected systematically. While the case-study methodology is very flexible, it must be clear how the data from various sources contribute to the overall aims of the study.
- You should not collect data randomly. There needs to be a purpose for which you are collecting certain data – refine your **research question/statement**, if necessary.
- Data must be stored in formats that can be referenced so that the patterns of information are clear.
- Researchers should be able to see causal factors associated with the information collected (how is X related to Y?).
- If changes need to be made to the data-collection procedure, these changes need to be recorded and documented.
- Anecdotes, comments and illustrations/examples might turn out to be vital pieces of qualitative information, so you need to be able to record them easily.
- Keep notes recording the thoughts you have about the evolving case study, such as a case diary.

Step 7: Analysing the data
Data are used to find relationships between the object of study and the research question(s) posed. A few pointers about doing this:

- You can quickly find yourself in a 'web' of complex data unless you have a clear research objective. Aim to seek data that answers this objective from as many different sources as possible. Don't try to establish 57 different things: establish one thing well with data from different areas that confirm it.

- Cross-check the facts and discrepancies in your data. Tabulate information so that it can be checked easily.
- Focus group interviews (in-depth interviews with a small number of individuals) may be needed to reconfirm existing data.
- Flow charts or other displays and tabulating the frequency of events are good ways of recording and analysing information.
- Quantitative data can be used to corroborate and support the qualitative data obtained, and vice versa.
- Multiple investigators can assist in seeing the patterns in the data. This can ensure confidence in the data. If there are discrepancies in how the data is viewed, then the researchers need to investigate again.
- You should also investigate *across* case studies (from one company or situation to another). Don't just settle on one example from one case.

Step 8: Preparing the report

The **report format** is generally followed in writing up case studies (see chapter 11). However, this format can be modified as appropriate.

- Qualitative data – stories, anecdotes, quotations, interview transcripts, artefacts, recordings, etc. – are placed in the **results** section, along with empirical data.
- Where possible, empirical evaluation techniques are used. The standard empirical report style is usually modified to make it clear how the data from different sources answer or illuminate the research question(s).
- Generally, the writer refers back to the research question(s) with quotations or other qualitative/quantitative evidence collected.
- The report also includes evidence from published literature that confirms and disconfirms the data collected. This is generally placed in the **discussion** section, and analysed carefully.

● 12 Summary

This chapter has given an introduction to the research process. All postgraduate education is preparing you for the world of academic research as well as the world of work. To advance in your postgraduate studies you need to demonstrate that you understand the scholarly issues associated with research. In addition you will often have to read journal articles about a piece of research. To be able to critically analyse it you have to understand what research is and how it should be conducted.

The second half of the chapter outlined what is involved in writing and analysing a case study. The advice on limiting your research aims is particularly important. Focus the case carefully, limit the scope, and investigate the company, or phenomenon under investigation, in as much detail as possible using alternative sources of evidence. In postgraduate study, depth of analysis is always better than breadth.

Part V

What About Me? Criticising and Analysing

8 Critical Thinking

● 1 Introduction

You have probably heard that one of the hallmarks of academic study is 'critical thinking'. This is considered particularly important in western universities. But what do we mean by 'critical thinking'? How do you do it? This chapter helps you to understand critical thinking and why it is important for higher-degree study. A good understanding of critical thinking will help you develop your skills in writing and the right kind of academic thinking style needed to succeed in your tertiary studies. Good critical thinking skills will also help you obtain higher marks for assignments. More importantly, it will equip you with the necessary skills for a future career – every employer likes evidence of an employee with good analysis and critical thinking skills.

● 2 What is critical thinking?

1 A definition of a critical thinker

A critical thinker is someone who *has an interest and ability to engage in intellectual arguments.* It is someone who thinks *actively,* and who *investigates* information carefully. He or she does not *accept* things without *analysing* the information and *checking* if it is true or not. Critical thinkers look carefully at *relationships* between ideas and consider whether the relationships are genuine and appropriate. They don't take *assumptions* for granted and weigh them carefully for *evidence.* We shall see a more precise definition shortly, but for now let's look at when critical thinking is needed.

2 When do you need to think critically?

You will need to think critically during various university tasks. For example:

- reading articles as part of your research;
- taking part in a tutorial;
- listening to a lecture; or
- writing assignments.

That is, you need to *analyse* and *evaluate* the academic work and contribution of others as well as your own work. Your grades will be influenced by how well you demonstrate the *skill* of critical thinking in everything you do at university.

● 3 How to think critically

1 Awareness of the position

When reading academic work, you should first be aware of the author's **position**. The 'position' of the author is their point of view, their attitude or – most importantly for critical thinking – their **argument**.

A person's attitude or point of view on some topic usually conceals an argument they hold that supports their attitude. For example, if I tell you: 'I believe that learning English is important for everyone', I am really not just expressing a belief. I am more than likely also concealing an *argument* behind that statement of belief. If you asked me to explain why I think 'English is important for everyone' I would probably explain my argument for my belief. This argument could look like this:

- ● *English is the world language, and it is necessary for obtaining work in the globalised workplace. Everyone wants to be able to obtain work somewhere in the world, so therefore learning English is important for everyone.*

This argument can be expressed very easily in an **argument map** like this, showing the premises for the argument leading to the conclusion of the argument (**premises** are the **reasons** given in an argument that support a **conclusion**):

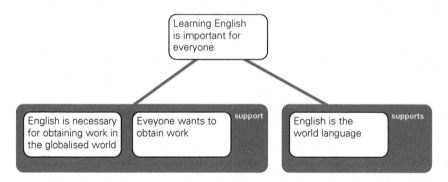

Notice that two of the points given are joined together. When premises are joined together like this, they are called **co-premises**. These are to be distinguished from arguments with connected but separate premises, where one reason is clearly different and independent from another reason. An example of an argument with two separate reasons is given below. There is also an **objection** provided to the position in this example. (In this example, notice also the **supporting points** given for each of the two separate reasons and the **rebuttal** or point *against* the objection.)

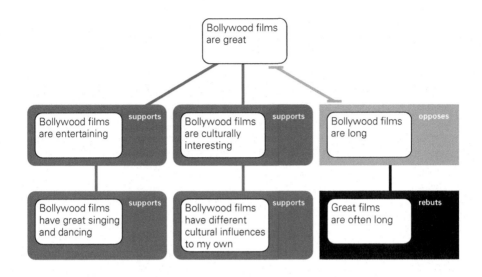

2 Making arguments explicit

Sometimes reasons and objections for an argument do not need to be stated clearly, like they are here. Often the position given is uncontentious (easy to accept) and no argument is needed. However, in academic work, more often than not, the argument needs to be made very clear. That's what the good critical thinker does. This allows the argument to be assessed and evaluated, and if necessary, *criticised*. Once you are clear about the author's position and the reasons given for the position – which may be implicit or explicit – you can begin to think seriously about it, and either agree or disagree with it, or partially agree and disagree with it. If the argument is not *explicit*, you can't do anything with it. So the first point to note is that good critical thinking involves **making arguments explicit**. The first step in doing this involves making the contention or position of the author very clear, as well as the premises for or against the contention.

Let's examine a more complex example. Someone may have the position *that research into genetically modified food (GMF) is a good thing.* (Note that positions or 'points of view' are best expressed verbally or in writing with 'that' clauses: 'I want to argue *that* research into GMF is a good thing.')

Person A believes this position because it enables disease-resistant crops to feed more people. By contrast, Person B has the opposing position because they feel GMF is untested and unsafe (e.g. 'I want to argue that GMF research is *not* a good thing'). Person C's position might be *qualified*: that research into GMF is acceptable in certain domains but not others (e.g. 'I want to argue that some GMF research on rice crops is a good thing, but GMF should not apply more widely to other food crops').

How does one deal with complex points of view like this? Without further information about the exact arguments behind these very different positions nothing more can be done. There is a stalemate. Person A will disagree with Person B, and Person C will insist his position is distinct from either A or B. What can be done with these very different claims on the same topic?

The answer is that you need to understand not just the positions being expressed, but the *argument* behind the positions. Sometimes this is clear in someone's writing or presentation, sometimes it isn't. This is where an ability to think critically is tested.

3 Awareness of the reasons supporting the position

As we have seen, the first stage in good critical thinking is being aware of the position(s) an author is expressing. As already suggested, the second stage in good critical thinking is to be aware of the argument that *leads to or supports* the position. This can sometimes be difficult to determine as some academics often do not make their argument very clear at all.

It is helpful when doing critical thinking to think in terms of **argument maps**. We have just seen examples of these. Recently developed software called *Rationale* has been developed at the University of Melbourne, Australia to allow argument mapping to be done with computers, but it can also be done with pens and 'butcher's paper'.

The position placed at the top of the argument map is called the **contention**. The branching statements leading to it are called the *reasons* or *premises* (or in some cases of a *negative* reason – i.e. against the contention – an 'objection').

In the GMF example just given, the position or contention is: *Research into GMF is a good thing.* (Note that the 'that' word is not needed in an argument map.) This statement goes at the top of the map like this:

Research into GMF
is a good thing

What reasons are given for this contention? One is easy to spot. This is: *Disease-resistant crops can feed more people.* However, if you put this as a reason linking to the conclusion it does not look right. Something is missing.

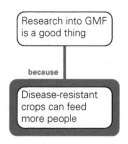

What is missing is the *link* between the reason: *Disease-resistant crops can feed more people* and the contention: *Research into GMF is a good thing.* This missing link is the unstated **assumption** that *GMF research can produce disease-resistant crops.*

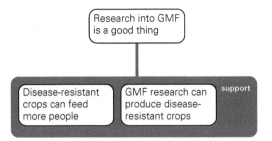

Note that these are **co-premises**, as they support each other. Consider the GMF argument again. Are there other reasons supporting this contention? If you think about it, there is another reason that is not stated explicitly. In fact, this reason is so obvious that it does not need to be stated and it is often forgotten. However, it is an important part of the argument being made. This is the claim that: *It is a good thing to feed people with disease-resistant crops.*

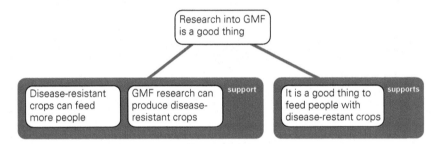

When you are doing argument maps and practising to be a good critical thinker, you need to formally express and state assumptions to arguments as well as the contention or position. This is because assumptions can indicate problems with the argument. Not all assumptions can be taken for granted. Some assumptions are completely false. If you can spot a false or misleading assumption in an argument you are doing well as a critical thinker!

In the diagram overleaf I have mapped the argument for GMF research in more detail, with a number of supporting reasons that might be given by someone agreeing with the contention at the top of the map. This map could be made much more detailed with further thinking and further research. Lighter-shaded boxes indicate objections *against* the contention, darker-shaded boxes indicate supporting points *for* the contention.

What about an argument map for a very different contention? I mentioned another possible contention: *Research in GMF is not a good thing.* We could produce a totally different map for this argument, or we could add 'objections' to the contention given in the argument above, as we have done here. More objections can be made to the supporting reasons given on the right-hand side of the argument as well. We will return to this example later.

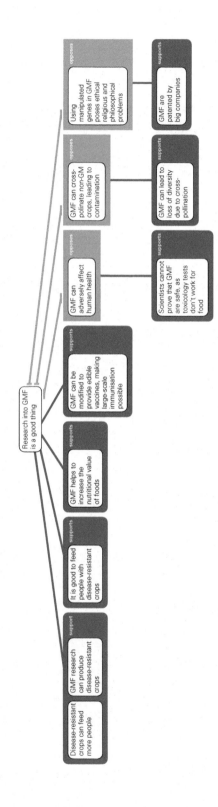

Research into GMF is a good thing

support — GMF research can produce disease-resistant crops
Disease-resistant crops can feed more people

supports — It is good to feed people with disease-resistant crops

supports — GMF helps to increase the nutritional value of foods

supports — GMF can be modified to provide edible vaccines, making large-scale immunisation possible

opposes — GMF can adversely affect human health
supports — Scientists cannot prove that GMF are safe, as toxicology tests don't work for food

opposes — GMF can cross-polinate non-GM crops, leading to contamination
supports — GMF can lead to loss of diversity due to cross-pollination

opposes — Using manipulated genes in GMF poses ethical religious and philosophical problems
supports — GMF are patented by big companies

4 Awareness of the objections to the reasons

Critical thinking therefore involves first being aware of contentions, and second being aware of all the *reasons* or *assumptions* for the contentions. The third factor involved in critical thinking is being aware of the *objections* to the reasons. This has several stages: (1) making sure the reasons are accurate or true (or at least believable); (2) assessing if the person making the arguments is biased; (3) assessing whether the *assumptions* lying behind the reasons are fair and reasonable; (4) determining if the arguments are valid; (5) assessing if the premises are relevant; and (6) deciding if there is enough evidence given for the premises. Let's take these steps in turn.

Are the reasons accurate or true (or at least believable)?
Critical thinking involves more than knowing the arguments being made and being able to 'map' them; it also involves being sure of the *accuracy* of the premises. Are they true? An argument with false premises can be questioned. The premises have to be at least plausible or believable. Can other explanations be given for the reasons that are different? I am sure you can all see that something is wrong with the argument below, even though its premises link well to the conclusion:

- *Tobacco is good for you because everything made from plants is good for you and tobacco is a plant.*

The problem with the argument is with one of the premises. It is false. Not all plants are good for you. This leads to a clearly false contention: *Tobacco is good for you.* I have shown this in an argument map along with 'basis' boxes providing evidence for the terminal points of the argument. The box with the tick in it indicates a 'commonly accepted view'. The other box indicates academic support for the reason, e.g. a scholarly paper discussing plants, such as tobacco, that are harmful to human health. The *Rationale* software allows for many different kinds of bases to be given to arguments, statistical evidence, definitions, and so on. Clearly, it is good if grounds for reasoning are based on academic support, and not just 'common opinion'.

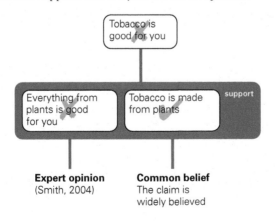

If an argument has one or more false premises its conclusion can be seriously questioned. Notice that one of the supporting reasons above is ticked because it is plausible; another is 'crossed' because we have supporting evidence from Smith, 2004, that it is false (we may know it is false without the supporting evidence, but it is better to provide evidence if you can because this makes your opinions much stronger!). On this basis, we can reject the contention as well.

Note, however, that the conclusion of an argument is not *necessarily* false just because one or more of its premises are false. In the following example we have a true conclusion based on false premises.

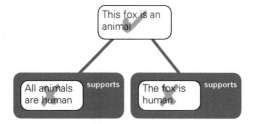

The contention is clearly true even though the supporting reasons are false. Is this a good argument or not? In one sense it is. The conclusion seems to *follow* logically from the supporting reasons. However, it is clearly not a good argument because the supporting reasons are false. This simple example shows that the logical structure of an argument (known by logicians as '**validity**') is quite a different thing from the truth or falsity of the premises of an argument (known by logicians as '**soundness**'). A good critical thinker will check the validity *and* soundness of arguments.

Is the person making the arguments biased?
Having established the truth or believability of the premises, you need to assess if the author/speaker had any reason to be predisposed to that position other than as a conclusion of their academic research. In other words, does the author have a **vested interest** or a prior bias to a certain position? For example, I would have a vested interest in GMF research if I were a GMF scientist or a farmer using genetically modified research to make my living. Everything I said about the subject would need to be scrutinised carefully. You need to keep this in mind as you analyse the work or arguments of others. Sometimes it is difficult to see bias in your own work, so care needs to be taken when presenting your own arguments.

> **Example:** You may question the neutrality of a medical researcher who produces an article in a medical journal claiming the wonders of a new drug if they are being paid to research the drug by the company that is planning to sell it.

Are the assumptions lying behind the reasons fair and reasonable?
We looked at assumptions in arguments earlier, now we need to consider whether they are reasonable, plausible or believable. Having mapped and assessed arguments for

accuracy and bias, you need to look at the (often unstated) assumptions lying behind the premises on which the position or argument is based. An assumption in an argument is something that is accepted or taken for granted as being true. We saw earlier than my argument about GMF had a concealed assumption that *it is good to feed people with disease-resistant crops.* This is a reasonable assumption. However, sometimes authors conceal assumptions that are not reasonable at all (e.g. *that everything made from plants is good for you*). The good critical thinker has to be constantly on guard against faulty or questionable assumptions.

Are the arguments valid?
You need to identify assumptions and assess whether arguments are *valid*. In a valid argument, the conclusion or contention *follows* logically from the premises given to support it. The argument above about tobacco is valid as the conclusion follows from the premises, despite the fact that there are false premises given. There is still a logical link between the premises and the contention. This logical link is called *validity.* As with well-founded assumptions, you have to be on constant guard for *invalid arguments.* If an author wrongly assumes that a conclusion follows logically from reasons given, then the rest of the argument falls apart. An example of an invalid argument is given below.

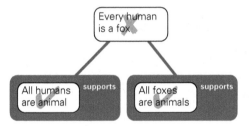

Here the reasons are true but they don't **connect** logically to the conclusion. Here is a more real-life, and possibly more contentious, example.

> **Example:** If you assume that the melting of icebergs leads to rising sea levels, and go on to argue that sea levels in 2020 will therefore rise by 'X' amount based on the amount of water contained within icebergs, then your figures will be disputed. In fact, only the melting of landmass ice/snow affects sea levels, as icebergs displace as much water in iceberg form as they add when they melt. Melting landmass ice, on the other hand, was not previously displacing water and so adds to the overall level of the sea.

Here a conclusion is being made about sea levels rising by a certain amount on the basis of evidence of water now contained in icebergs. But this ignores certain facts about water displacement and different kinds of icebergs (on land as well as in the sea). The questionable nature of this argument and the objection to it can be seen more easily if the argument is mapped out:

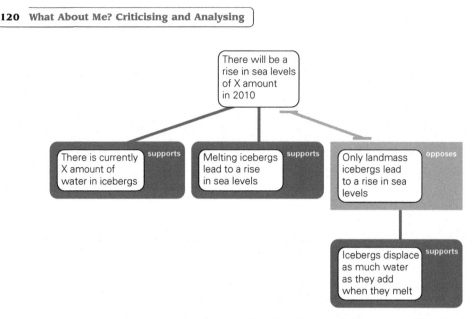

An argument, or any piece of reasoning, involves an **inference**, a **link** between reasons and conclusion. There are thus really two questions involved when we ask: 'Is this a good argument?'

● The first concerns the *basis* of the reasoning. It asks whether the *premises are true.*
● The second is concerned with how rational or *logical* the inference is. It is concerned with whether the conclusion *follows logically* from the premises, or is at least *sufficiently supported* by the premises.

Are the premises relevant?
If the assumptions are fair and reasonable, there is no bias, and the argument is valid, then you then need to assess whether the reasons given for an argument are really *relevant* to the position being taken. Is the position reached *as a result* of relevant points being made? Are the reasons relevant to the conclusion? Sometimes arguments are valid (well linked), but the premises are irrelevant.

> **Example:** The statement that males outperform females on spatial maths problems is correct. However, to therefore conclude that only males can solve spatial maths problems or be engineers is not relevant, and ignores the many females who are just as capable in these areas, and the males who are not.

Is enough evidence given for the premises?
You need to ensure that an argument is supported with appropriate evidence. Unsupported or insufficiently supported arguments, no matter how good, are unacceptable as they lack academic justification and credibility. Arguments need concrete support, to clearly illustrate and back them up.

This is where academic research comes in. As a student you will be referring to experts in your field of study to support your arguments. Other authors and speakers will also do this, as any work is only part of a body of knowledge that builds on other people's ideas. Academic research is quite different from other kinds of research (e.g. commercial research) in that the better (and the more) the evidence advanced, the more seriously the arguments are taken. No easy guidance can be given on what is acceptable as 'research evidence', as to some degree this is discipline-specific. In the sciences only empirical and repeatable experimental research is taken seriously. In other disciplines, different criteria are used. In general, the use of peer-reviewed, **refereed** articles citing research work will help you in supporting your arguments and in criticising the arguments of others.

> **Example:** If an author writes that the rapid growth in the Chinese economy is fuelling the natural resources boom around the world in the twenty-first century, few people would question it. However, in an academic paper, you would expect such a statement to be backed up by comparative export figures from countries that are rich in natural resources. You would need to show the percentage of natural resources being exported to China, compared to other countries, and present figures that reflected the situation before China's economy boomed. You would also expect a discussion about the consequences of this phenomenon, again backed up by evidence.

Where an argument is supported, you need to assess the *quality* of the evidence. Do this with your own work too. Is the evidence from a reputable source? Are they a recognised authority in this area? Is the information cited up-to-date (i.e. published in the last five years or less)? Is it published in a reputable, **peer-reviewed journal**? Details like this will matter in terms of the grades you obtain in a postgraduate assignment. Lecturers are generally not impressed with old information, non-peer-reviewed information (e.g. from newspapers or the internet) or unsupported information (e.g. your own opinion).

> **Note:** Supporting an argument with articles from newspapers is not enough. Nor is it sufficient to use the opinion of an authority in one area to support an argument in an unrelated area. Both you, and the authors that you read, need to use evidence that comes from an expert in the area, and which is written up in a reputable journal or academic text.

How many references?

I am often asked how many references are needed in an academic assessment task. 'How long should my reference list be?' This depends on the length of the work and what you are trying to achieve.

A good piece of well-supported research is not determined by quantity, but the *quality* of the research cited and how well it is *integrated and explained* in your own writing. That said, as a very general rule, a page or two of peer-reviewed articles is sufficient for most postgraduate assessment tasks. Some lecturers will stipulate how many articles you need to cite. If they don't tell you, use the 'one- or two-page rule' as a very rough guide.

Let's return to the argument for GMF research given above. Look separately at each reason given. It is hard to think of objections to the premise that *It is a good thing to feed people with disease-resistant crops*. This seems sound. However, an objection might be made to the premise that *Disease-resistant crops can feed more people*. What is the evidence for this claim? Who provides the evidence? Is it evidence that is based on well-tested research? Is the evidence biased (e.g. is it evidence from GMF scientists with a vested interest?) Is the claim itself reasonable? After all, crops susceptible to disease – potatoes, apples, etc. – have been feeding humanity very well for thousands of years. Does making a crop disease-resistant automatically mean that it will be more productive? Seeing the evidence for this is important for establishing the truth of the claim, and therefore the reliability of the argument overall.

Another objection might be made to the premise that *GMF research can produce disease-resistant crops*. Are there any other ways in which crops can be made disease-resistant without modifying their genes (selective breeding, for example)? Is it acceptable to assume that GMF research will *necessarily* produce disease-resistant crops? What is the evidence for this? Opponents to GMF research argue that a danger of GMF research is not being able to manage the process of genetic manipulation properly and allowing 'faulty genes' to escape into the environment. If this is true, GMF research might cause more problems than it solves.

Finally, be aware of poor reasoning. Generalisations based on limited observations, faulty logic and oversimplification are easy traps to fall into. To help you avoid these, the next section deals with 'academic arguments'.

● 4 How do I recognise an academic argument?

If you are constantly being told by your supervisor or lecturer that your work 'is not critical enough' or 'doesn't argue the point', this does not *necessarily* mean that you are wrong in presenting your data, or that you have the wrong facts – the facts you provide might be accurate in every detail! It usually means that you haven't organised the facts/data in a logical way. This could mean a number of things. For example, your work might be criticised for:

- being a mere **collection** of facts (with no synthesis or analysis of the material at all);
- being **insufficiently** argued (there is some argument, but not enough to be convincing);
- being **wrongly** argued (your argument could actually be faulty/fallacious – despite your facts being accurate).

What exactly is an academic argument? This is not easy to answer. Some statements look like arguments, but they are just assertions (unsupported claims); some statements look like **assertions** and are really arguments in disguise (the 'English' example given earlier). Some writing is so jumbled and difficult to read that the arguments get lost in the process. It is your job as a student to make your arguments, and the arguments of others, *very clear.*

Engaging in presenting an academic argument means doing several things:

- attempting to arrive at *conclusions* about some matter of academic interest by debate;
- *questioning* and *criticising* the conclusions of others in this debate in order to make that view more accurate;
- pointing out problems with the *assumptions* that may influence the conclusions;
- recognising how well-argued conclusions and assumptions might *influence* one's own opinions about the matter being debated (to be *challenged* by the debate);
- being prepared to *change* one's own views as a result of the debate.

Engaging in an academic argument is not meant to be hostile or insensitive, but rather should be:

- stimulating for all parties to the dispute;
- useful for *everyone,* regardless of educational level;
- helpful to your own research and the independent research of others;
- impersonal (it is the *idea* that is being debated, not the person who thought of it);
- ongoing/endless (once you stop doing it, you become dogmatic!).

Arguing in an academically acceptable way is not the usual sense of 'argument'. It does not mean attacking someone personally, raising one's voice, swearing, or trying to win a fight with someone.

> **A definition of 'academic argument':** to be engaged in an intellectual dispute with others over the truth/falsity or relevance/application of some claim to scholarly knowledge – with the aim of arriving at a more accurate version.

Of course, this is not to say that people in universities don't become defensive about their opinions or do not become upset when their views are criticised – they very often do. But within universities people are *less* likely to respond in this way because they all recognise that their work is part of an important ongoing critical debate. Participating in this critical debate is the most exciting part of being at university – and your work as a postgraduate student can be a part of it.

From reading the preceding section we can begin to see how arguments are understood. In an argument, we present a conclusion based on a number of premises or assumptions. An argument is a series of **connected** statements which *lead* to a conclusion. Importantly, when we present the conclusion of an argument, we don't just state it, we also have to give **reasons** for stating it. There are thus three components of an argument:

Parts of an academic argument:

1 the premises (or assumptions);

2 the conclusion;

3 the *inference* (or link) from the premises to the conclusion.

Any of these will *usually* indicate the presence of an argument. If none of these are present, you haven't got an argument – only an assertion or statement. Here's a simple example of an argument:

If metals expand when heated, and 'X' is metal, then 'X' will expand when heated.

It is easy to see what is being concluded here. The conclusion is: *'X' will expand when heated.*

The assumptions that lead to this conclusion are as follows:

All metals expand when heated and
'X' is a metal.

The inference being made is from the assumptions to the conclusion. You can write this argument out like this to show the progress of the argument from assumptions to conclusion:

P1: All metals expand when heated
P2: 'X' is a metal
C: 'X' will expand when heated.

P1 and P2 above stand for 'premises' 1 and 2 – **premises** are statements/assumptions in an argument which help in arriving at a conclusion (they are called the 'major' and 'minor' premises in this example). 'C', of course, stands for 'conclusion'.

This is even clearer when presented as an argument map:

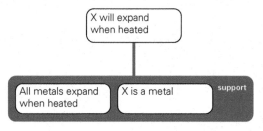

Here are some useful definitions:

- Premises can be defined as statements which are used to infer a certain conclusion. They are statements you argue *from* to a conclusion.
- Conclusions can be defined as statements which are inferred from certain premises. They are statements you argue *to* from premises.

Beyond these definitions, there are several ways of recognising arguments. However, none of these *guarantees* that you have an argument – they are just guides. Here are some rules that will help.

Rule 1: Look out for conclusion indicators

Conclusions are often signposted by the use of indicator words. The following words indicate that they are *likely* to be followed by the conclusion of an argument:

- *let us conclude that ..., we conclude that ..., we can conclude that ..., concluding ..., thus ..., therefore ..., so ..., consequently ..., hence ..., then ...*

Rule 2: Look out for premise indicators

These words indicate that a premise of an argument is to follow:

- *since ..., as ...; for ..., because ..., assuming that ..., supposing that ..., given that ..., for the reason that ..., if such and such ....*

Rule 3: Look out for argument sequence indicators

There are also indicators which signal that what goes before is a premise, and that what comes after is a conclusion.

e.g. (premise) ... then ... (conclusion)
e.g. *If we heat water then it will boil.*

Other words used in this way include: *shows that ..., indicates that..., proves that ..., entails that ..., implies that ..., establishes that ..., allows us to ..., infer that ..., gives us reasons for believing that ...*

Rule 4: Look out for conclusion sequence indicators

Indicators can also signal a reverse sequence: that a conclusion that comes before has as its premises some statements that come after:

e.g. (conclusion) ... then ... (premise)
e.g. *If the streets are wet, then it must be raining.*

Other phrases used in this way include: *is shown by ..., is indicated by ..., is proven by ..., is entailed by ..., is implied by ..., is established by ...*

Of course, not all arguments use sequence indicators.

Let's look at another example.

- *If men have obtained advantages through past discrimination in their favour, then we may discount men's advantages when selecting people for jobs.*

This statement is intended to give a **reason** for discounting men's advantages in employment. Therefore, it should be regarded as presenting an argument in favour of that conclusion. The conclusion is based on the assumed premise that men have in fact obtained advantages from past discrimination in their favour. But in this example there is no conclusion indicator present. However, we can put one in to make it clear. It can be rewritten as:

- P1: If men have obtained advantages through past discrimination, then we should discount men's advantages when selecting people for jobs.
- P2: Men have obtained advantages in the past from discrimination in their favour (assumed).
- C: Therefore, we should discount men's advantages when selecting people for jobs.

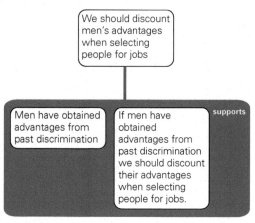

The lesson here is: don't be fooled by indicator words when you are looking for arguments and don't assume that the lack of indicators means that there is no argument.

Academic writing involves understanding arguments, which distinguishes it from novels, newspaper articles and other forms of writing. These other kinds of writing are often just 'opinion' pieces (i.e. claims for which no reasons or evidence are given). However, academic arguments are much longer and more complex, and reasons and evidence are expected.

Sometimes the arguments made in academic articles will not be obvious. Part of your job during lectures and when reading is to try to recognise these arguments and break them down into their own discrete parts. You then need to analyse the different parts and make sure that they are performing the function that they are supposed to perform in the argument. You should consider all the issues associated with critical thinking mentioned earlier. This will take a lot of practice, but should also be a part of your classes, where your tutor will work through these steps via a series of questions and exercises.

To show the potential of argument mapping, consider the following map. The argument makes the case for obese passengers on aircraft receiving additional seats at no charge:

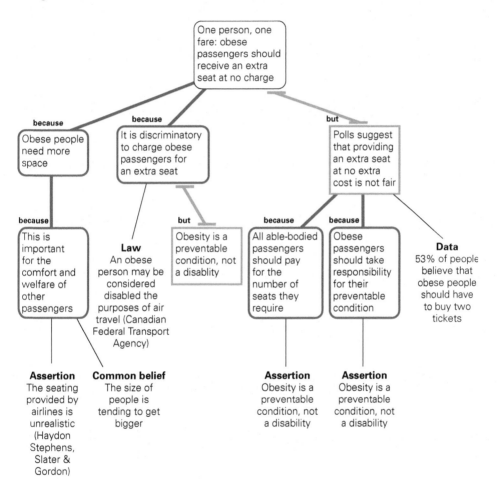

● **5 Critical thinking and writing**

A natural question to ask is: 'So what? What does this all have to do with being a post-graduate student?' As explained in chapter 1, you are **assessed** on how well you present arguments and criticise arguments in your assignments. Critical thinking is very important. Indeed, it is the most important skill after paraphrasing.

To see how to apply critical thinking, consider the following real postgraduate essay topic from a class in International Business:

> Michael Porter's schema of industry analysis is a powerful tool for managers to think strategically about the relationships their firm has with their external environment.
>
> Is the industry in which a firm for whom you have worked (you can disguise its identity if there are issues of commercial confidentiality or you can choose another company if you feel that your employment experience does not help you with this question) 'attractive' or 'unattractive'? **In making your argument** you must address each of the 'Five Forces' identified by Michael Porter. The **second** part of the question is to **make an argument** about whether the current state of industry 'attractiveness' will stay as it is or whether it will change over the next 3–5 years. Take care to explain why you expect this outcome.

The essay topic asks you to 'make an argument' in two places. Indeed, if you study the task carefully you will see it asks you to do four things:

1 **describe** Porter's industry analysis schema;
2 **outline** whether your industry is 'attractive' or 'unattractive';
3 **discuss** whether your industry's level of attractiveness will change or stay the same;
4 **explain** why you expect this.

In addition, you are requested to 'make an argument' about parts 1–3. The words in bold are **direction words** telling you what to do (sometimes they are made *explicit* in assignment topics and sometimes they are not). We will learn more about these words in chapter 12. (We will also return to this example in chapter 13.)

First you go to the library to learn more and obtain information to help you devise an argument. Let's imagine you have worked in the manufacturing sector and you are an international student from Thailand. It's usually a good idea to use your work experience as a postgraduate as much as possible. Suppose, in response to the first two parts, you eventually decide (after a lot of reading and thinking, and remembering your work history) that Porter's Five Forces theory is only of **limited** importance for explaining the attractiveness of the manufacturing industry in Thailand. This is due to a variety of sound reasons for which you have good evidence. This becomes your **thesis statement**, contention or position on the topic. *But it is not yet an argument.*

The easiest way to make sure you are making an argument is to choose a **valid deductive argument form** from a logic book. Logic books are books that outline the forms and patterns of acceptable and unacceptable reasoning. They are common enough in western university libraries. This is because logic was a western invention, developed by the Greek philosopher Aristotle and refined by other western philosophers and mathematicians. An example of a valid deductive argument form is as follows:

> *If A then B*
> *Not B*
> *Therefore not A*

This simple argument form can be used to frame your argument:

> P1: If Porter's industry analysis is to adequately explain the attractiveness of an industry it needs to be X.
> P2: Thailand's manufacturing industry *is not* X or *does not* indicate X [evidence needed].
> C: Therefore, Porter's industry analysis does not adequately explain the attractiveness of the Thai manufacturing industry [evidence/support needed].

This format is very clear but it is not very suitable for a written assignment which needs to be in flowing English prose. However, you can use the basic argument 'form' and 'dress' it in language like that given below (underlined phrases are connecting phrases to assist in linking the parts of the argument). The argument below is not complete and would need to be supplemented by providing some discipline-specific points:

> In this essay it will be argued that while Porter's Five Forces, especially the third, are important for most industries, they are not crucial in explaining the attractiveness of the manufacturing industry in Thailand. For Porter's Forces to be crucial in explaining attractiveness, they need to be .... However, in the case of the manufacturing industry, this is not the case due to the following three factors: ... (1) ... (2) ... (3) ... Therefore it will be claimed that Porter's Forces are of only limited relevance to the manufacturing industry in Thailand.

But this introductory argument could be even better. As we shall see in chapter 13, an introduction should be shaped like an inverted 'funnel'. It should begin with the general topic, narrow down to the specific topic, isolate a research gap, give an argument or 'thesis' statement, and then signpost the essay ahead (i.e. give an outline). It could also be supported with a few in-text citations. We will see the final version of this introduction in chapter 13.

From this initial argument you can build a more complex and convincing case in your essay. In chapter 1 we saw the following structure:

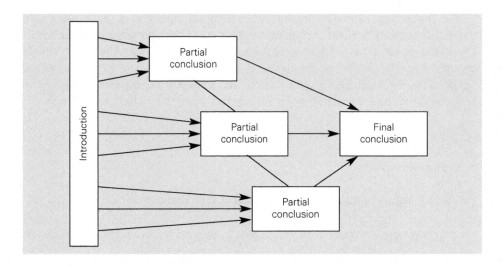

The argument structure mentioned above can be 'defended' though your essay as follows:

- In **partial conclusion 1** you argue why, of Porter's Five Forces, only the third is most important to the case you are considering, namely, the manufacturing industry in Thailand.
- In **partial conclusion 2** you argue that if Porter's Five Forces theory is to explain attractiveness of an industry, it needs to explain certain characteristics or features.
- In **partial conclusion 3** you argue why Porter's Five Forces are not crucial in explaining the attractiveness of the manufacturing industry in Thailand for three main reasons.
- This builds to the **final conclusion** that Porter's theory is only of limited relevance to the manufacturing industry in Thailand.

6 Summary

Critical thinking is a complex and difficult skill. One of the main reasons for doing a postgraduate degree is to refine this skill. This learning never stops; one is always improving. This chapter has outlined several definitions of critical thinking and explained its importance in the tertiary context. Several things that good critical thinkers need to identify about arguments were explained in some detail. Examples of premise and conclusion indicator words were outlined. Several arguments were given to show inferential relationships between premises and conclusion. Finally, a suggested method was provided to put arguments into introductions of assignments. You might wish to consult further books on critical thinking, such as Cottrell (2011).

Part VI

Putting Pen to Paper: Writing for Assessment

9 Writing Style and Language

● 1 Introduction

International students commencing postgraduate studies are naturally worried about their English language skills; in particular, that their writing skills are not good enough. However, *everyone* can learn to improve their writing skills. This is very much a part of graduate-level education.

The following points should encourage all students who feel that their English is 'not good enough':

- Everybody (including your lecturers) is constantly working on improving their writing – literacy is a life-long commitment for all, native speakers included.
- No one who writes well does so because they are 'naturals' – they have worked hard at it.
- English is a very complex language with many different influences. It has a vast vocabulary drawn from many sources (see *The Adventure of English*, 1999). The *Longer Oxford English Dictionary* – the authoritative guide to meaning and pronunciation – runs to 20 volumes and takes up an entire library shelf! If you are finding English difficult, it is entirely to be expected.
- Your commitment to learning how to write better is vital for your future career – regardless of subject area. Good English literacy is truly a '**generic**' skill that is as important – possibly more important – than subject knowledge acquired. Your efforts will eventually be rewarded.

This chapter outlines some suggestions for improving your writing style. This chapter is not intended to be a substitute for a specialist ESL textbook. It covers some of the recurring writing mistakes that I regularly see as a postgraduate learning adviser. These mistakes can be remedied with some simple suggestions and advice.

● 2 Eight tips for better writing

1 Use short and simple words where possible

Many students think that complex, multi-syllabic words sound sophisticated and 'academic'. To some extent they can, but they can also make your work unnecessarily hard to read.

> **Compare**
>
> ✘ A considerable multitude of invited participants enquired about the location in which they could purchase beverages.
>
> ✔ Many guests asked where they could buy drinks.

Your lecturer may find more to tick on your work if you make your points clear by using simple vocabulary.

2 Use abbreviations in moderation
Abbreviations can include:

- *Acronyms:* words formed from usually the first letters of a series of words, such NASA and UNICEF, which are pronounced as regular words.
- *Initialisation:* usually the first letters of a series of words that don't read as new words (UNSW = University of New South Wales; HRM = Human Resource Management).
- *Shortened forms* such as Assoc. = associate or association; Feb. = February; Intl = International; Grad. Dip. = Graduate Diploma; and etc. = etcetera.

> **Compare**
>
> ✘ In Feb. 2008, MMSP of UEB, Ian Appleton, spoke about HRM use of the MBTI.
>
> ✔ In February 2008, Associated Management and Marketing Senior Professor of the University of East Borneo, Ian Appleton, spoke about Human Resource Management use of the Myers-Briggs Test Indicator.

Your readers might not know all of the abbreviations you use or they might find it hard to remember what they stand for. In addition, your readers might find shortened forms too informal and 'lazy-sounding'. Lecturers particularly dislike 'etc.' which, while clear, sounds less formal than language to introduce examples, such as 'for example', 'for instance', or indeed, 'such as'. In general, it is far better to give a *full list of items* than simply writing 'etc.' (see the 'Writing for a selfish reader principle' below).

3 Don't overload the sentence
Good writing never *overloads the reader's memory.* Bad writing frequently does. Avoid using lots of noun phrases, compound nouns (nouns added to nouns), adjectives and adverbs in one sentence. Make sure there is a **main verb** in every sentence (often the verb explains to the reader what is *happening*) and a **main subject** that explains *who or what* is doing the action. We shall look at some examples below.

4 Don't write long sentences
A simple way to fix bad writing is to *shorten your sentences.* You can't write a good long

sentence if you can't write a good short one. Keeping the sentences short minimises grammatical mistakes. You have better control over short sentences. Many international students have the idea that to write in an academic manner they have to write long, complex sentences (as well as using long complex words). This is certainly not the case, and this attitude can lead to disaster.

5 Keep the subject of the sentence at the start with the main verb nearby
You would be surprised how this simple rule can help. Read the **Example** of a student's work below. The subject is 'globalisation' but this word is not in the sentence. Now read the second version. It begins with the main subject and the main verb close together at the start of the sentence (underlined). Doesn't it make a big difference?

6 Don't copy what you read
Sometimes you read articles that are written *by* professionals *for* professionals. Sometimes academic articles by professionals are *not that well written*, but have good ideas. (Academics call them '**seminal**', i.e. key or most important, articles, and sometimes the first time a particular idea has appeared in print.) However, such articles may be full of jargon and language that do not clearly convey meaning to a non-expert. Trying to copy this style will lead to disaster. Instead concentrate on **clarity**, while maintaining formal language. Communicating what you want to say clearly is more important than trying to 'sound academic'. No lecturer will expect an international student to 'sound academic'. They *will* expect clear, understandable writing. Students who master clear writing invariably receive better marks than students who do not.

7 Use the active voice
The passive voice ('be' + past participle) can sometimes make writing sound 'scientific' or 'academic'. However, overuse will make your writing seem boring and difficult to understand, or sometimes silly.

Compare
✗ It is believed by many lecturers and tutors that inadequate care is put into writing by too many students.
✔ Many lecturers believe that too many students put inadequate care into their writing.
✗ It was found that he wanted to be an engineer.
✔ Brian wanted to be an engineer.

8 Edit your work
Good writing is subject to **constant editing**. Native speakers who write well always have to edit their writing. This is critical to good expression (see chapter 15).

> **An authentic example of a problematic piece of postgraduate student writing**
>
> Because the economy of each country is becoming a close relationship and every country need depend on some aspect of the economy in other country more or less every country needs these people who have the experience of studying overseas in order to develop the business with other countries.
>
> This is neither clear nor well written.
>
> **Suggested rewrite**
> <u>Globalisation has</u> affected the relationship between different countries and their economies. Each country's economy has a close relationship with the economies of other countries. Every country needs and depends on some aspect of the economy of other countries. For example ... [incomplete]
>
> There are two main reasons why globalisation is important. Every country needs people who have the experience of studying overseas. This experience helps to develop business with other countries [and this, in turn, improves local businesses]. Secondly ... [argument continues]

Notice how each sentence in the rewrite is short and begins with a noun phrase with the main verb nearby.

● 3 Misunderstandings about writing

As noted above, international students who use ESL often mistakenly believe that writing in an 'academic' way and writing in a complicated way are the same.

Nothing could be further from the truth. Clear writing is *always* best. Academic ideas are complex enough. Don't make them more complex by using too many embedded clauses that you cannot grammatically control. *No lecturer will ever fail your work for being too simple and clearly expressed.*

Of course, as you develop your writing skills, you will eventually be able to control your sentences better, and this will lead to more complex sentence structure. While you are learning, though, always **keep things simple**. The structure of a good English sentence is as follows:

Subject–Verb–Object (sometimes the object is not present)

If you keep to this structure and you keep your sentences short, you will inevitably produce much clearer and more coherent sentences. An added advantage of this approach is that grammatical mistakes are easier to spot and avoid.

The selfish reader

Often international students have very different expectations about the style and purpose of writing. They bring these expectations to their postgraduate studies overseas. Look at the two diagrams below:

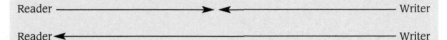

The first diagram represents the reader making some attempt to understand the writer's meaning by **interpreting** his or her work. This might be called the **'writing for a generous reader' principle**. The second diagram represents a situation in which the reader makes no attempt to understand the writer's intended meaning. Everything has to be made perfectly clear for the reader. The reader does not think or work at all. This might be called the **'writing for a selfish reader' principle**.

In western countries, academic writing is usually evaluated on the basis of the 'selfish reader' principle. This attitude by readers is not meant to be mean-spirited and nasty. Lecturers often evaluate how clearly students can communicate ideas and how well they can make something complex really simple and clear. Students are graded accordingly. If lecturers have to work hard at trying to understand the students' thoughts or sentences, they deduct marks or fail the assignment. Later we shall see that there is a useful fiction that can be adopted in ensuring you write for the 'selfish reader'. (See the high school test, below).

4 Writing sentences: readability

What does it mean when lecturers complain that your work is 'unreadable'? It means that your work 'doesn't flow'. But what does this mean? There are several causes for lack of readability and we have already covered some of them with the eight tips, above, but more tips can be added. Here is a comprehensive list of the causes of unreadability:

- there are too many unnecessarily complex and long words;
- abbreviations are used which are unknown or unclear;
- sentences are overly complex and long;
- the passive voice is overused;
- subjects appear too late in sentences;
- pronouns are used confusingly;
- noun phrases are positioned badly;
- punctuation is used incorrectly;
- there are no clear connections between sentences themselves;
- paragraphs and text structure are weak;
- font choice, spacing and other presentation issues make comprehension difficult.

Poor readability is often the reason why students fail assignments. Let's have a look at some of these reasons in detail.

Often the cause of unreadability is the misplacement of noun phrases.

What is a noun phrase?

A noun phrase can be:

1 a noun
2 a noun + modifier combination
3 a pronoun

Any of these can function as the subject of a sentence. Examples (noun phrases are in *italics*):

- *Carbon emissions* are on the way up.
- *A barrister* earns a lot of money.
- *The increase in terrorism* will continue for some time.
- *Excessive attention to your share portfolio* may mean that you miss other investment opportunities.
- *We* are not going to press the point in the meeting.

Noun phrases carry the main subject or information of the sentence. Because of this they are essential for good readability. However, the placement and number of noun phrases in a sentence is critical.

Each underlined unit in the sentence below is a noun phrase. However, the example below is overloaded. Notice how much information is contained in these noun phrases.

An example of an unreadable sentence

One of the <u>first things</u> that should be done in <u>the evaluation of structural equation models</u> is an <u>assessment of the adequacy of input data</u> and <u>the statistical assumption underlying any estimation methods</u> used in <u>the analysis</u> (Bagozzi & Yi , 1988, p. 76).

Note that this was written by a native English speaker! I'll return to this example and improve it. Right now, let's look at what makes for a more readable sentence.

1 Put given information before new information
- *Given information* = noun phrases in a sentence that refer to concepts/objects already mentioned or understood from the context.
- *New information* = noun phrases that refer to concepts/objects not yet mentioned.

Given information before new information

When we read and/or listen, we constantly try to attach new information to old information. However, our short-term memory can only hold seven (+ or - 2) pieces of information at one time before it gets overloaded. The trick with sentence writing is not to overload the reader's memory.

Example
Version A below overloads the reader's short-term memory because: (a) the sentence is too long; (b) there are too many noun phrases; and (c) it is also hard to tell the new information from the old information.

Version A:
   Many procedures to assess the adequacy of input data and test underlying assumptions of estimation measures were taken.

Version B:
   Many procedures were taken to assess the adequacy of input data. This included testing underlying assumptions and estimation measures.

Why is **Version B** better? Firstly, it comprises two sentences rather than one. This reduces the problem of compounding nouns. Another reason is that the given information and new information have been separated. The given information is the 'procedures'. The new information is what was involved in the carrying out the procedures (i.e. testing underlying assumptions and estimation measures).

   Many procedures were taken to assess the adequacy of input data [given information]. This included testing underlying assumptions and estimation measures [new information].

2 Put 'light' noun phrases before 'heavy' noun phrases

Noun phrases vary in length and complexity. 'Light' noun phrases are short and simple. Examples:

- *Carbon emissions* are on the way up.
- A *barrister* earns a lot of money
- *We* are not going to press the point in the meeting.

'Heavy' noun phrases are long and complicated:

- *A measure of the distance in multidimensional space is known as Mahalanobis distance, which is the distance of each observation from the mean centre of the observations.*

To make sentences more readable, place light noun phrases before heavy noun phrases whenever possible.

- *Mahalanobis distance* [light] is a *measure of observations taken and where they are taken from* [heavy]. To be specific, *it* [light] is *the distance in multidimensional space of observations* [heavy]. This *measurement* [light] is normally taken from *the mean centre of observations* [heavy].

> Notice how much more readable the text is when there are several shorter sentences rather than one long one, and when light noun phrases are placed before heavy noun phrases.

Now let's return to the example given before:

- One of the *first things* that should be done in *the evaluation of structural equation models* is an *assessment of the adequacy of input data* and *the statistical assumption underlying any estimation methods* used in *the analysis* (Bagozzi and Yi, 1988, p. 76).

I'd suggest the following, putting light noun phrases before heavy ones and splitting the sentence into two:

- One of the *first things* [light] that should be done in the *evaluation of structural equation models* is an *assessment of the adequacy of input data* [heavy]. Another *important consideration* [light] is the *statistical assumption* underlying any *estimation methods used in the analysis* [heavy] (Bagozzi and Yi, 1988, p. 76).

3 Unclear use of pronouns

Sentences that begin with a direct reference to the subject are often clearer than those that begin with a pronoun.

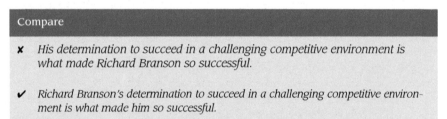

Compare

✗ *His determination to succeed in a challenging competitive environment is what made Richard Branson so successful.*

✔ *Richard Branson's determination to succeed in a challenging competitive environment is what made him so successful.*

Richard Branson is the subject. Don't make the reader work through lots of text to get to his name, and be careful with pronouns replacing his name. This is especially important in long sentences.

Students often make the mistake of thinking that the reader will understand everything they are talking about, and they assume that they can leave out details. Unfortunately, this often results in incomprehensible work. An example of this is not ensuring a clear connection between pronouns and their associated nouns.

> *The list consists of the names of Australian importing companies, their addresses, telephone numbers, and the person to contact. The details are important for many reasons.*

Which details are important? The names of companies? Their addresses? Their telephone numbers? Or all of the details provided? It is better to **specify the subject**, in this case:

> *The list consists of the names of Australian importing companies, their addresses, telephone numbers, and the person to contact. The names of the companies are important for many reasons.*

4 Put the subject of the sentence early in the sentence

Many problems in readability arise from having long clauses before the subject of the sentence. This can only be done well if one is very confident and capable in the English language and if one does not overload the reader's memory. It is usually better to make the subject of the sentence clear by putting it early in the sentence.

> <u>*In order to go through how the information system influences the investors' decisions,*</u> *an example will be given to display the whole process of decision making.*

The subject of the sentence is 'an example'; the long embedded clause before the subject is underlined. A better rewrite of the sentence involves **repeating the subject** in a new sentence, as follows:

> *An example will be given to display the whole process of decision making. This example shows how the information system influences investors' decisions.*

Putting the subject earlier in the sentence, near the main verb, greatly improves readability. It is a good idea to begin your sentences with your subject. Keep the main verb right next to the subject. You can start a sentence with a short word or phrase like 'however', 'firstly' or 'to begin with' before the subject, but while you are learning to write clearly, **avoid long embedded clauses** before the subject of the sentence.

I have found that this advice reduces grammatical problems greatly. Many grammatical problems simply **disappear** when students write simple sentences. This is because students can **control** these sentences better. Well-controlled and clear sentences ultimately mean better marks!

Remember these rules for readability

- put given information before new information;
- put light noun phrases before heavy noun phrases;
- put the subject early in the sentence and repeat the subject in a new sentence if necessary;
- ensure a clear connection between subjects and their pronouns;
- have several shorter sentences rather than one long sentence.

● 5 Writing paragraphs

Everyone thinks that they can write a paragraph. After all, it is one of the basic things we learn at school. However, in helping students with their work, I often see evidence that paragraphing skills have been forgotten, or at least not learnt well. Bad paragraphing is intimately connected with bad writing. This section is designed to remind you of these important skills.

1 What is a paragraph?

A paragraph is a unit of *ideas:* there should be only *one* new idea in each paragraph. Good paragraphs exhibit two features:

- **Coherence**: everything in the paragraph fits together; there are no 'loose' or disconnected sentences.
- **Unity**: there is only one main idea.

These features are not as easy to achieve as it might seem. I frequently see paragraphs that start well but then lose focus and go off at a tangent. This can also be seen in the work of native English speakers. I will give some examples in this section.

Paragraphs

- are the <u>building blocks</u> of writing;
- provide <u>logical breaks </u>in subject matter;
- <u>aid reading</u> by breaking up the text into units;
- <u>develop ideas.</u>

---

2 Key features of a well-written paragraph (1)

- A topic sentence is present. This sets up expectations for the reader.
- Only *one* idea is developed in a good paragraph, i.e. the paragraph has <u>unity</u>.
- The sentences follow each other in a logical sequence in a good paragraph. i.e. the paragraph has <u>coherence</u>.
- The sentences in a good paragraph develop the topic sentence by giving evidence, facts and examples (i.e. the paragraph contains <u>support</u>).

3 Key features of a well-written paragraph (2)

- The length of paragraphs can vary considerably depending on the purpose and length of the document overall.
- Paragraphs that are too long are hard to read.
- Paragraphs that are too short make writing 'choppy', like a shopping list.
- Sentence lengths within a paragraph should vary.

Test of a paragraph

Do this little test. Put all your sentences in a paragraph in your essay or report on the left. A well-written paragraph should be a mixture of longish (but not too long!) sentences and short sentences.

It should look like this: *Not* like:

_____   _____
_____   _____
_____   _____
_____   _____
_____   _____
_____   _____
_____   _____

A simple example

- In an imperfect capital market share prices across firms are different. Some studies prove this empirically. Dyl and Elliot (2006) examined cross-sectional share-price variation in 1976–2001 in the US markets. While other academics study Hong Kong, New Zealand and Swiss equity markets in 1994 (Angel, 1997), Dyl et al. (2002) also examine cross-sectional share-price variation traded on the Australian Stock Exchange in 1995. Based on a sample of 468 firms in the Australian market, they show mean and median stock prices to be $2.80 and $1.58. This is a significant finding. They also show that there is a large percentage difference between share prices that are greater than $3 and less than $1. This is also a significant finding. This cross-sectional variation across markets and countries shows that firms do not choose the level of share price arbitrarily.

The above paragraph starts with a clear **topic sentence** (underlined) that guides the paragraph. This sentence has only *one* idea: *In an imperfect capital market share prices across firms are different.* The paragraph has *unity*. It does not discuss the trading of shares or the impact of share prices, or anything else. The supporting sentences give examples of *share variability*. This is *all* the paragraph discusses. The paragraph has *coherence*. The examples given are the **supporting sentences**.

> **Note:** As in this example, all academic writing requires support for the claims made in topic sentences, unless this information is obvious or well known.

In addition, the sentences in the paragraph are a mixture of long and short sentences (*long, short, long, short, short*). It is a good and elegant paragraph.

Topic sentences can *occur anywhere* in a paragraph, not always at the beginning. They can even occur at both the start and finish. However, if you are learning how to write well in English it is best to keep the topic sentence at the start of the paragraph, until you get more confidence in using the language.

Compare the examples: which is best?

- (A): Human Resource Management (HRM) policies affect certain immediate organisational outcomes and have long-term consequences. For example, policy choices made by managers affect the overall competence of employees, the commitment of employees, the degree of congruence between the goals of employees and those of the organisation, and the overall cost-effectiveness of HRM practices. These four Cs are not exhaustive of the criteria that HRM policy-makers may find useful in evaluating the effectiveness of human resource management. However, they are reasonably comprehensive.

- (B): Post-heroic leadership still requires many of the attributes that have always distinguished the best leaders – intelligence, commitment, energy, courage of conviction, integrity. But here's the difference: it expects those qualities of just about everyone in the organisation. The time when a few rational managers ran everything with rational numbers, it seems, was just an anomaly, or part of an era very different from the fast-paced, continually shifting present. Now we are back to the real **self-reliant** democratic stuff of the kind envisioned by Jefferson and his friends when they were trying to craft a new reality out of chaos and change. As in that era, those who cling to the past are in danger of losing their way, while the pioneers who forge ahead are most likely to claim the future.

We can see that (A) has some unity and coherence. The topic sentence is *the consequences of HRM policies:* otherwise known as the four 'Cs':

- <u>HRM policies affect certain immediate organisational outcomes and have long-term consequences.</u> For example, policy choices made by managers affect the overall *competence* of employees, the *commitment* of employees, the degree of *congruence* between the goals of employees and those of the organisation and the overall *cost-effectiveness* of HRM practices. <u>These four Cs are not exhaustive of the criteria that HRM policy makers may find useful in evaluating the effectiveness of human resource management.</u> However, they are reasonably comprehensive.

Paragraph (B) goes off at a tangent to discuss all kinds of things unrelated to the idea of *the attributes of leadership*. It discusses changes in management styles, the 'shifting present' (whatever that is), the pace of change, American President Jefferson, the attempt to craft 'new reality out of chaos', the dangers of 'clinging to the past'. Read it again carefully:

In reading example (B) it is natural to ask oneself: *what is the point?* If this question cannot be answered it is likely that the paragraph is badly written.

Concluding sentences are optional in good paragraph writing but it is sometimes very helpful for the reader (especially if the paragraph is long, complex or detailed). It is always better to write shorter and clearer paragraphs. This avoids the need for concluding sentences.

6 Paragraphing rules

There are no firm rules on how to organise paragraphs in an essay, but the following ideas are good advice:

- aim for three to five or more sentences per paragraph;
- include on each double-spaced page about two handwritten or three typed paragraphs (as a guide);
- make your paragraphs proportional to your paper. If you are writing a 100,000-word Ph.D. thesis your paragraphs can often be longer and more detailed than if you are writing a 1000-word essay;
- if you have a few very short paragraphs, think about whether they are really parts of a larger paragraph and can be combined, *or whether you can add details to support each point and thus make each into a more fully developed paragraph.*

How to develop a paragraph

There are many ways to develop a paragraph, limited only by your imagination and your purpose. The following are common:

- using examples and illustrations ;
- citing data (facts, statistics, evidence, details and other data) ;
- examining testimony (what other people say, i.e. quotes and paraphrases);
- using anecdotes or stories;
- defining terms;
- comparing and contrasting ideas;
- evaluating causes and reasons;
- examining effects and consequences;
- analysing the topic;
- describing the topic;
- offering a chronology of an event.

7 Kinds of paragraphs

The following kinds of paragraphs are common in academic writing. Different language is used for each, and examples of each are given below:

- classification;
- comparison and contrast;
- process (sequence);
- definition;
- description;
- choice;
- explanation;
- evaluation;
- a combination of methods

Classification and comparison/contrast

Classification	Comparison/contrast
is a kind of ...	is similar to ...
can be divided into ...	On the other hand ...
is a type of ...	both ...
falls under ...	However ...
belongs to ...	but ...
is a part of ...	while ...
fits into ...	In contrast ...
is grouped with ...	As well ...
is related to ...	differs from ...
is associated with ...	Unlike ...

Process and definition

Process	Definition
First(ly)/second(ly) ...	Is a kind of ...
Recently ...	Can be defined as ...
in the beginning ...	Is like ...
Previously ...	Is similar to ...
Before ...	
Afterwards ...	
Then ...	
When ...	
After ...	
Finally ...	
Lastly/ at last ...	
Subsequently ...	

Description and choice

Description	Choice
Resembles ...	In my opinion ...
Above the ...	I like/dislike ...
Below the ...	I believe ...
The purpose of ...	In my view ...
Besides the ...	I feel ...
Next to the ...	My understanding is ...
Is like ...	I think that ...
	I consider that ...
	It seems to me that ...
	I prefer ...

Explanation and evaluation

Explanation	Evaluation
Because ...	I suggest ...
Therefore ...	I recommend ...
Since ...	I advise ...
Thus ...	In my view ...
as a result of ...	Comparing this shows ...
Consequently ...	
is due to ...	
hence ...	
it follows that ...	
if, then ...	

8 Transitions between paragraphs

The transition from one paragraph to the next should 'flow' smoothly. There are two ways of doing this:

- take an idea from the end of one paragraph and use it to start the next;
- use transition words to signal the direction your writing is taking.

Example

Unlike in many European countries, multiple voting shares do not exist in Thailand. Thai law prohibits the issuance of such shares. Therefore, when I identify who owns and controls the sample firms, I focus only on <u>three control mechanisms</u>, namely, direct, pyramidal, and cross-shareholdings.

<u>The first form of control mechanism,</u> 'direct ownership', refers to the ownership of shares by a shareholder who owns shares under his own name or via a private company owned by him. 'Indirect ownership' is when a company is owned via other public firms or a chain of public firms. ...

(In this example, the first form of control mechanism has been carried over to the second paragraph, thus creating a smooth transition.)

Indentations between paragraphs

There are two methods of indentations between paragraphs. If your lecturer does not specify a preference, choose one of these methods and use it consistently. Do not use both together.

Either at the start, 1 cm indent   *or* space between

_____   _____
_____   _____
_____   _____
   _____
_____   _____
_____   _____

To sum up:
- keep paragraphs unified and coherent;
- have one topic sentence per paragraph and stick to the topic;
- mix the length of sentences;
- don't write paragraphs that are too long (around 3 paragraphs per double-spaced page);
- use transition signals in and between paragraphs (and 'carry over' the idea);
- provide an indent OR space between paragraphs.

● 9 Using English tenses

Why are English tenses so hard to learn?

Many of the writing problems international students have concern the misuse of tenses. This is not surprising. English tenses are complex. The language has three main tenses (present, past and future), though these are made more complex by the presence of simple, perfect and continuous forms.

International students find English tenses hard to use because *some languages do not use tenses*. Mandarin, for example, indicates the time of an event: they say the English equivalent of 'I go to shop **yesterday**', instead of 'I *went* to the shop', or 'I *have already been* to the shop'. It makes the time of an event clear by the addition of the adverbs 'today' or 'yesterday'. Japanese and Korean use adverbial particles. Other languages use word order to indicate time.

English has a complex system of tenses that must be learnt. This complex system is one reason why English is such a powerful and precise language. Find a grammar book that explains the different tenses in a way that is readily accessible to you. Keep it close by when you are writing and consult it whenever you are unclear about what tense you should be using or how to use a particular tense.

There are, however, some uses of English tenses particular to academic writing that are worth mentioning here.

When the past is 'present'

In academic writing, we often use the present tense to describe literature that has been published in the past. The rationale for this is simple: if it is ideas we are discussing – not experiments, surveys, or things that are 'finished' or completed – and the ideas are still being evaluated or used, then they are considered 'present' (even if they were published a long time ago). If these ideas are still being discussed it is normal to use the present tense for this.

> Jones (1998) argues that ... (not 'argued')
> Smith (1966) claims that ... (not 'claimed')

It is assumed that Smith and Jones still believe their own ideas, even now! By contrast, if Smith or Jones did experiments in 1998 and 1966, we would use the past tense for this, because, unlike their ideas, their experiments are completed events:

> *Jones (1998) used three subjects in his experiment. Results indicated that ...*

This practice is not consistent in some academic journals. For example, in some Finance journals, the present tense is sometimes used even for past, completed events:

> *In their experiment, Jones and Harris (1990) find that the yield spread between the long rate and short rate is an optimal predictor of future changes of short rates over the life of the long bond.*

Keep the normal conventions of 'present' for ideas, and 'past' for completed things, as noted above, but, if in doubt, follow the tense conventions of your subject. Check the academic journals in your subject to see what tense conventions they use.

There are countless websites available on English tenses. Below is a selection of sites that I consider worth investigating. They include useful links, diagrams and even cartoons. The last one listed is an excellent interactive CD-ROM:

- Englishpage (URL: http://www.englishpage.com/index.html);
- English grammar online for you (URL: http://www.ego4u.com/en/cram-up/grammar/tenses);
- English tenses with cartoons (URL: http://www.englishtenseswithcartoons.com/);
- Tensebuster (URL: http://www.clarity.com.hk/program/tensebuster.htm).

10 Summary

Perhaps the most serious problem that international postgraduate students have with their writing is producing long sentences that are unreadable. Often this arises from the idea that 'academic' writing must be complex, long and sophisticated. Writing long, complex and sophisticated sentences often leads to disaster for students who are weak in English. Correcting this problem leads to clearer sentences and clearer assignments. Other common problems that affect the clarity and readability of international students' writing are poor paragraph structure and the incorrect use of tenses. Focusing on these key areas of improvement will dramatically improve your writing style, and give you higher marks.

10 Writing Critical Reviews: A Step-by-Step Guide

● 1 Introduction

A critical review (sometimes called a **summary and critique**) is similar to a literature review (see chapter 14), except it is a review of *one* article. This is an important piece of assessment that is more difficult than it may appear.

The process of critically reviewing an article can seem intimidating. How, you may worry, can you think of things to say about an article written by an expert? What if you can't find anything to 'criticise'? How will you avoid just producing a summary? Also, how should you structure the review? This chapter provides step-by-step instructions on how to do this.

● 2 A procedure for writing a critical review

Step 1: Skim read the article to get a general idea of what it is about. (This should take you about 10–15 minutes or less (see chapter 4).

Step 2: Discuss the article with someone else. Write down its general ideas or themes. Discussing the article may clarify your understanding and trigger some initial ideas.

Step 3: Read the article again and take notes of the important details: the *subject/s* of the article, the *conclusion/s*, and the *arguments* and/or *data* that the writer uses to reach these conclusion/s. Then check your notes with someone else. Make a note of differences and similarities in the points you have written down, and if there are major differences, go back and check the article.

Step 4: Look at the main points of the article once more. Check that your notes 'agree' with the points raised by the author – you should be able to point to passages from the text confirming that your notes are accurate. Draw a 'flow' diagram of the article, using the main points of each paragraph. The aim of the diagram is to show the relationships between the main points in the article. You might consider doing an argument map (see chapter 8).

Step 5: Put the article aside and think about what you have read. Good critical review writing requires careful deliberation and clear thinking. Don't be afraid to have a strong response to the argument of the article.

Step 6: Reread your notes and look at the diagram you have made. Are there any *criticisms* you can make about the article? (These can include questions, doubts, disagreements, and so on.) You are *not* criticising the *author* here, only the points raised in the article. These criticisms could include:

- the theoretical claims being made;
- the evidence used;
- the case method used;
- the statistical support used;
- the use of other writers' arguments.

Now, can you think of anything you *agree with* in the article? Perhaps you can think of a further application of one of the writer's ideas, for example. Any strong response that you have to the article is generally useful. When you have finished, check your criticisms and agreements with those of another person. Note that for *every* academic article there is always something to clarify, criticise or take issue with. No piece of writing is ever perfect, even if it is written by international experts.

Step 7: Start writing the introduction to your review. This should constitute about ten per cent of the total word count of your review. It should be short and largely in your own words.

3 What to include in a critical review

You will need to include in the introduction:

- a *general overview* of the article;
- an overview of *your review* (your approach to the article);
- an anticipation of *your conclusion* (what will you say about the major ideas expressed in the article).

In introducing the article, you should mention the author's name and the title of the article, as well as referencing the article using a conventional referencing system. (A bibliography listing the complete reference details should be included at the end of your review).

> In this paper I will discuss chapter 2 of Ballard and Clanchy's book: *Study Abroad: A Manual for Asian Students* [*give reference*]. Ballard and Clanchy's chapter is about [*say what it is about*]. In particular, they argue that [*list the main points*]. After summarising Ballard and Clanchy's main points, I shall be claiming that [*give a general overview of your main criticisms* – ***don't*** *give any details here*]. In concluding, I shall show that [*give a quick outline of* ***your*** *conclusion about the subject*].

Note that there are many variations in the kind of expression that can be used here, but they must make essentially the same points: (1) introduce the material being reviewed; (2) sum up the main idea discussed in the review; (3) point out the evidence for the idea discussed; (4) outline your criticisms of that idea and the evidence for it; (5) state your own conclusion on the topic.

Step 8: Next, write the body of the review. This must consist of both summary and criticism sections in roughly equal proportions. The summary of arguments of the writer must come first, followed by the critique (as you need the summary to understand the critique), although some critical reviews split their review up into an overall summary of the position of the writer, and then detailed summaries of specific arguments; i.e. they summarise an argument and then critique it, before moving on to the next argument and critique. The important thing is to *balance* your criticisms with an adequate summary of the author's work.

● 4 Nine things to remember in writing your critical review

1 You need to demonstrate that you have read the article, so it is useful to give quotations from or paraphrase a part of the article. However, remember: don't make the quotations too long and don't quote too often. Only quote when you can't say a point better in your own words, or when you are trying to prove to the reader that the writer did in fact say something. As we saw in chapter 5, a quotation should not normally exceed three lines of text.

2 Ensure that you summarise the main points in the article fully. If the author has 1 major theme and 5 sub-themes your summary should show this.

3 Don't just write 'X says that ... but I think that ...'. Provide details of the work and spell out each point fully, using your own examples where possible. If you can think of implications that you think follow from the ideas, spell these out too. However, make it clear when you are summarising the *writer's* ideas and when you are stating using your *own* ideas! (See 'Critical review language', later in this chapter).

4 When spelling out the points don't assume that the reader has also read the article and knows what you are referring to. Your review must be able to **stand on its own**. The reader should be able to gain a reasonably full understanding of the contents of the article by reading your critical review.

5   Don't be afraid of *criticising* the text. If you think that a point is wrong, say so and give reasons. Equally, don't be **hypercritical** (critical of everything). If you agree with point X but disagree with point Y, say so. Similarly, if you agree with a point but only to a certain extent, say so. In fact, a good part of your summary should be devoted to *distinguishing* those points that have merit and those that do not. Remember that no article is perfect on all dimensions! Every article has both something wrong with it as well as something that is good about it.

6   The body should make up 80 per cent of your review. Dedicate at least one paragraph to each main point and use topic sentences, examples/elaborations and concluding sentences in each paragraph. You should easily be able to write one page, but do not write empty sentences or repeat yourself. If you can't think of anything to say, look at your notes or read the article again.

7   Use critical review language (see later in this chapter) *almost to the point of excess.* The language will prevent you from simply writing a summary. Try to use *at least* two critical review phrases in each paragraph.

8   Use connectors ('firstly', 'secondly', 'moreover', 'furthermore', 'on the other hand'). Make sure you guide the reader through the body of your review. The reader should never have to wonder 'Where is all this going?'

9   The body of the review is the place for solid details and argument. Write as fully and completely as you can.

Step 9: Once you have written the body of the review, you need to write the conclusion. This should constitute about 10 per cent of the review and should include a brief recap of the main points raised in the body of the review, noting where you have agreed and disagreed with the author. You may also use your conclusion to give suggestions for further research work, or the contexts in which the work you have reviewed can be used. See the example below. **Note the change in tense**.

> In this review, I have discussed Ballard and Clanchy's book: *Study Abroad: A Manual for Asian Students.* The review covers several points [*give list of points*]. I have argued that while they are right that [*give examples of where you agree with them*], this does not mean that [*give your criticisms*]. My overall view of Ballard and Clanchy's paper is that [*sum up your main views*].

Step 10: Leave your critique on your desk for a day or two before looking at it again. Carefully edit and proofread it before submitting it (see chapter 15).

> **Note:** Make sure that you are clear about the use of surnames. Bibliographies are always alphabetical by surname, so you must put the surname *first*. When you write literature reviews or essays, you always *refer* to people by their surname: 'Smith argues ...'; 'Jones claims ...', etc. This is always true, unless, of course, you are introducing them: 'Professor John Smith, Head of the Department of Engineering claims that ...' (afterwards, you just say: 'Smith'). For how to identify surnames and given names in the library, see the chapter on **Information Literacy** on the website.

● 5 Example of a critical review

Look at the example below. It is an excerpt from a summary and critique of chapter 2 of the widely read book *Study Abroad: A Manual for Asian Students* by Ballard and Clanchy (1984). Borrow this book, read the chapter, and then read the critical review below (note that another example of a critical review on this topic is available at http://arts.monash.edu.au/aallu/resources-good-crit-review.pdf).

Notice four things about the review below:

- It is carefully balanced, with approximately 50 per cent for summary and 50 per cent for critique or criticism. (The summary comes before the critique, otherwise the critique would not make sense).
- The review is written for people who have not read the original article. Note the clarity of expression and the short sentences.
- Note that not all the criticism is unfavourable: some of the responses are generally positive, suggesting that Ballard and Clanchy have a good point, but it needs to be refined.
- Note that the language used is very forceful and direct. There is no vagueness or uncertainty in what the author wants to argue.
- *Surnames* are used for reference identification, *not given names.*
- Notice the use of critical language and the directness of the point of view being expressed by the writer. I have underlined this use of language for you.

Note: I have written 'summary' and 'critique' to show where the different parts of the review occur, though this would *not* normally appear in the final version.

Summary

In chapter 2 of their book *Study Abroad: A Manual for Asian Students* (1985), <u>Ballard and Clanchy argue that</u> international students 'often bring different purposes to their thinking and learning'. <u>They claim that</u> such students look at academic tasks differently from their lecturers at western universities. <u>They use an example of</u> a Japanese economics student's response to an essay topic. The student's essay topic was: *Compare Friedman's views of economic policy in post-war Europe with those of Samuelson.* How would a Japanese student and their western instructor approach this topic?

<u>Ballard and Clanchy show</u> that the Japanese student's response to the topic was very different from how the lecturer themselves would respond to the topic if they were writing about it. Whereas the lecturer would have responded to the topic by evaluating and analysing the respective views of the theorists, the student's response was merely an outline of bibliographic data about the theorists. They provided no coverage of their theoretical ideas. The difference in approaches was stark. <u>Ballard and Clanchy explain that</u> the student felt that his way of approaching the topic was consistent with how he

would be expected to do the task in a Japanese university. This was very different from the expectations required by their western instructor ... .

Ballard and Clanchy claim that, in Asian countries (but also other countries), there is an emphasis on only the 'reproductive' approach. International students, such as those from Japan and other Asian countries, are required to change their learning styles when they move to a western country to study. In particular, they are required to become 'more critical' and 'analytical' in their approach to assignments. Ballard and Clanchy view this difference as one of the central, and most difficult adjustments that international students have to face when studying overseas.

The authors use the work of Robert Kaplan to justify their assertions. Kaplan (1966) is famous for arguing that there exist five intercultural variations in expository paragraphs. The English pattern is 'linear' and moves directly from the central idea or 'thesis statement' to explanations and examples supporting that thesis. By contrast, the Oriental pattern he describes as an 'approach by indirection'. Kaplan shows that the Oriental approach involves 'sentences moving round the topic ... and avoiding any explicit judgement or conclusion'. According to Ballard and Clancy, Kaplan's idea of intercultural variations partly explains the differences between the Japanese student's approach to the essay topic, and the expectations of the lecturer. Asian students, they claim, tend to write 'around' a topic using extraneous details (e.g. bibliographic information of theorists), and avoid tackling the topic head on. By contrast, Westerners, using the English style of paragraph writing, approach topics very directly, concentrating on classifying the main arguments and assertions into groups and assessing the evidence for them. They avoid extraneous detail.

Ballard and Clanchy assert that international students who intend to study in an English-speaking country have to do more than come prepared with adequate English skills. According to them, they need 'to develop a more analytical and critical approach to learning'. This involves learning a different approach to writing, and a different approach to thinking. Emphasis needs to be placed on criticism of ideas and analysis of information. International students need to move from 'reproductive' learning to 'analytical' learning.

Critique

Are Ballard and Clanchy right? Do Asian students think in a very different way from their western instructors? What is the evidence for this view? The case studies provided by Kaplan are interesting, but the examples he provides are very small in number, only a few examples of each intercultural variation in paragraph structure are outlined and discussed. Is the example of the Japanese student typical or atypical? What evidence is there that Kaplan's intercultural profiles are widespread? Would a group of Vietnamese students, for example, respond in a similar way to the Japanese student? Clearly a systematic analysis of the alleged variations in thinking and writing patterns needs to be made using large groups of students from different cultural backgrounds. Kaplan does not do this, and Ballard and Clancy rely on Kaplan's work to assert their claims about international students.

A second point to note is that, even if there are intercultural differences in types of expository paragraph, as Kaplan asserts, it does not follow that there are intercultural differences in *thinking* patterns. Writing styles and thinking styles are arguably very different. Plausibly, international students may still *think* the same as their western counterparts, but not write in the same way. This would be unsurprising given that English is not their native language.

It can also be argued that there is an implied cultural bias in Ballard and Clanchy's work. Their tacit point appears to be that the western education system is superior to the Oriental system. Their claims about their model of learning styles provided are tantamount to suggesting that Asians are 'stuck' in 'reproductive' learning and westerners have advanced to 'analytical' and (sometimes) 'speculative' learning. This means, by implication, that Asian students are less intellectually developed than western students. But what is the evidence for this view? Does this necessarily follow from Kaplan's work?

(critique continues)

6 Critical review language

A common complaint lecturers make of students' work is that the student's 'voice' is not clear. By this, lecturers mean that students fail to state their perspectives and opinions directly, and that they don't incorporate the ideas of others in ways that indicate critical distance and analysis. At the same time, some lecturers criticise the use of the word 'I' in texts ('I think ...', 'I will present ...') and consider it inappropriate in academic writing. So, how can you write in a way that makes your voice clear?

1 Four tips for making your voice clear
1 Follow genre conventions
Follow genre conventions for assignments such as the essay, the literature review, the report, and the guidelines specified by your lecturer. In an argumentative essay, for example, you can do this by presenting your central argument and outlining your main supporting points in the introduction. (For genre conventions, see the sections of this book on the essay, literature review, report and annotated bibliography.)

2 Use appropriate connectives
The appropriate use of connectives ('first', 'likewise', 'therefore', 'indeed') can help, as they act as 'signposts' for the reader.

3 Use a variety of reporting verbs and expressions
This section provides you with a variety of terms and expressions you can use to introduce your positions and to refer to the ideas of others. Using this language will not only make your writing appear more critical; it will also help you to become more

critical about texts. It will mean you do more than just refer to ideas ('he states ...'/'she states ...'), and instead develop a habit of supporting, attacking, synthesising, questioning, summarising and contrasting ideas. This is what lecturers and supervisors want!

4 Appropriate use of language
As you consider the language presented below, pay close attention to the often subtle but significant differences between terms. Be aware also that some of these examples will be considered inappropriate for some disciplines (e.g. social science and empirical science subjects tend to avoid expressions using the first person.) You may need to consult written work in your own discipline to be sure which examples are acceptable.

2 Reporting verbs
Use a range of reporting verbs to indicate your ability to analyse the views of others:

	discusses	
	examines	
	explores	
	investigates	
	questions	
	undermines	+ noun phrase
	refers to	
	attacks	
	supports	
Author's surname	presents	
	dismisses	
The article		
	states	
He/she	asserts	
	argues maintains	
	explains	
	claims	
	implies	
	affirms	
	assumes	+ that + clause
	notes	
	accepts	
	acknowledges	
	adds	
	admits	
	agrees	
	concedes	
	denies	
	predicts	

Present tense or past tense?

The verbs listed above are all in the present simple tense, because the **present simple** tense is most often used when referring to the ideas of others. Writers generally use the present simple even when the information was published a very long time ago and the writers are dead. The *ideas* are still alive, that is, they are still being used or evaluated and are therefore still considered present.

Using the past simple ('Smith presented') is not always wrong, however, and it is necessary for some action verbs (*discovered, realised*) and for references to experiments, surveys and other actions that took place *in the past*. When proofreading your work, always check you have used tenses correctly and consistently.

3 Reporting expressions

The expressions presented in this section are useful examples to help you write critical reviews and literature reviews. This chapter provides a 'checklist' for you – make sure that you have used *at least some* of the following terms in your own work. Make sure that you *vary* the examples in your own work – don't just use one or two. The following expressions are commonly used when reporting the ideas of others or expressing your own views on the ideas of others.

> **Note:** where >>>>>> appear, the variations given in the example above it can also be used. Square brackets [...] indicate that words can be either used or omitted. Obliques (/) indicate that any one of the given alternatives is acceptable.

Learning tip

There are thousands of other variations used in critical review language. Consult academic textbooks to see and learn more!

1 Stating your own position
'The aim of this paper is ...
'I shall be arguing/claiming/showing/highlighting/demonstrating that ...
'I want to argue that/claim that/show that/ highlight that/demonstrate that ...
'It will be argued in this paper/review/thesis that ...
'The point of this article is [to claim that] ...
'The view presented in this ... is that ...
'The argument/point of view expressed/put forward in this ... is that ...
'The conclusion I will be presenting is that ...
'The point of view argued for here is that ...
'The perspective presented here is that ...

2 Stating somebody else's view on a topic
'Jones thinks that ...

'Jones claims that ...
'Jones argues that ...
'Jones's claim is that ...
'Jones's point is that ...
'Jones's argument is that ...
'Jones's conclusion is that ...
'Jones's point of view is that ...
'According to Jones ...
'From Jones's point of view ...
'The point of Jones's article/paper is that ...
'The substance of Jones's article/paper is that ...
'The upshot of Jones's argument/paper/article is that ...
'Some theorists, such as Jones (1989) think that ...
'It is thought by some theorists, for example, Jones (1980) and Smith (1989) that ...'
'Jones's work/data allows him to draw the conclusion that ...
'Jones's work/data leads him to the conclusion that ...

3 **Attributing a view to another person (if you are not quite sure)**
'The point of Jones's article seems to be that ...
'Jones seems to be claiming that ...
'Jones's argument seems to be that ...
'Jones's claim seems to be that ...
'Jones's conclusion seems to be that ...

You can use any of the examples in (2) and add 'seems to'. There are a few **exceptions**: This cannot be done for the examples: 'From Jones's point of view ...', 'According to Jones ...' and 'It is thought by some theorists ...').

4 **Drawing a conclusion using the work of others**
'The conclusion of [all] this is that ...
'The result of [all] this is that ...
'A consequence of this is that ...
'An outcome of this is that ...
'An upshot of this is that ...
'... it can be seen/shown that ...
'Looking at Jones's work/argument [in detail] ...
'Analysing Jones's data shows that ...
'When Jones's argument is analysed, it can be seen that ...
'When Jones's work is looked at closely, it is seen that ...
'The following argument can be brought out of Jones's work ...
'The following point can be brought out of Jones's work ...
'Developing Jones's work/argument to its logical conclusion shows that ...
'Using the work of Jones (1980) and Smith (1989), it can be shown that .../argued that ...

'From Jones's work it can be determined that ...
'Using Jones's work, it is possible to show that .../argue that ...
'One possible consequence of Jones's work is [that] ...
'One outcome of Jones's work is [that] ...

5 Disagreeing with the views of others
'I do not agree [with Jones] that ...
'My argument against Jones is that ...
'My disagreement with Jones is that ...
'I will argue/shall be arguing against Jones's view that ...
'Against Jones, I will/shall be claiming/arguing/presenting the view that ...
'In contrast to Jones's view/argument/data ...
'Contrary to the views of Jones, I will/shall be/it will/shall be ...
'The argument being advanced here is opposed to that of Jones ...
'Unlike Jones, I want to suggest/claim/argue/propose ...
'Jones's arguments do not seem to work for the reason that ...
'Jones's data/arguments are faulty for the reason that ...
'It does not seem to follow from Jones's work/data that ...
'Problems arise in Jones's work [when it is seen that] ...
'Analyzing Jones's work in this way, it can be seen/one can see that ...
'The point I am making/being made [here] is that Jones's argument/data/conclusion
does not follow.

6 Agreeing with the views of others
'I agree with Jones's point [that] ...
'As Jones says ...
'This is also Jones's view ...
'Following from Jones's point ...
'Here I am following the work of Jones ...
'I will argue a similar view to that of Jones here.
'I agree with Jones in so far as ...
'In this matter, I am [largely] in agreement with Jones (1980).
'I agree with Jones in respect of his point [that] ...
'The argument being put forward/espoused here is similar to that of Jones (1980).
'Not unlike Jones (1980), I am suggesting/proposing/arguing ...
'The view I am putting forward here is largely in agreement with [that of] Jones.
'Along the lines of Jones (1980), I am suggesting/claiming/arguing/putting
forward ...

7 Pointing out assumptions
'This assumes that ...
'The following assumption is being made here ...
'The point being assumed here is that ...

'Jones assumes that ...
'Jones's assumption is that ...
'Jones's argument depends on the assumption/assumes one thing: ...
'One/An assumption of this view is that ...
'The assumption behind this view is [the point that] ...
'The assumption on which this depends is ...
'Assuming ... [then] it follows that ...

7 Annotated bibliographies

An **annotated bibliography** is similar to a critical review but far less detailed. In fact, an annotated review is usually only a summary (a **descriptive annotation**) but can sometimes contain a very brief critical one- or two-line commentary (an **analytical annotation**). A single annotated bibliography entry is written in the present tense and does not normally exceed 150 words.

The aim of an annotated bibliography is to provide more than simply a list of sources. It is to write something summarising the main point of each source. An annotated bibliography is therefore different from a critical review in that it provides a much shorter summary of a number of sources, sometimes hundreds. Think of an annotated bibliography as being a form of writing that is in-between a critical review (of one article) and a literature review (of many articles) (see chapter 14).

Descriptive annotations
Jones, Jeffrey M. (2000), 'The Assessment Debate'. *Parent Soup*, 6 December.

In this article the author supports the standardised multiple-choice test. He believes the professional test makers know how to create a good test for all students. He believes the tests are valid and reliable and can be trusted, as opposed to performance tests. Performance tests include essays that, as the author concludes, take too long to grade and cannot cover a wide variety of subjects. The format should be kept the same, and the high-stake associated with the test should remain in place. He believes people will complain, no matter what the format.

Analytical annotation
Hammer, M. (1990), 'Reengineering Work: Don't Automate, Obliterate'. *Harvard Business Review*, 68(4), pp. 104–142.

Hammer asserts the possibility of huge efficiency gains by eliminating unnecessary work activities through process analysis and redesign. The piece contains much strategic sense (the building of a resource-based organisation, with excellent capability advantages), and justly emphasises the primacy of 'process'. The author underestimates the socio-technical complexity of multidimensional organisational change, however, and gives unfortunate impetus to the phenomenon of downsizing (Beecham, 2006).

8 Summary

This chapter has outlined how to write critical reviews and annotated bibliographies, two of the common forms of assessment given to postgraduate students in university. Critical reviews and annotated bibliographies are not easy to write. They demand careful thinking and consideration. Each word is decided upon very carefully. The aim is clarity and succinctness. It is also very important to have some simple points that *you have thought about yourself.* Always remember that, as a postgraduate, originality in ideas will be a key determinant of your grade.

11 Writing an Empirical Report

● 1 Introduction

The report format is standard in style. It is important to be clear what a particular lecturer means by the word 'report' before you begin writing, as it is sometimes used ambiguously by lecturers. It is common in management subjects for 'report' to mean an argumentative essay (see chapter 13). In some subjects, such as Accounting, Physics or Biology, the report format described here is sometimes called a 'research paper', an 'experimental report', a 'formal report' or a 'formal project'.

● 2 The structure of a report

Your lecturer will probably show you what a typical report should look like, and how the sections should be organised. There may be particular requirements in different disciplines. You must follow your lecturer's requirements exactly. This chapter provides general information only.

Generally, reports have the following sections (weightings given are approximate only):

- **front matter** (this may include a confidentiality clause, table of contents, list of figures, list of abbreviations, etc.)
- *abstract* (or 'executive summary') [**5 per cent**]
- *introduction* and *literature review* (can be separated) [**20 per cent**]
- *methodology* (and sometimes, *procedure*) (can include a theoretical model) [**10 per cent**]
- *results/findings* (and sometimes, case study to make the results clear and practical) [**20–25 per cent**]
- *discussion/analysis* [**25–30 per cent**]
- *conclusions* and *limitations of research* [**10 per cent**]
- *recommendations* (can be combined with conclusion) [**10 per cent**]
- *appendices* [**0–5 per cent**]
- *reference list/bibliography*

The precise structure of a report will depend on the purpose for which it is intended. The above sections would cover the typical 'experimental' report format. If your report is a 'business report', or a 'case study-style report', then the 'literature review' and 'methodology' sections may not need to be included. If you were writing a business report for Bill Gates at Microsoft, it is unlikely that he would be interested in what the literature says. He is more likely to want a problem in the company solved, and want to know the cheapest way to do it! An empirical report differs in style from a business report and a case study-style report, as shown in the following diagram. (Major sections are included only, and the relative weighting of each section is approximate.) Note the similarities and differences:

- all reports have a separate abstract (usually called an executive summary in corporate reports);
- all reports have a proportionally large discussion or analysis section;
- corporate-style reports and case studies generally have 'recommendations' which are based on the analysis. Empirical-style reports do not possess these;
- empirical reports have literature review and methodology sections.

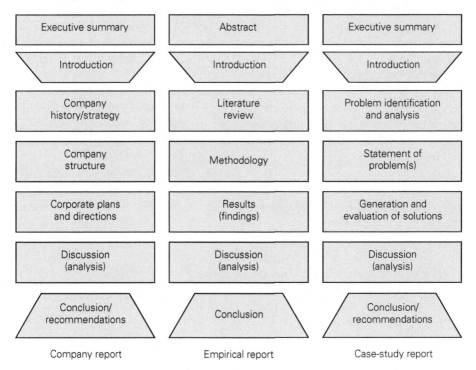

| Company report | Empirical report | Case-study report |

We will look at the general 'shape' of assignment writing, including writing funnel-style introductions and conclusions in chapter 13. For now, notice the following points which distinguish report writing from other assignments.

The report contains *objective* items (facts) in the **results** or **findings** section, and your justified and supported *opinions* in the **analysis** or **discussion** section. The **recommendations** section can also contain your personal viewpoint, but only on the information supported by the conclusions you have reached. Don't mix up findings, conclusions and recommendations, as they serve quite different functions (see 'conclusions and limitations' and 'recommendations', below).

Make sure the pages look attractive and ensure they are easy to follow. Include a lot of white space, spacing between sections and wide margins on each page. Separate each main section by using a new page.

Take a great deal of care in the preparation of the report. Ensure the section headings are numerically accurate and follow sequentially. Use cross-references (e.g. 'See section 4.3 below'), but note that it is very easy for these cross-references to become inaccurate if you are making lots of changes to your document. *Edit them carefully* (see chapter 15).

Use numbered headings and sensible titles for different sections. Use indentation and different fonts to show the different levels. You should easily be able to follow the hierarchy of ideas and locate major sections, subsections and minor units by following the system of numbering, indentation, and use of bold type and underlining. Style guides, such as the Australian Government's *Style Manual*, explain the correct way to do this using different heading styles (AGPS, 2002).

The language of a report is concise and direct. You make your points simply and in a no-nonsense fashion. Use short sentences, using, e.g. 'This report outlines ...', 'This report presents ...', 'See Section 3.2 for details on ...'. The reader wants information quickly in a minimum number of words.

There is no use of 'I', 'me', 'we' or 'you' in reports, and no personal comment is given (e.g. your 'beliefs'). Use the passive and third-person forms where possible, unless these are obviously unsuitable (e.g. 'It was found that the author of this report wanted to be an engineer'). If you have to refer to yourself, write: 'The writer of this report', 'the author', 'the present author', etc., but avoid personalising, if you can.

Some information appears in reports in the form of listed bullet-pointed facts, instead of as complete sentences (unlike in essays). Use 'lead-in phrases' before such lists, e.g. 'The following items were presented to the Board of Directors for their consideration:' followed by a bullet-pointed list.

All facts and information gained from other sources should be referenced in the normal way. Even lists of information in bullet-point format should be sourced if they are from a publication obtained elsewhere (Nutting & White, 1990).

Now let's look at each section of the report in more detail.

1 The front matter

The front matter consists of the title page as well as the following items (each on new pages). It is customary to paginate the front matter with Roman numerals (i, ii, iii, iv, etc.) and start the introduction – which forms the main text of the report – with Arabic numerals (1, 2, 3, etc.). The **abstract** or **executive summary** can appear before the **table of contents** and is generally not numbered.

Title page
Apart from the title itself (what the report is about), the following information should be shown on the title page:

- the author's name;
- the person (or body) for whom it is written;
- the purpose of the report, with its limitations (sometimes called 'terms of reference' in corporate reports);
- the date the report was requested;
- the due date of the report.

Other front matter

A **confidentiality clause** is sometimes given, if the report describes commercially sensitive material. This may specify a 'release date' for the report. This is seldom needed for graduate-level reports, but they are common in commercial reports.

As reports are generally organised into main sections and sub-sections, the **table of contents** sets this out in detail: 3, 3.1, 3.2, 3.2.1, etc., with associated titles (Nutting & White, 1990).

- Don't overdo subsections (no more than 3–4). If you need more than four levels, reorganise your sections to avoid this.
- Note that Word has a **table of contents function** which automatically updates titles and pages as needed. It is well worth learning how it works.

> ### Example
>

- Sometimes a list of tables and/or a list of figures are included. These should be listed in the table of contents. The list of tables and the list of figures should be presented clearly, identifying the page number where each table or diagram occurs. Use a separate page for each.
- Any abbreviations used in the report are outlined on a separate page.

2 The abstract or executive summary

An abstract (sometimes called a 'synopsis', 'summary' or – in the professions – an 'executive summary') is a very condensed summary of a formal report, research paper or thesis. It is placed on its own at the start of the document. Some writers distinguish abstracts from executive summaries in terms of length (abstracts are shorter) and purpose (abstracts summarise research findings; executive summaries provide an aid for decision making for managers).

The purpose of the abstract is to enable the reader to get a broad overview of a paper to help them decide whether to continue reading. The length of the abstract can depend on the length of the report. Between 100 and 350 words is usual, and it would be uncommon for an abstract to form much more than 5 per cent of the entire text of paper.

An abstract is quite different from an introduction. An introduction can be longer, it can provide a clear background to the research focus, and it generally moves from the general to the specific (see chapter 13). An abstract must be written after all other sections are completed to ensure it as concise and precise as possible. If an abstract is well written you should be able to follow the main idea of the paper without having to read the paper itself.

The structure of an abstract
In the case of a formal report, there are generally five main sections. The abstract of a report mirrors these stages:

- the background;
- the purpose/principal activity;
- the methodology used;
- the results obtained;
- the conclusions and recommendations.

Note, however, that not all abstracts follow this exact structure. The abstract for a report that does not involve experimental research may not need a methodology section, and rather than summarise findings you will more likely stress the *purpose* and *focus* of the report. This kind of abstract is more common in the humanities and social sciences.

Abstracts follow the structure of the article. The following abstract structures are common in the literature:

- background, methods, results, conclusions;
- background, methods, findings, interpretation;
- context, objective, design, setting, participants, interventions, main outcomes, measures, results, conclusions;
- background, objective, design, setting, participants, measurements, results, conclusions;
- objective, design, setting, participants, interventions, main outcomes, measures, results, conclusions.

Any given abstract need not have all the sections listed above, and they need not be in this exact order.

In broad terms the key sections can be understood as follows:

- **background** = the general topic area or issue;
- **context** = another word for 'background', but also the surrounding circumstances at the time and what others think in the area;
- **methods** = the formal approach taken in the research to collect data;
- **findings** = what the research discovered;
- **interpretation** = the ways in which the researchers made sense of the findings;
- **design** = how the experiment was set up;
- **objective** = what the researchers were hoping to determine or find out;
- **setting** = the situation in which the research or experiment was carried out;
- **participants** = the people or subjects involved in the study;
- **measurement** = the thing measured when data are collected;
- **interventions** = how the experimenters changed the experimental set-up to obtain their results;
- **main outcome measures** = how the conclusions were tested;
- **results** = what the experimenters discovered after analysing their findings;
- **conclusions** =the interpreted results of the study.

Example

[1] In the academic literature and the business press, there seems to be a lack of guidance and lack of cross-cultural models to support companies' localization strategies on the Web. [2] To address this deficit in literature and to provide marketers and Web designers with insights into website localization, [3] this paper conducted a comparative analysis of the [4] US-based international companies, domestic websites and their Chinese websites. [5] A framework to measure cultural adaptation on the Web is presented. [6] Forty US-based Fortune 500 companies are surveyed to investigate the cultural adaptation of their Chinese websites. [7] Content analysis of the [8] 80 US domestic and Chinese websites reveals that [9] the Web is not a culturally neutral medium, but it is full of cultural markers that give country-specific websites a look and feel unique to the local culture.

The parts of this abstract are listed below.

[1] background	[6] participants (more detail)
[2] objective	[7] method (more detail)
[3] method	[8] measurement (more details)
[4] measurement	[9] results
[5] main outcome measures	

Verb tenses used in abstracts

The tenses used in abstracts typically mirror the tenses used in different sections of the report. Look at the following example:

Background information (present tense/past tense/present perfect)
- 'Accreditation of ISO 9000 <u>continues</u> to grow. ... Whilst manufacturing organisations <u>were</u> early adopters, in recent years, many organisations from the service sector <u>have pursued</u> accreditation.'

Principal activity (past tense/present perfect tense)
- 'In this paper, attitudes towards the standard <u>were compared</u> to determine if there <u>were</u> significant differences between the views of manufacturing and service organisations.'

Methodology (past tense)
- 'Empirical data <u>were taken</u> from a survey of 149 service and 160 Australian manufacturing organisations.'

Results (past tense)
- 'Results showed that differences <u>were not insignificant</u>, particularly in terms of the benefits sought.'

Conclusions (present tense/tentative verbs and modal auxiliaries)
- 'The implications of the results <u>suggest</u> that service organisations <u>need</u> to be careful when applying the lessons learnt from the experiences of the manufacturing sector to overcome the problems associated with the implementation of ISO 9000. Further, the results of this study <u>lend support</u> to the argument that the standard is not universally applicable and may need industry-specific tailoring.'

What not to include in an abstract

The following elements are generally considered inappropriate for an abstract:

- vague generalisations;
- complex sentence structures and vocabulary;
- detailed facts and figures, and information presented in graphic format;
- abbreviations and contractions;
- citations (however, there are discipline-specific variations on this).

Steps for writing an abstract

Take the following steps when writing an abstract:

- reread your paper/report for an overview;

- read each section and reduce the information to one or two sentences;
- read these sentences again to ensure that they cover the major points in your paper;
- ensure you have written something for each of the key points outlined above for either the descriptive or informative abstract;
- check the word length and cut out unnecessary words, or rewrite using fewer, more succinct sentences;
- edit for flow and expression.

3 The introduction

The introduction provides necessary background information. You can outline what is covered in the different sections of the report here and mention the purpose and scope of the report. You can explain technical terms used in the report and identify the hypotheses you are testing. You can do the following in the introduction:

- outline the broad problem/issue to be investigated;
- provide the background and rationale for the study;
- outline the problem investigated in the study, and the research questions/hypotheses tested;
- discuss the nature and type of the study, the time horizon of your study, the study setting and the unit of analysis.

In the literature review (which may form part of the introduction) you review the work of others in this topic area. You do the following in the literature review section:

- define the 'gap' (what others have done; what you will do);
- outline the company, policies, resources, and the need for research.
- outline the purpose/justification for the research.

Here is an example of a report-style introduction with the sections identified. I have highlighted and provided titles for the key sections to help make the structure clear. The research 'gap' is underlined:

[general area] In recent years economic imperatives have provided the pressure for governments to reassess their relationships with universities. Governments are no longer prepared to accept unquestioned institutional autonomy and the culture of self-regulation that have for so long been features of these relationships. Governments are now concerned that universities be more publicly accountable, productive and efficient than in the past. As a result, the move to increase student retention in our universities in an era of rapidly increasing enrolments has become a key goal and easing the transition from school to university is seen as a signifi-cant element in this process.

[other research] The focus on retention and transition has been reflected in the recognition that an emphasis on how students learn and the complex interactions that take place in the learning process are as important as the traditional focus on teaching methodology (see for example Barr & Tagg, 1995). School leavers face a number of challenges in making the adjustment from school to university (Jones, 1999; Smith, 2003). They are expected to learn challenging material and to be capable of independent thought, and to adjust to different teaching styles and an expanded social environment. [**gap in research**] Until recently, in many disciplines, including the Commerce-related disciplines, little attention has been given to student learning and the effects of teaching on the learning process.

[**purpose of research**] The Faculty of Economics and Commerce at the University of Melbourne conducted two surveys of the first year Bachelor of Commerce intake in 1999 as part of a programme to ease the transition of students from school to university and to improve the quality of the teaching and learning environment. [**justification of research**] The surveys were seen as a first step in gaining a better understanding of student perceptions of their approaches to learning and their expectations and experiences in their first year in the Faculty. In order to gain an understanding of their perceptions of their previous year of education and their expectations of the learning context at university, students were surveyed after they had enrolled, but prior to the start of semester. A second survey was conducted towards the middle of the second semester to gather student perceptions of the Faculty environment and to compare these perceptions with those reported in the first survey. [**overview**] This report presents the results of the surveys and discusses the implications of these for first year teaching and learning.

Source: Johnston, C. (2001). Student Perceptions of Learning in First Year in an Economics and Commerce Faculty. *Higher Education Research and Development, 20*(2), 169–184, Routledge/Taylor & Francis. Reprinted by permission of the publisher (Taylor & Francis Group, http://www.informaworld.com).

It is customary to review some of the literature briefly in the introduction to provide a context. If the literature is extensive, have a separate section following the introduction for a more detailed review (see chapter 14 for more information on how to do this).

4 The literature review

In the literature review, which may be part of the introduction, you review the work of others in this topic area. You may do the following in the literature review section:

- compare and contrast different authors' views on an issue;
- group authors who draw similar conclusions;
- criticise aspects of methodology;
- note areas in which authors are in disagreement;
- highlight exemplary studies;
- highlight gaps in research;
- show how your study relates to previous studies;
- show how your study relates to the literature in general.

When reviewing literature, you can group information in the following ways:

- *Difference of approach:* While Jones (1982) argues ..., Smith (1990) ... claims that ...'
- *From distant to closely related:* 'Smith (1991) and Jones (2001) both showed that ... However Hutchison (2002) demonstrates that ...'
- *Chronologically:* 'Early marketing theory owes its development to ... Many studies contributed to ... for example, Jones and Smith (1986). Hunt (1987) was recognised for ... but later Jamison (1999) showed that ...'

Use different ways of reporting data so that your literature review does not read like a shopping list ('Smith claims that ... Harry says that ..., etc.) (for more details on how to write a literature review, see chapter 14).

Note: The past tense is used for completed work and the present tense for work that is considered still 'current' (even if it may have been published in the past).

5 The methodology/procedure section

In this section, you describe the **method** you used to carry out your research. This can be an empirical methodology (e.g. surveys, questionnaires), statistical methodologies, or case method. *You do not discuss your results in this section, only the method you used to obtain your results.* You may, for example, highlight:

- where this methodology has been used elsewhere or previously;
- what was involved with setting up the methodology (issues of design and applicability, etc.);
- the scope and limitations of the methodology;
- research design issues (i.e. why you chose your research method);
- population and sample issues;
- the variables and measures used;
- the data-analysis techniques used.

Sometimes a **procedure** section is included in the Methodology section; sometimes it is given in a separate section. The Procedure is how you *applied or used* the type of analysis in question. In the Procedure section, you do the following (note the use of the **past tense**):

- describe the stages of the experiment step by step ('The survey was distributed to all company employees at 10.15. After an interval of 10 days a second survey was administered', etc.);
- outline the day and time when the experiment was conducted and any follow-up experiments, surveys, etc.;
- mention how the results were collated and tabulated, etc. ('Data were collected by means of an initial interview recorded on tape followed by soliciting the opinion of managers in an internet-based survey').

In the methodology and procedure sections, be sure to describe materials in a logical order. Start with an overview and then narrow down to specifics:

- overview (**present tense**): 'The choice of sampling method for this experiment <u>requires</u> great care, 'Participants <u>are</u> crucial for the success of the ...';
- description of parts/samples used in the experiment (**past tense**): 'A measuring device <u>was used</u> to ... A sample <u>was taken</u> ...';
- the spatial/functional organisation of the experiment (**past tense**): 'The surveys <u>were conducted</u> under strict conditions ... Firstly the ... was ... then the ... <u>was</u> ...

Choose whether to use the active or passive voice to describe procedures:

- use the passive voice if no human agent needs to be mentioned ('The monitor <u>is placed</u> in a suitable location and turned on ...');
- use the active voice if it is important to mention the human agent ('The survey <u>was presented</u> to all employees ...'). Use the passive if this is not important: 'The team <u>presented the survey</u> to all employees.'

6 The results/findings section

The body of the report describes essential information and alternatives gained from such diverse activities as interviews, research reading, personal observation and questionnaires. It is a detailed and balanced account of reliable, relevant facts and should therefore be easily verifiable (see chapter 7).

The language should be presented clearly and without jargon. If you introduce technical words, they should be clearly explained.

Illustrations: Use well-captioned illustrations (drawings, photographs, etc.), tables and graphs to assist you in making your meaning clear. They should be numbered and inserted in the text in appropriate places. Be careful to use an identifying phrase in the text to 'point' the reader to the diagram. For example: ('see figure 3'), ('see table 5.1'), and so on. The figures and tables should also be clearly labelled (e.g. figure 3, table 5.1) and include a short descriptive caption. The label and caption should be centred below the figure or table.

For example:

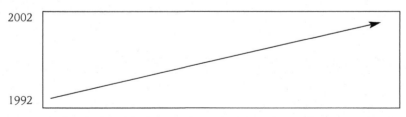

Figure 1: Line diagram showing the increase in enrolments in the Faculty of Humanities over 10 years.

Make sure you identify the kind of figure or graph you are using: histogram, line graph, pie or scatter chart.

Note that if the graphics or tables are very large, it is better to place them in an **appendix**. You then need to put a phrase in the text that refers to the appropriate part of the appendix. For example: '(See Appendix 4.)' The appendix should be labelled appropriately and described in a similar way as diagrams in the text. Don't leave your reader to identify the purpose of the diagram. Make it clear for them.

When discussing the tables or diagrams in the report, use statements which:

- locate the results/diagrams/figures (**present tense**): 'There are no obvious features in Table 1 which indicate groupings associated with age, sex, language or schooling. ... ', 'Figure 3 shows that ... ';
- present the most important findings (usually the **past tense**): 'The immediately noticeable feature was the rise in. ... '. 'As can be seen, there were three ways in which ... '; 'The results also showed that ... ';
- comment on the findings (usually the **present tense + modal auxiliaries or tentative verbs**): 'These results suggest that ...', 'Another interesting fact seems to be the ... '.

Quotations: Short quotations can be included in the text. Longer quotations should be indented from the left-hand margin of the text. All quotations should be enclosed in single inverted commas and cited appropriately (for information on using quotations, see chapter 5).

Numbering: The numbers and headings that appear in the table of contents should reflect the numbers and headings that appear throughout the report. Two schemes can be used: the decimal system and the numeral and letter system. The former is easier to manage and refer to. Whatever scheme you decide on, you must maintain it consistently.

7 The discussion

The discussion is where you evaluate your findings. It should contain the following elements:

- reference to the purpose/hypothesis of the study (**past tense**): 'The principle of ... was not followed in conducting the research. We originally assumed that physical decrements would be more apparent in speed jobs than in skilled jobs. However, we saw that ... and that there was a ... ';
- review of important findings (**past and present + modals**): 'We found that ... . Results showed that participants might be less inclined to assist managers, if ... . This seemed to show that ... ';
- possible explanations for, or speculations about, findings (**present tense + modals**). 'Results seem to indicate that there was a ... . This suggests that ... . On the other hand, there may be a ... ';

- limitations of study (**present tense**). 'While there <u>is</u> little chance of ... . The study <u>is</u> not concerned with establishing ... the aim <u>is</u> not to ... but to ... . We do not <u>attempt</u> to ... only to <u>look</u> at ...'.

8 Conclusions and limitations

In the Conclusion, you must provide clear, unexaggerated, objective statements summarising the information given in the body of the report. No new matter may be introduced at this stage. The conclusions should be comprehensive so that they can serve as an adequate basis for the recommendations to follow (for how to write a conclusion, see chapter 13).

The **limitations** of the study can be added in this section. Here you identify, in an unbiased and objective way, what your report *could have done better,* any flaws in methodology or problems associated with the gathering of data. For example, if you were reporting on a case study, you might highlight that, because the company was going through a takeover, the managers and employees may have been behaving differently – and their responses may have been different – from their normal behaviours and typical responses.

9 Recommendations

Recommendations are statements provided by the writer on: (a) what is to be done; (b) who is to do it; and (c) how it is to be achieved. Sometimes alternative courses of action are proposed, then reasons are given for the chosen recommendations. Sometimes timelines for action are provided in recommendations section.

Recommendations should be specific, clearly and simply written and *based on the conclusions.* The most important should be given first, followed by the others in descending order of importance.

Stages in the conclusion, limitations and recommendations
   Summing up (present perfect + modal auxiliaries)

- This report <u>has looked</u> at the importance of marketing management to the farming industry. The report <u>has provided</u> a practical ...which <u>seem</u> to ...

Implications of the study (present + modal auxiliaries)

- Results from the experiment <u>seem to indicate</u> that, if managers adopt a ... they will <u>more than likely</u> develop a ... .This <u>suggests</u> that ... (the main results or findings only – put details in the discussion)

Limitations of the study (present perfect + modal auxiliaries)

- While this report <u>has </u>... . It is noted that the date <u>could have been</u> different in the following situations: ...

Recommendations for future research (present + modals)

- While the report <u>did not</u> discuss the … there are clear implications for … . It does <u>seem to suggest</u> that, if … then … . This <u>may give rise</u> to more … in future. The following course of action is proposed: … <u>should be</u> provided to … . The CEO <u>should</u> then …

> **Note:** Students often confuse findings, conclusions and recommendations:
> - *findings* are factual and verifiable statements of what happened or what was found.
> - *conclusions* are your own ideas that you deduce from your findings.
> - *recommendations* are what needs to be done in the future.

10 Reference list (bibliography)

Use referencing conventions as described in chapter 6.

11 Appendices

The appendices section includes tables and diagrams, graphs and charts, lists, etc., that are peripheral (less essential) to the main content of the report but are considered of interest to the reader.

You provide a new page for each appendix and number each one sequentially. Provide a title for each, e.g. *Appendix 4: Bus Timetable for St. Kilda Residents.* Be sure that your table of contents lists each of the appendices. References in the body of the report should 'point to' the relevant appendix, e.g. ('see Appendix 5 for more information'.)

● **3 Style and language in report writing**

Reports must be presented in an impersonal, objective manner and are therefore usually written without using the personal pronouns 'I', 'we' and 'you'. Ways of avoiding these personal pronouns include (Nutting & White, 1990):

1 Using passive sentences

Instead of:	*Write:*
We examined the evidence.	The evidence was examined.
I interviewed five managers.	Five managers were interviewed.

2 Using third-person pronouns

Instead of:	*Write:*
I found …	It was found that …
I recommend that …	It is recommended that …

3 Eliminating pronouns

Instead of:	*Write:*
My report looks at ...	This report examines ...
In this section I want to ...	This section analyses ...

4 The correct use of tenses

International students often get very confused about the use of tenses in report writing. In written reports, **past-tense verbs** *are used to explain all prior events.* Since the study itself is completed, and is now being reported, all references to it are in the past tense. For example, the introduction could read as follows:

- The purpose of the study was to ...
- The scope included ...
- The methodology used ...

The findings section of the report is also written in the **past tense** (because the study is finished):

- The study revealed ...
- It was found ...

In contrast, **conclusions** and **recommendations** are written in the **present tense**, because they discuss the circumstances at the present time. That is, the findings, conclusions and recommendations are still true now even though the study itself is finished.

- The findings are ...
- The findings show ...
- The findings indicate ...
- The conclusions drawn are ...
- The recommendations are ...

(Nutting & White, 1990)

> **Note:** You should write all your reports objectively, using the passive voice as much as possible. However, when this would be inappropriate you can use the expression: 'The author of this report'..., 'The writer believes ...', for example, where you are stating your opinion or offering your personal recommendations. Sometimes subjectivity is unavoidable. However, use expressions such as: 'It is claimed/suggested that ...', 'It is thought that ...' wherever possible.

4 Summary

This chapter has outlined some basic guidance on empirical report writing as an assessment task. The report format is a complex one which should not be underestimated. It is very formal in style and specific language structures are needed for specific sections. It is strongly recommended that you consult reports written in discipline-specific journals for more detailed models and examples of writing style. While there is no 'right way' to write a report, there are certainly common conventions. I have outlined the most important of these here.

5 Report-writing checklist

Use the following checklist to help you determine the strengths and weaknesses of research reports. Be aware that not all research reports will feature all of the elements listed below.

A The report format

	Yes	No
Title page		
• Author's name	☐	☐
• Person or body for whom it is written	☐	☐
• Purpose of the report/terms of reference	☐	☐
• Date report was requested	☐	☐
• Date report is due	☐	☐

	Yes	No
Table of contents		
• Main sections/subsections listed	☐	☐
• List of tables and figures	☐	☐

	Strong	Weak
Abstract		
• Background	☐	☐
• Purpose	☐	☐
• Methodology	☐	☐
• Results	☐	☐
• Conclusions/recommendations	☐	☐

	Strong	Weak
Introduction		
• Outline of problem/issue	☐	☐
• Definitions of terms	☐	☐
• Background and rationale	☐	☐
• Purpose/research questions/hypotheses	☐	☐
• Nature of study, time horizon, study setting/unit of analysis	☐	☐
Literature review		
• Logically sequenced discussion of key literature	☐	☐
• Comparison/contrast of key literature	☐	☐
• Identification of gaps/flaws in literature	☐	☐
• Establishment of the need for further research	☐	☐
Methodology		
• Research design issues	☐	☐
• Mention of prior use of methodology	☐	☐
• Methodological scope and limitations	☐	☐
• Population and sample issues	☐	☐
• Variables and measures used	☐	☐
• Data-analysis techniques	☐	☐
Procedure		
• Stages of the experiment/dates	☐	☐
• Collation and tabulation of results	☐	☐

	Strong	Weak

Results

- Objective and clear description of main findings | ☐ | ☐ |
- Numbered and captioned tables, graphs and diagrams | ☐ | ☐ |
- Appropriate references to visual information in the text | ☐ | ☐ |

Discussion

- Reference to purposes/hypotheses of study | ☐ | ☐ |
- Review of key findings in relation to purposes/hypotheses | ☐ | ☐ |
- Possible explanations for, or speculations about findings | ☐ | ☐ |
- Limitations of study | ☐ | ☐ |

Conclusion

- Summary | ☐ | ☐ |
- Limitations of the study | ☐ | ☐ |

Recommendations

- What/how/by whom | ☐ | ☐ |

Appendices

- Clearly titled and presented list of relevant appendices | ☐ | ☐ |

Reference list

- Comprehensive list of sources | ☐ | ☐ |
- Appropriate formatting | ☐ | ☐ |

B Language, referencing and presentation

	Strong	Weak
Paragraphing		
• Sequencing of paragraphs	☐	☐
• Topic sentences	☐	☐
• Supporting sentences	☐	☐
• Relevance of all points	☐	☐
• One main idea per paragraph	☐	☐
• Linking of points within paragraphs	☐	☐
• Length of paragraphs	☐	☐

	Strong	Weak
Language, fluency and cohesion		
• Grammar	☐	☐
• Sentence structure	☐	☐
• Vocabulary (accuracy and formality)	☐	☐
• Conciseness	☐	☐

	Strong	Weak
Referencing and citations		
• Acknowledgement of all sources	☐	☐
• Paraphrasing, summarising and quoting	☐	☐
• Use of critical review language	☐	☐
• Format of in-text citations	☐	☐
• Bibliography/reference list	☐	☐
• Appendices	☐	☐

	Strong	Weak
Presentation		
• Fonts, margins, spacing	☐	☐
• Spelling and punctuation	☐	☐
• Capitalisation	☐	☐
• Titles	☐	☐
• Tables, graphs, photographs, illustrations	☐	☐

12 Preparing the Research Essay

● 1 Introduction

In normal circumstances, postgraduate students only get a few weeks to complete an essay. I have advised in chapter 5 that, with careful strategic planning, you can find out in advance the likely topics you will have to write about in assignments. However, the process of writing an essay usually begins when your lecturer gives you an essay question. Each essay question involves topic and direction words.

● 2 Direction words

Direction words, such as 'compare', ' list', 'outline' and 'contrast', *tell you to do something*. It is essential that you familiarise yourself with direction words as these are used regularly at university. Your lecturer will often use them when advising you, and they will expect you to know what they mean.

Direction words in essay topics

Usually you will find direction words in lists of essay topics. For example:

- **Compare and contrast** the Marxist account of society and social change with the capitalist account. Which is more plausible?
- **Discuss** the role of principals in schools.
- **Analyse** three models of marketing. Which one best fits small business?
- **Trace** the history of nursing. **Show** how earlier nursing methods have been adapted to fit into modern hospitals.
- **Evaluate** the role conservation now plays on farms and its contribution and suggest why it has been embraced by some farmers and not others.

These are examples of realistic essay questions that you might have to answer. Clearly, if you don't know what 'compare and contrast', 'discuss', 'analyse', 'trace', and 'evaluate' mean, you will be stuck! See the website for an exercise to help you to understand and use direction words.

3 Narrowing down your research question

Lecturers often deliberately set essay questions that are too general. Look again at the examples provided above. 'The Marxist account of society and social change' is a very broad area. So is 'the role of principals'. What do they really want to see? What *aspects* of society? What *particular kind* of role?

Part of the assessment process in evaluating essays may involve identification of whether students can *narrow down the essay topic* to a more manageable one. To do this, you have to reformulate the topic into your own **research question** to focus the topic and develop a clear essay plan. The research question is different from the essay question: the essay question is usually very general and sometimes quite vague, whereas research questions are very focused and clear. Clever students will narrow the essay question to a very precise research question. These set limits for the subsequent research.

1 Beginning to refocus

To refocus your assignment topic you can turn it into a question. This is an effective way to begin an essay. 'Discuss the role of principals in schools' can be approached more easily if it is written as a question: 'How does the role of principals in schools impact on society at large?'

Alternatively, you can refocus an assignment question using direction words. For example, if your question was: '*What* are the security issues raised by computer crime in the e-commerce industry?' try adding a different direction word and see how it changes the focus. ('*How* are the security issues raised by computer crime a problem in the e-commerce industry?' '*Why* are the security issues raised by computer crime a problem in the e-commerce industry?').

What is the focus that *you* want to have? Your lecturer cannot help you here as it is a personal choice. But they will be impressed if you narrow the scope and tell them in the introduction why you are doing this.

2 Narrowing your scope

Begin to spell out for yourself the *scope* of your research, that is, what you will do and what you won't do. For example, what other industries might you look at *in addition to* the e-commerce industry? Can you make comparisons with other areas? What will you *limit* your discussion to? For example, you might choose to compare e-commerce and traditional commerce security in the sale of books and household groceries.

A *good essay* will make *connections* between different areas of knowledge and different disciplines. An *average essay* will rehearse something that is already commonly known. A *bad essay* will repeat the lectures or the book you used in tutorials. A *good essay* will go that extra step and do something different. An *exceptional* essay will educate your reader using recently published information. A **good essay** will look like a complex, ingeniously constructed spider's web joining related areas of study; a **bad essay** will look like a predictable 'shopping list' of familiar points.

3 Don't be too general or too specific

Make sure that your research question or statement *is neither too general nor too specific.* If it is too general, you will not know how to make a plan or where to start. If it is too specific, you may find it hard to find enough resources. Getting this right is a matter of practice.

Which topic is easier to start work on right away?

- 'The nature of computer crime' or:
- 'Distinguish between the security issues raised by computer crime in the e-commerce industry and the security issues in traditional industries.'

The first topic is too broad and it will be hard to find relevant information about it. It has no focus. The second topic is far more researchable. This is because it is narrow. The narrower the question, the easier it is to find information about it and start to do research. If the second question above is the one your lecturer has given you, you can narrow it down *even further* by limiting your research to **time** (i.e. computer crime over the last two years only), to **place** (i.e. computer crime in Australia or the UK) or to **type** (i.e. involving a certain type of crime; e.g. embezzlement of funds from banks). The narrower your focus the more likely it is you will be able to find specific information as well as say something interesting.

When you have devised a suitably narrow topic, you can underline the noun phrases, write a search string, and search the databases. (For more information on this, see the online chapter about library skills.)

4 Give your essay an all-encompassing title

Once you have refocused your research question or statement, you need to think of a title that captures the whole area of your research. A title is very important as it helps you to frame your research area. You may decide that a question best captures your topic:

Can Computer Crime Be Prevented in E-Commerce Industries?

Or you may think of a good statement. The use of colons (:) is good for this purpose. For example:

Security and Computer Crime: A Comparison between E-Commerce and Traditional Commerce in the Wholesale Grocery Industry.

A combination of question and statement can also be very effective:

Can Computer Crime Be Prevented? A Study of E-Commerce in the Wholesale Grocery Industry.

Note: In titles, capitals are often used for all words, with the exception of prepositions and conjunctions (this is called maximal capitalisation or title case).

5 Have a thesis!

An essay is a waste of time if it does not have a 'thesis statement' or point of view.

Students are often frightened about having their own point of view. However, there is nothing to be worried about. A point of view need not be *completely original*. You can make reference to writers who support your views.

It is easiest to start thinking about a thesis for your essay topic, by using a *that* phrase: 'I will argue *that* ...' or, even better: 'This paper argues *that* ...'.

The thesis statement may mention opposing, or modifying, positions in a dependent clause. The following table reads from left to right and top to bottom.

While Although Despite the fact that Even though In spite of the fact that	it has been argued that ... it is true that ... ... (can lead to ...) some theorists argue that ... (...) is not always ... many people assume that ...	[+ counter argument or modifying clause]
Your position X Y Z	for three main reasons. has two causes. in five methods. can be distinguished in four main ways. + perhaps a list of these actual areas to be addressed.	

● 4 Essay-writing attitude

Essays are used not only for assessment but also so that you can learn from the exercise of writing them. This section aims to give you the general principles of essay writing. In particular, it tries to suggest the best attitude to have when beginning an essay, and how to carry this through to successful completion. Some of these points have been adapted from a document given to me when I was an undergraduate by Associate Professor Stan van Hooft from Deakin University. However, the original source of this document is now lost to time. In the discussion below I am recalling useful points from this document.

General principles

1 Take it seriously

The essay is a very difficult genre. Professors and lecturers also write essays but they call them 'papers'. Academics may spend weeks, and even months (sometimes years!) working on a paper, because they are trying to advance knowledge with new ideas.

International students have difficulties with writing papers for very different reasons. Naturally they have difficulties with English, which is for them a second or third language. Another part of the difficulty for international students is that it is important to say exactly what is required in a limited number of words. Most people could cover the topic with an unlimited word-count and unlimited time. Being succinct, and yet covering everything that needs to be covered, is often a challenge (this is also true for lecturers and professors).

Given this, it is absurd to think that you can rush the process of writing an essay. The student who 'throws an essay together' at the last minute may be lucky to get a good grade once or twice, but they will never do well in the long run. Treat the essay genre with respect. Make sure you allow at least four weeks to complete a standard 3,000-word essay:

- week 1 for research and writing the first draft;
- week 2 for 'laying down' time (you can still do additional research during this period);
- week 3 for correcting and revising the first draft;
- week 4 for correcting and polishing the penultimate draft.

Plan your time strategically so you can have longer to complete your assignments (see chapter 2).

2 Don't be a perfectionist
While you should take essay writing seriously, you need not be your own worst enemy. A 'perfect' essay doesn't exist in reality. None of us can write a perfect essay, but that doesn't mean that we can't get better by trying. The more work that you put into writing essays, the more you will improve, both in terms of style and substance. The process of gaining a degree makes you better at writing essays, but you *never* stop improving your essay-writing skills.

What not to do when writing an essay

1 Don't write for your lecturer!
When writing an essay, *do not* think of yourself as writing for assessment, or for a highly scholastic reader such as your lecturer. Why not? If you write *for* a lecturer or professor you will probably make yourself nervous. You might start to think that you are writing for 'experts'. For example, you might think that you need to use big words that you may only half-understand. You might also imagine that the lecturer/tutor already knows everything about the subject and that therefore you can leave out lots of details and write in a complicated, 'wordy' academic style.

This approach leads to incomprehensible writing, poor grades and much misery. Pretend you are *not* writing for assessment and this problem evaporates. Who, then, should you write for? See '**Write for an imaginary audience**', below.

2 Don't merely reproduce what you think the lecturer wants
Essays are not exercises in reproducing and rehashing 'correct' answers – unlike some exams, for example. Essays test your ability to *question and criticise ideas* – **including** the ideas of your lecturers. A good essay shows the reader that you can develop coherent *arguments* and *counter-arguments* and provide *evidence* for an idea or proposition. Some lecturers take great delight in reading good, well-argued criti-

cisms of their own ideas. It shows them that they have a good student who can think for themselves.

This is not to say, of course, that you have to show disagreement with what the lecturer says. Rather, you should approach ideas from all sources with a critical attitude. Take nothing for granted unless you have good arguments or evidence. Agree in part with things that you think have *some* evidence, and so on. Give reasons in your essay.

What the lecturer really wants to see is to see how well you can 'think' on paper. It is quite irrelevant whether you agree or disagree with them. Of course, they will not be impressed with poor arguments criticising their ideas. You need to do better than that!

3 Don't leave the essay to the last minute
Writing essays requires considerable abilities in reasoning, scholarship and literacy. It takes time and effort to do a good job. Rushing it will virtually ensure that you won't make the grade. *Don't rush it.*

4 Don't be a soloist; use others for support
Working on your own can be lonely and miserable. You may be convinced that you know exactly what to do and don't need help. However, collaborative scholarship occurs at the highest levels, so it is odd to think that you don't need it too. Form a study group, share your work and take advice from others. Your work can only benefit from their input. The learning skills unit in your university is also there to help you and will give you feedback.

We have said what *not* to do. Now let's look at *what* to do.

What to do

1 Writing for an imaginary audience
Imagine yourself writing for an intelligent, friendly but uninformed audience. Imagine yourself being asked to write for a group of students similar to your tutorial group, for example. The students are not familiar with your subject, but they are intelligent and interested. Imagine you are standing in front of them and reading your essay to them. Doing this, you will feel the necessity of being clear and systematic in a way that does not produce anxiety in you. This strategy does, of course, involve a slight fiction. Remember the '**writing for a selfish reader principle**' in chapter 9. Lecturers will ask themselves:

- 'Is this essay clear?'
- 'Does it communicate the ideas well?'
- 'Would anyone who is intelligent be able to follow this?', and so on.

They will *not* ask themselves:

- 'Is this essay using big academic words?'

- 'Does this essay use long and complicated sentences?'
- 'Has the writer carefully hidden their meaning?'

A word of advice: for the fiction to work you really do need to *take it seriously*. First close your eyes and imagine the students in front of you. Start to write your essay (after you have prepared your outline and your notes). As you write every sentence of your essay ask yourself if the students would understand it. Perhaps you need to simplify your main points. Perhaps you need to add an example to make this point or that point clear. When you redraft the essay imagine them listening to you read (see 2 below).

2 Ask yourself questions
Ask yourself these questions after you have written a paper:

- 'How much could I learn from reading this essay?'
- 'How could I have made certain points more obvious and clear?'
- 'Does this point follow from the previous one?'
- 'Do my points follow each other logically?'

Assume that your audience is, by nature, a sceptical one: you should imagine that you need to be *convincing* in the material you are presenting. This will help you produce a better piece of work. How would you make your points more convincingly? More evidence? More examples? Clearer arguments? A better structure?

3 Recognise the need for redrafting
You would never present a difficult idea to a student audience successfully on the first attempt. You will need to redraft your work carefully. This procedure helps you to recognise lack of precision in your paper, and this helps you to improve your writing. Indirectly, of course, it assists you in a better understanding of the topic or issue you are presenting. You may need to rework and revise your essay several times. Do the best you can and don't get depressed about the process. Remember: there's no such thing as a 'perfect' essay.

4 Use lots of examples
It is critically important to use examples. If a point is difficult or subtle, it is essential to illustrate it with an example or an analogy. You can either think of examples yourself, or draw them from your research (with acknowledgement, of course). An example will always help your imaginary audience – and your lecturer – understand what you are trying to say.

Never underestimate the value of a well-placed example or two. Remember that you are writing for an intelligent but uninformed audience. They need examples to understand your main points. The more complicated your argument is, the more you need to step back from the flow of your argument and support your points with **examples**.

5   *Give reasons for what you say*

Essay writing involves careful and rigorous reasoning and detailed argumentation. You should not rely on tradition, authority (including the lecturer's), faith or a hunch. Distrust bold assertions for which no reasons or arguments are given. *Academic* essays are not works of fiction, personal monologues or statements of your beliefs. They involve the presentation of *arguments* and the *support* for those arguments, and/or the *criticism* of other arguments (see chapter 8). Consider making an argument map before you begin writing.

The good student should not be dogmatic but rather always be willing to *evaluate* arguments to arrive at a conclusion based on his or her deliberations. Make sure you *always give reasons for what you say.* Ask yourself: 'Would my imaginary audience accept this point, or do I need to give reasons?' The more you do this, the better your grade will be.

6   *Apply what you learn from others*

Try to apply what you learn from the lecturers and from the various ways that points of view are argued in class in the presentation of your essays. Learn how to *think* like an accountant, a biologist, an IT professional, and so on. Classes in specialist subject areas are designed to model the kinds of thinking required in essays. If necessary, seek the assistance of books on logical methods and critical thinking in your subject area.

Be aware that professional texts in the discipline, while useful as models for arguments and a source of ideas, are *not* always useful as *models for writing* for students. Journal articles are written by professionals *for* other professionals in the discipline: they are not intended to be essays. Sometimes professionals in the discipline write in an idiosyncratic (strange or unusual) style. Sometimes they leave out details (they know their audience will understand their point). Many famous articles in discipline journals are famous because of the *ideas* expressed, not because of the style or the presentation. To model your writing on these articles is often a mistake. Professionals use criteria for 'quality' that do not apply to graduate or undergraduate students. The criteria that apply to you include:

- clarity of arguments;
- brevity and succinctness;
- coherence and cohesiveness;
- a formal academic structure;
- the correct citation of others;
- relevance to the question.

Journal articles do provide a rich source of ideas. Learn to recognise 'good' arguments and 'bad' ones. Be aware of the many informal fallacies that are commonly made in writing and speech. When you think that a particularly bad argument is being used to support a certain position, criticise it forcefully using these techniques of reasoning and analysis.

7 Be clear about the expectations of different 'academic tribes'
A good essay in one subject is not necessarily a good essay in another. Science essays are not written in the same manner as essays for the humanities. There are variations within Faculty areas too. In the Faculty of Economics and Commerce in most universities, essays for Accounting require different styles and conventions than essays in Management and Economics, for example.

However, the point of most academic essays is to try to solve a certain problem or resolve an issue. The aim is to try to come to a satisfactory understanding and resolution of these problems and the assumptions underpinning them. The conceptual tool used in this process is the evaluation of arguments by clear and precise methods of reasoning. What each subject regards as 'good' reasoning, and the methods of reasoning used, can vary.

Inform yourself of these different methods and use them in your essays. With practice and application, the process of writing an essay for a particular discipline area, and the different requirements for each discipline, will begin to make sense.

8 Be relevant
A common complaint by lecturers of students' work, especially the writing of international students, is irrelevance.

Always *stick to the point* when you are writing an essay. If you are asked to 'critically assess' such-and-such a position or argument, you should give a brief statement of the positions or arguments concerned, then proceed to a consideration of arguments for or against that view. You should *not* waste time with bibliographical sketches of the proponents of the position to be discussed, or the historical details of the development of the view – or anything else not directly connected to the topic.

If you refer to the views of a writer on an argument you are discussing, make sure that you only discuss those views that are relevant to the issue in your essay. Don't sketch his/her whole theory. You are *not* being asked to do that, and points that wander off the main topic will be seen as 'irrelevant' by the lecturer. Your imaginary audience of students will be puzzled if you do this too. Narrowness of focus, and sticking to the point, are critical.

Remove all unnecessary information that clutters the first draft of your essay: literary frills and fancies, side issues, unargued points about the lecturer's preferences for a certain theory, etc. Get rid of any obscurity (see 'Clarity and precision', below.)

Remember, you are not being asked to write everything you think or know about a topic. You are being asked to focus on the essay topic. Narrowing the topic down to a research question helps to avoid rambling and irrelevant responses. Attempt to be as *succinct* as possible and concentrate on your central arguments and/or criticisms of other arguments. *Make these detailed points powerfully.* It is challenging to be **clear and precise** with complex academic ideas. If you are finding it easy there is something wrong!

9 Be coherent
Plan your essay so that your reader will always know where he/she is being led. The

reader should *always* be informed about how what you say at any point in the essay fits into your overall theme or argument.

In the introduction, state what you want to cover in the essay. Use precise and direct language:

- 'In this essay I will discuss X and Y.'/'This essay will discuss X and Y.'
- 'Firstly, I will .../This paper will ...'
- 'Secondly, I will .../This paper will ...'
- 'Finally I will .../This paper will ...'

Then go on and do it. Do *nothing* else!

In the body of the essay, guide the reader from point to point. Again, use very direct language:

- 'The next point I will discuss is .../The next point is ...'
- 'Now let us move on to look at .../The next issue is ...'
- 'I now want to make the following point .../The next point is that...'

The reader should *never*:

- have to ask themselves how something is connected with what you said before;
- have to try to work out where the essay is going;
- have to ask themselves how a paragraph in your essay relates to what you say in a previous section (see the **'writing for a generous reader principle'** and 'writing for a selfish reader principle' in chapter 9).

Cultural differences in essay writing are a cause for confusion for many international students. Some international students are used to a very different essay writing 'style'. Some cultures require *the reader* to make an effort to understand the paper without the writer's help. In the English-speaking academic tradition this is evidence of a poor and inconsiderate writer. Make everything absolutely clear to your reader.

Consider using headings, sub-headings and numbered paragraphs to make clear how your points are to be understood. Use the 'Imaginary audience' test when you write a section: 'Would the audience understand it?' 'Do I need to make it clearer?' If you don't do this, coherence can suffer and your actual reader – your lecturer – can get lost. The result? You will get a bad grade.

Another good strategy is to use 'signposts' in your essays to guide your reader through the points that you are making. Examples of this are expressions like 'Following from this point ...', 'Given this argument ...', and paragraph starters such as 'Firstly', 'Secondly', 'Thirdly', etc. (see chapter 10). Making deliberate use of signposts will also help you gather your thoughts on the essay topic. This is a most useful technique. Lecturers look for it in your essays.

10 Make your argument clear

Essays should begin with a clear statement of the position or argument that you are to discuss. Always make it clear at the outset whether you propose to attack or defend that position or argument. This is known as the **thesis statement**. You can do this by writing in the introduction:

- 'In this essay I will argue that .../'This essay will argue that ...'.

You should always indicate your position in regard to *any* argument that you raise or present in your discussion.

You might feel that you are not an expert and, because of this, you are uncomfortable giving your opinion about an issue. Yet you are not expected to be an 'expert'. Remember that the essay is for assessment as well as *an opportunity for you to learn.* Being prepared to give your point of view in relation to a topic and then going on to argue for it and defend it is an important part of this process. It is also a vital skill to acquire. *This* is what you are being assessed on. Lecturers don't care much *what* you argue. In fact, they will give excellent marks for well-argued views that they completely disagree with! They *do* care if you have a clear argument and thesis statement in your essays.

11 Demonstrating clarity and precision

This is critically important: it is a reason for passing or failing essays. To write good essays you must be clear and precise with your expression. A few tips:

NEVER USE WORDS IN ESSAYS THAT YOU ONLY HALF-UNDERSTAND

Technical terms should all be explained and used consistently. Inconsistency will be noticed and corrected by lecturers. Also, be aware of that many different positions can be held under general technical labels. Don't make uninformed statements about such terminology, because you may be quite wrong. If in doubt, look up such words in a dictionary or a discipline-specific encyclopedia (not a general encyclopedia – these are not detailed enough). To the extent that it displays misunderstanding, lack of familiarity with key terms in the discipline can be penalised.

TAKE CARE WITH YOUR USE OF THE ENGLISH LANGUAGE

Academic disciplines emphasise detailed use of language. Make sure that you use the English language well in your essays. This applies particularly to punctuation, grammar and syntax. Poor expression can cause ambiguity (many possible meanings) or be responsible for work being meaningless and unreadable (see chapters 9 and 15).

DON'T TRY TO IMPRESS BY USING COMPLICATED WORDS AND SENTENCES

Strive for simple, uncluttered and clear expression.

Do not attempt to emulate obscure, convoluted or technical professional writing. Avoid secondary texts that confuse you. Instead, find other material that is more accessible. Explain the subject matter of your essay in a manner that is comfortable and familiar to you. Remember the 'imaginary audience' test.

One of the worst things that students can do is to try to 'sound academic'. Often students have the impression that this will impress their reader. Students sometimes try to 'sound academic' before they have mastered simple and clear writing. Usually this results in lack of clarity and the writing seems 'woolly' and 'vague' to the professional reader. Think of it this way: before a good musician can play their instrument well, they need to practise their scales. It is the same with writing. Before you can write in a convincing 'academic' way, you need to master the basics of clear writing. This clarity is what you are being assessed on when you write essays.

If an issue is complex, try to make it simple by choosing your words and phrases carefully. Be careful when constructing your sentences. Do you mean this? Or that? *If the sentence is unclear, rephrase it until it is clear.* This may be difficult but aim to do it as well you can.

BE PRECISE ABOUT WHAT YOU MEAN AT ALL TIMES

Make sure that you know exactly what position you are arguing for or against. Often students waste time on arguments for or against an idea that sounds much like – but is actually different from – the idea that they are supposed to be writing about. What **exactly** is the essay question asking you to do? *Check carefully.*

The conclusion in your essay should mirror the precision in your arguments. Make sure you don't get confused about what your arguments demonstrate. Conclusions should *follow* from your arguments. 'You conclude X in your essay, but your arguments support Y' is a common complaint by lecturers of students' work. Failure to recognise and avoid problems like this results in a lower grade.

12 Show independence of mind

You will be expected to think carefully about the issue(s) discussed in your essay. If you are given an essay question you must try to *make up your own mind* on the question, even if your conclusions are only tentative.

You may find certain arguments cause you to rethink long-held, unargued and assumed views on an issue. It may be that they cause some conflict with other beliefs incidental to these views. Don't be afraid of changing your mind. This is really what university study is all about – the critical exchange of ideas and arguments, and the assessment and *reassessment* of them. This is what it means to *educate* yourself. If you are unwilling to accept better arguments for something you are being dogmatic. If you continue to hold a belief about something that you no longer agree with – or for which you have no convincing arguments – perhaps you need to seriously consider why you continue to believe it.

13 Being consistent

It is fine to change your mind as your read and consider arguments by others when you are planning and preparing an essay, but don't change your mind *during* an essay. The essay must exhibit a single, clear and unambiguous point of view.

Be *consistent* in the conclusion you are aiming for, look at it from a number of angles and try to defend it from attack from other arguments. The situation may arise where you are just not sure which of two conflicting views is correct, and cannot come down on either one side or the other. In this case, consider the conflicting views as best you can, and then show why you personally regard the reasons for both being equally valid or important. If you have to 'sit on the fence' at least be *consistent* in doing so. Do not write giving the impression that you think theory X is better than theory Y but hedge your bets in the conclusion because you are afraid to be 'wrong'. The chances are that there is no 'right answer'. Remember: the lecturer is more interested in how you *think through* the issues and arrive at a conclusion based on your arguments than in your conclusion. It does not really matter what you conclude. It *does* matter whether you are consistent or not.

14 Use the work of others – but always use your own words

Your work must be just that: *your* work. You can borrow ideas from others with acknowledgement, but you need to do more than that if you want a good grade. Don't just summarise the views of the lecturer, or one or more of the authors you have looked at. Let these things *influence* your conclusions, but your arguments and conclusions must be *your own*. Extend or develop the ideas of others and relate them to your particular topic.

Above all else: *do not merely reproduce the views of some author in their own words.* This is never acceptable and can be considered to be plagiarism (see chapter 5). An essay that contained large sections lifted straight from a reference book would fail badly. This does not mean that one cannot use quotations. Moderate use of quotations can be effective, but you should always use them only after having put forward the view in your own words, or after having explained the meaning of the quotation as you understand it. Always *integrate* quotations into your argument (see chapter 5). Never use quotations for anything more than an additional articulation of the position that you support or do not support, and never try to 'prove' anything simply by an appeal to someone else – it is simply not good scholarship. You need an *argument* as well as support from the literature.

15 Follow arguments to their conclusion

A good essay is not merely a documentation of certain positions on an issue. You are expected to *think through* different perspectives on a topic and come to some conclusion. A good essay will *extend* an idea to new areas, or *make connections* between different ideas and pieces of evidence.

The conclusion you arrive at may be conventional, or it may be unusual and unconventional. What will be assessed is whether your arguments and the reasons you have advanced have been thought about and carefully presented. You will also be assessed on whether you have demonstrated an understanding of problems and possible solutions in the area of study. Your conclusion will be evaluated in terms of *how well it follows* from your arguments and your reasons for them: *what* you conclude is less important than *how* you arrive at your conclusion. No lecturer will give you a good grade if you simply agree with them. Exceptional students are sometimes awarded good grades by taking issue (disagreeing) with the lecturer's point of view and advancing good arguments that convince the lecturer they were wrong. This does not mean that you should take a contrary position for the sake of it. It means that if you genuinely have strong arguments and evidence supporting a different point of view from the one advanced by your lecturer in class, do not hesitate in presenting it in your assignment.

16 Genuine originality
This is very rare in academia. It is prized highly when it occurs. Lecturers and tutors do not, of course, demand of you that you produce answers to problems that no one has ever thought of before. Originality is not expected of postgraduates (unless they are completing a Ph.D.). If you believe, however, that you have a genuinely original position to take on a topic – a completely unconventional approach – you would certainly do best to put it forward after you have given reasons for dismissing the more conventional positions on a topic. Only develop something new after you have looked at, discussed and criticised other points of view in the literature. New ideas are welcome in academia, but you won't be taken seriously unless you have shown why other approaches are inadequate.

Further, you will have to give reasons for why your own approach should be considered. Certainly, any grand claims on your part will require substantial defence. Bold assertions of originality will be scrutinised very carefully. Be extremely careful about what you are claiming.

A word of warning: make sure that you have **read all you can** on the subject (including journal articles) before you claim that a particular position is your own. It is usually the case that students are not familiar enough with the literature to know that 'their' idea is, in fact, decades or centuries old. A. N. Whitehead once said: 'The entire history of western thought is only a footnote to Plato!' Your lecturers might kindly inform you that 'your' idea is actually quite old, and they may advise you to read certain articles.

On the other hand, in chapter 8 we saw that a minimal degree of originality can be achieved by almost any student if they can integrate examples from their work experience into an argument. In chapter 13 we will revisit this example and see how a student might narrow down an essay topic on Porter's Five Forces theory by limiting it to something he had experience of; namely, the Thai manufacturing sector. This is an example of 'originality'. It is likely that a student has 'insider' knowledge in such cases, knowledge of issues within the sector, and access to useful publications and company documents.

17 Stay within word limits
Part of the exercise of writing an essay is to assess your capacity to argue cogently for a certain position *within a certain word limit*.

This is very hard. Most people would do well at arguing for some point of view if they had an unlimited time frame and no bounds on the length of the document. But even so, quantity never equals quality: a long essay is not necessarily a better one. Long manuscripts can be 90 per cent filler and 10 per cent content. Learn to be your own best critic, and edit your essay heavily if it does not make the points convincingly, or if the content seems confused. (Use the 'imaginary audience test' above.)

18 Swap with others' learning
You may even like to swap essays with someone else who is writing on a different topic, for a fresh appraisal of the relevance of your essay. Collaborative scholarship is an excellent way of improving your writing and understanding of an area. Someone with a fresh approach to your essay might challenge you to revise what you actually thought was relevant to the topic. You will be surprised how honest and constructive critics can find mistakes in your work. Note that, to be useful, this advice requires students to be *critical* of one another's work, and not simply accepting of everything fellow students produce. Some international students are culturally uncomfortable with being critical of others. Yet this skill is important for academic success.

19 Show acknowledgement
In all essay writing, you must show the sources from which you have obtained material (see chapters 5 and 6). All books and articles that you use in your essay should also be listed in a bibliography.

20 Present your essays professionally
Presentation does influence your overall grade. Check with your Faculty or department for presentation requirements; the following are commonly used. Leave a **wide margin** on your papers (about 2 cm all around). This leaves room for the person marking your essay to add comments. This is also true for **double spacing**, which also makes your essay easier to read. Provide a **blank page** at the end of your essay for additional comments. The reference list, table of contents (in reports), abstract, and title page all require separate pages.

21 Enjoy yourself!
Make sure you enjoy the process of essay writing. Don't leave things to the last minute, take lots of breaks, discuss your work with others, and do the best job you can.

● 5 Summary

This chapter has looked at how to prepare for the most common of all postgraduate assignments, the research essay. Essays are a very difficult genre, and – regardless of your level of education – you never stop learning how to write better essays. Several steps need to be taken in preparing to write an essay. The first thing to do is to clarify the topic given to you in terms of the direction words given. Then narrow down the topic into a precise research question or statement. Go to the library and search for relevant material, including journal articles. After finding some articles to read on the topic, use the advice given in terms of writing style and structure to prepare a first draft. Further advice on essay structure is given in the next chapter.

13 Writing a Research Essay

● 1 Introduction

This chapter provides basic advice for essay writing, and includes a formal, staged procedure for preparing an essay. Essay writing is difficult and demands dedicated practice. I have suggested that you try to allow about four weeks to complete an essay of average length. Your essay-writing ability will continue to improve over your lifetime. There are many dedicated texts that provide very useful advice on essay writing, including Greetham (2008). To assist you, there is a model example of a postgraduate-level essay on the website.

● 2 A formal procedure for writing an essay

Let's suppose that you are faced with an assignment topic, such as the one given below, and you are required to write an essay. My suggestion is to break the task down into a series of manageable stages (Davies, 2009). To do this I will use the example of an essay task that we saw in chapter 8.

1 The analysis phase

In *the analysis phase*, the nouns and noun phrases are isolated. The noun phrases are underlined in the example essay question. The task falls into two parts: the preamble to the task and the task itself:

> Michael Porter's schema of industry analysis is a powerful tool for managers to think strategically about the relationships their firm has with their external environment.
>
> Is the industry in which a firm for whom you have worked (you can disguise its identity if there are issues of commercial confidentiality, or you can choose another company if you feel that your employment experience does not help you with this question) 'attractive' or 'unattractive'? **In making your argument** you must address each of the 'Five Forces' identified by Michael Porter. The **second** part of the question is to **make an argument** about whether the current state of industry 'attractiveness' will stay as it is or whether it will change over the next 3–5 years. Take care to explain why you expect this outcome.

Nouns/noun phrases
- Michael Porter's schema of industry analysis
- a powerful tool for managers
- the relationships their firm has with their external environment
- the industry in which a firm for whom you have worked ('attractive' or 'unattractive')
- the current state of industry 'attractiveness'
- stay as it is or change over the next 3–5 years?
- this outcome

Many students receive poor grades for assignments simply because they have not been covered one or another main point. Taking a deliberate strategy of underlining and listing the noun phrases can avoid such oversights. The analysis phase ensures that all key terms are itemised and nothing is missed out.

2 The representation phase

The representation phase involves a graphic representation of the required parts of the essay. This helps you to see the general shape of the essay that you have to write. Points 1, 2 and 3 in the list above apply to the first box; point 4 applies to the second box, and so on. This is a simple essay topic, but you may imagine how complex such diagrammatic representations can be with more complex essay topics. Some students like to use concept maps or argument maps at this stage (see chapter 8). Concept and argument maps are similar to the diagram below, but are generally more structured.

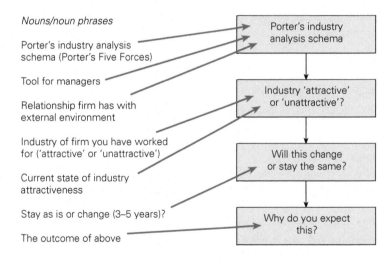

Now note what needs to be done in each of the sections. The first box calls for a *descriptive* account of Porter's Five Forces theory. The second and third boxes require the writer to make a judgement on the basis of an *argument*. (The importance of the argument is emphasised in bold in the original essay topic.) The fourth box requires evidence for the arguments in the second and third boxes. (This could be incorporated into the arguments devised in this section, or treated independently.)

3 The issues phase

The areas of investigation can be further looked at in terms of things to discuss in the essay. This moves you into *the issues phase*. For ease of understanding, the discussion points can be listed under the two main directions given in the essay question (the issues marked with an asterisk below are central to answering the essay task; the non-marked issues are important but not critical).

1 *Industry: 'attractive' or 'unattractive'?*

- Define/clarify/outline what is meant by 'Porter's industry schema and the Five Forces'. Why are they important and useful? How are they measured/assessed?
- Outline your industry in relation to the model (refer to the external environment).*
- Is your industry 'attractive' or 'unattractive' and why? (evidence/argument needed).*
- To what extent can Porter's Five Forces model be applied in your firm/industry to explain the above? (Refer to each of the Forces.)*
- Which of the Five Forces is more appropriate and why? (Evidence/argument needed.)*
- What do different theorists say about Porter's schema regarding 'attractiveness'/'unattractiveness'? (Use readings and class discussions.) Do you agree/disagree?

2 *Industry: change or stay the same over 3–5 years?*

- Outline your industry in relation to the future.*
- To what extent will it stay same/change? (How assessed? Evidence?)*
- How do you justify this position?* (How assessed? Evidence?)*

4 The research phase

One simple way to clarify your response to the issues raised in an essay is to use *research questions* (see chapter 12). Examples of research questions are given below:

- What is the influence/importance/relevance of Porter's Five Forces model in explaining the 'attractiveness' or 'unattractiveness' of [your industry] in [your country]?
- Will this 'attractiveness' or 'unattractiveness' stay the same or change over the next 3–5 years? Why?

This moves us into *the research phase*, in which you go to the library to find information.

The first step is to read widely. Find relevant articles addressing a general question such as: *Is Michael Porter's Five Forces model still a useful framework?* As you find articles and books, list them as either 'useful' or 'not useful'. Those listed in the 'not useful' column are discarded. We saw this table in chapter 4.

Useful	Not useful

It is helpful in this phase not only to rephrase your topic as research questions, but also to note the degree to which you might respond to each question during the research phase.

You must also establish what you need to find out during the research phase. Let's return to our example.

What is the influence/importance/relevance of Porter's Five Forces model in explaining the 'attractiveness' or 'unattractiveness' of [your industry] in [your country]?

What do you need to do?
- look at the published literature;
- study the importance of each force to the industry chosen;
- make an argument;
- become clear on the extent to which the information and evidence you find supports the research question, i.e. is Porter's model:

Very important —WHY?
Somewhat important —WHY?
Unimportant —WHY?

Will this 'attractiveness' or 'unattractiveness' stay the same or change over the next 3–5 years? Why?

What do you need to do?
- look at the published literature;
- make an argument and give an account of the situation of industry attractiveness in relation to the literature;
- become clear on the extent to which the information and evidence you find supports the research question, i.e. will the state of the industry change?

Yes it will —WHY?
No it won't —WHY?
Partial answer (it will and won't) —WHY?

In the example in chapter 8 we assumed that you are a student from Thailand and wished to use your experience in the manufacturing industry. Suppose, after a great deal of reading and thinking, you decide on the following.

> *Porter's Five Forces model is only* **marginally important** *for explaining the 'attrac-tiveness' of manufacturing industry in Thailand.*
>
> *The 'attractiveness' of their industry will* **not** *stay the same over 3–5 years.*

The claims become the **thesis statements** with respect to the major parts of the essay question. The responses require evidential support from the literature, and may also involve the use of personal experience from your work history.

In the next part of the research phase you should use your research questions to construct a search statement, and then begin reading the literature. (For explicit guide-lines for constructing search statements, see the Information Literacy chapter on the website.) To decide to what extent the articles and books are useful, use the 'Yes-BUT' approach to reading.

A strategy for reading the literature: the 'yes-BUT' approach

Write your research questions on the top of the page, then divide the page into six columns:

- *YES*
- *Yes, but*
- *Yes, BUT*
- *No, BUT*
- *No, but*
- *NO*

- *YES:* the author *completely agrees* with your proposed thesis statement(s).
- *Yes, but:* the author *mainly agrees* with the statement but has minor disagreements.
- *Yes, BUT:* the author *mainly agrees* with the position you wish to defend; however he or she has some major disagreements.
- *No, BUT:* the author *mainly disagrees* with the position you wish to defend; however he or she has some major agreements.
- *No, but:* overall the author *disagrees* but has minor agreements with some aspects of the statement.
- *NO:* the author *completely disagrees* with your thesis statement(s).

Using an appropriate information-management strategy, write under the columns where the authors agree or disagree, giving full citation information and page numbers so you do not forget these later.

In the example, your initial thesis statement could be reworded as follows (using letters as placeholders for the key terms of the argument):

> *Porter's Five Forces model – especially the third force – is of some importance in explaining the 'attractiveness' of the manufacturing industry in Thailand because of A, B and C. However, it is not very important because of D, E and F.*

5 The argument phase

With the research done, the thesis statements devised, and evidence for the thesis statements adequately derived from the literature, you can move into *the argument phase*. This involves using a standard argument form to guide the connection between the premises and the conclusion. A sound argument, in part, is a valid deduction with true premises, e.g.:

> *If A then B*
> *Not B*
> *Therefore not A*

As we saw in chapter 13, you only need to choose a valid argument pattern to guide the argument you wish to make. The argument form above is clear in the reworking of your thesis statement and might be expressed in an argument below:

> *P1: If Porter's industry analysis is to adequately explain the 'attractiveness' of an industry it needs to X.*
> *P2: Thailand's manufacturing industry is not X or does not indicate X.*
> *C: Therefore Porter's industry analysis does not adequately explain the 'attractiveness' of the Thai manufacturing industry (support needed).*

6 The writing phase

The *writing phase* requires putting 'clothes' on the basic argument form given above. This requires the use of 'connector words and phrases' or 'critical review language structures', i.e. phrases commonly used in English to express a logical inference. ESL teachers usually provide such structures for their students as a way to model good 'critical thinking'. As we noted in chapter 13, this is done in two ways: (1) using connector language to make the argument structure read better; and (2) developing the introductory paragraph to include an 'inverted funnel' shape. The passage below is an example of the kind of language required for part of the introduction in an essay.

> **Sample introduction with connector language added**
>
> <u>In this essay it will be argued that</u> while Porter's Five Forces, especially the third, are important for most industries, they are <u>not crucial</u> in explaining the attractiveness of the manufacturing industry in Thailand. For Porter's Forces to be crucial in explaining attractiveness, they need to be ... . However this is not the case for the manufacturing industry, <u>due to the following three factors: ...</u> . Therefore <u>it will be claimed that</u> Porter's Forces are of only <u>limited relevance</u> to the manufacturing industry in Thailand.

But this introductory argument could be even better. Introductions should be shaped like an inverted 'funnel' (see later in this chapter). They should begin with the general topic, narrow down to the specific topic, isolate a research gap (in *italics* below), give an argument or 'thesis' statement, and then signpost the essay ahead (i.e. give an outline of the parts of the assignment to follow). It could also be supported with a few in-text citations. With a little reworking the essay introduction might read:

Sample introduction with inverted funnel format

[general outline]
↓

Porter's Five Forces industry analysis has been used as a conceptual tool for more than ten years (Franklin, 1999; Jones, 2000). Its relevance is undisputed in modern industrial western societies (Harrison, 1997). **[gap]** *However, while it has been applied to a number of industries it has not been extensively used in the industrial sector in developing countries such as Thailand* (Higgens, 2002).

[thesis]
↓

In this essay, it will be argued that while Porter's Five Forces, especially the third, are important for most industries, they are <u>not crucial</u> in explaining the 'attractiveness' of the manufacturing industry in Thailand. For Porter's Forces to be crucial in explaining attractiveness, they need to be ... . However, this is not the case for the manufacturing industry, <u>due to the following three factors: ...</u> . Therefore, it will be claimed that Porter's Forces are of only <u>limited relevance</u> to the manufacturing industry in Thailand.

[outline of paper]
↓

The essay is structured as follows: ... . In the first section, the essay outlines ... . In the second section, the paper looks at ... [and so on].

Now you have a good introduction with a clear argument. The hard part is over. The rest is a matter of supporting this argument with appropriate evidence from the literature and doing what you say you will do in each section of the assignment. The extent to which you do this with evidence will determine the grade you receive. The procedure outlined allows you to have a clear structure and argument. My example is general in nature but can be applied to all academic discipline areas.

● 3 Essay structures

There is little variance in how academics write essays. Learn the structure and you will make life easier. Below is a diagram of the structure in a simplified form. (Note that another, more detailed, version of this diagram has been developed elsewhere in Rao, Chanock & Krishnan, 2007.)

This structure can be used as a template for the majority of academic essays in almost every academic subject area. Essays always have an introduction (around 10 per cent of the essay) and a conclusion (also around 10 per cent). Introductions 'narrow down' to the central thesis statement or argument. Conclusions restate the main points and 'broaden out' to a general statement to finish.

Another thing that makes essay writing easier is the method of organisation in the body of the essay. The main approaches are **block style** and **chain (concept) style**.

1 Block-style structure

In **block style** all of one group of ideas is discussed in the first part (block) of the essay, then another group of ideas is discussed in the second part (block). For example, a *compare and contrast* essay asks you to 'Discuss the similarities and differences between medical intervention in the delivery of babies in Australia and Holland'. In a block style, you would discuss the situation in Holland in full in the first block, and in the second block you would discuss the situation in Australia, drawing attention to the similarities and differences with Holland. In your discussion in the third block of your essay you would critique the two systems.

2 Chain-style structure

In the **chain style** you discuss one idea at a time, and move from point to point. (Chain style is also known as 'point-by-point' organisation.) In a chain-style approach to 'Discuss the similarities and differences between medical intervention in the delivery of babies in Australia and Holland', you would discuss one part of the medical intervention at a time. Your first point might be what the medical system instructs a pregnant woman to do when she first goes into labour in Holland. You would then compare and contrast that to what she is told to do in Australia. After that, you would discuss the implications of the medical system's initial advice, before moving on to your next point, which may be which medical professional carries out the first assessment of the pregnant woman. Again, you would compare and contrast what occurs in Holland and Australia and discuss the implications.

Different essay topics may be more compatible with one style than another. Also, you may feel more comfortable writing in one of the styles.

3 A diagram of a simplified academic essay structure

See the diagram on following page.

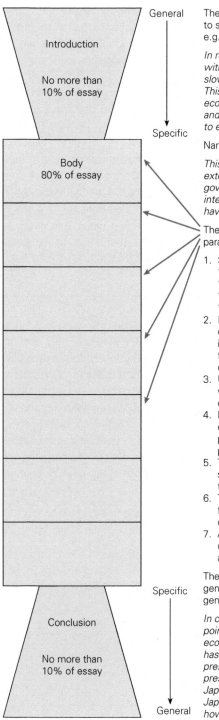

General

The introduction always moves from general to specific. Start the introduction very generally: e.g.,

In recent years, Japan has experienced problems with its economic growth. Its economy has slowed and this has led to 15 years of stagnation. This has made it hard for Japan to regain economic prosperity. There are several internal and external problems that have caused Japan to experience slow economic growth.

Specific

Narrow this down by the end of the introduction:

This essay will discuss the internal and external problems, and the effectiveness of government policies. This essay will argue that internal pressures are the major problems that have caused 15 years of economic stagnation.

The body of the essay should be divided into paragraphs. Each paragraph makes a new point.

1. Signal each point using words such as: 'Following this point ...', 'Given this ...', 'Firstly, ...', 'Secondly ...', 'Therefore, ...', 'In conclusion ...', 'Thus ...', 'Consequently ...'.
2. If you have three main things to say in the essay, divide the essay into three sections; if you have five things to present have five equal parts in the body. Use block or chain style.
3. Use numbered sections and sub-sections with titles for each section to make each part of the essay clear.
4. Don't waste words. Make your points with economy and clarity and move on to the next point. The reader always knows when you are padding things out.
5. The body is where you argue for or against some point of view and/or attack or defend the views of others.
6. The body is where you weigh up evidence for something and/or present two or more competing theories about something.
7. Avoid irrelevant ideas; technical jargon; your own 'beliefs' or appeal to authority (without argument).

Specific

The conclusion always moves from specific to general. Start by summing up and then end with general remarks:

In conclusion, the essay has made three main points: 1)...2)...3)... Japan has faced slow economic growth for a long period of time. This has been caused by internal and external pressures. This essay has shown how these pressures have been mishandled by the Japanese government. Further analysis of the Japanese economic situation might shed light on how these pressures can be alleviated in the future.

General

4 Models for the body of an essay

How should you structure the body of the essay? Below I have provided three models of a structure for the body, but there are many variations on this, depending on the topic you are writing about and the depth of your analysis. In general, an essay that looks at both sides of an issue and comes to a well-argued conclusion is much better than an essay which only looks at one side of an issue. To help you structure your thoughts for the body of the essay, you might like to consider using the argument-mapping approach mentioned in chapter 8.

Model 1

Introduction
Body
1. First supporting argument
2. Second supporting argument
3. Third supporting argument
Conclusion

Model 2

Introduction
Body
1. Summary of counter-arguments + rebuttal of counter-arguments
2. First supporting argument
3. Second supporting argument
4. Third supporting argument
Conclusion

Model 3

Introduction
Body
1. Counter-argument 1
   + Rebuttal of this counter-argument
2. Counter-argument 2
   + Rebuttal of this counter-argument
3. Counter-argument 3
   + Rebuttal of this counter-argument
Conclusion

● 4 Organisation of essays

As we saw in chapter 9, a paragraph is a collection of sentences about one topic and tends to have three main parts: the topic sentence, the body (supporting sentences) and perhaps a concluding sentence. Similarly, an essay is a group of paragraphs about one topic and also has three main parts: the introduction, the body and the conclusion. This makes it easy to learn essay structure. A paragraph and an essay have the same basic structure. An essay is just much longer (Oshima & Hogue, 1999).

In structural terms, the relationship between an essay and the paragraphs in an essay looks like this:

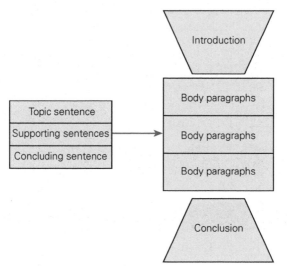

(Based on Oshima & Hogue, 1999)

1 The introductory paragraph

The introduction begins with a statement about the general area of research or the general topic. It also engages the reader. It then 'funnels down' to the most specific sub-topic. An **exceptional essay** will then outline the research '**gap**' – what others have done and what the writer is going to do (this is optional, but demonstrates that the writer knows the literature well). It then poses a precise research question to be investigated. The '**thesis statement**' comes next, which anticipates the argument in the essay and gives a tentative answer to the **research question**. Finally, a very brief **outline** of the essay body is provided (this can be reversed with the thesis statement coming after the outline). The diagram below shows all the key elements in a good, but not exceptional, introduction.

> **Model introduction (for complete essay see the website)**
>
> **general outline**
> ↓
> In the twenty-first century, countries in every region around the world are becoming more economically integrated. This integration is a way of solving economic problems. Economic integration varies from reduction of intra-group tariffs to common economic policies and common currency. Free-trade areas, such as

NAFTA and AFTA, are integrated to remove intra-group tariffs. The well-known European Monetary Union (EMU) has common economic policies with an intensive degree of cooperation. For example, a new single currency, the Euro, has been created within the member countries.

specific topic
↓

The EMU was formed with four main purposes. The first purpose was to bring European people more closely together. The second purpose was to create cooperation between European people. The third purpose was to create Europe's single market to benefit European economies from stable prices, more competitive companies, varied choices of goods and services for the consumer and faster economic growth. The last purpose was to increase the Euro's role to be an important currency in the world economy (*Euro Guide*, 1998, p. 24).

One significant role of the Euro currency is that it is used as an official reserve currency. Since the creation of the Euro, many economists have claimed that the Euro will quickly compete against the US dollar as a reserve currency (Bergsten, 1997, p. 29; Bertaut & Iyigun, 1999; Hanes, 1999).

outline of essay
↓

In this essay, I will firstly outline the historical background of the EMU. Secondly, I will discuss the importance of a reserve currency. Thirdly, I will give the required qualifications of a reserve currency. Fourthly, I will describe the reasons that the dollar became an important reserve currency. Finally, I will examine the prospect of the Euro as an official reserve currency.

thesis statement
↓

I will argue that the Euro cannot currently compete against the US dollar as an international reserve currency because of the incumbency of the dollar and incomplete integration of the EMU.

If this introduction were to be improved, I would suggest that it follow the elements outlined below. This might require that the student do more academic research to uncover a research 'gap'.

General area or topic
Specific area of focus
Research 'gap'
Research question to be answered
Thesis statement (answer to question)
Outline of essay to follow

An introduction can do a number of things (and MUST do what is marked*):

- give an overview of the general topic area;*
- put forward the reasons for writing the essay;
- define the key terms;
- introduce the question(s) the essay will be discussing;*
- demonstrate your research in the area and include references;
- explain the reasons for answering the question in a particular way;
- relate the writing to other work in the field;
- present the central idea (the 'thesis statement');*
- give an indication of the structure of the essay or assignment (outline);*
- state the specific topic of the essay;
- list the sub-topics of the main topic;
- outline the method of organisation in the body of the essay.*

2 The body paragraphs

The body of the essay is made up of several paragraphs, as noted earlier. Each of these paragraphs has a topic sentence, supporting sentences and, sometimes, a concluding sentence. Each of the body paragraphs supports the thesis statement (Oshima & Hogue, 1999). Read the body paragraphs of the model essay provided on the website. Note how each paragraph introduces new ideas related to the Euro as a currency. The sub-sections assist in this. Underline the topic sentence in each paragraph and the supporting sentences provided. Note the linking language between each paragraph.

3 The concluding paragraph

The conclusion of an essay can do a number of things (it *must* do the things marked*):

- round up the essay by bringing together all the main points;*
- summarise the arguments developed in the essay;*
- point to areas of further research if this is relevant to the writing task;
- refer back to the question to demonstrate how it has been answered;*
- show what the essay has answered and what it has not addressed;
- show that the writer did what he or she set out to do in the introduction;
- put forward a point of view supported by the evidence presented;
- provide a solution to the problem posed in the introduction.

Conclusions should never introduce new ideas or arguments. If something is important enough to be added, it should be in the body of the essay. The first part of the conclusion always summarises the main points or repeats the thesis statement using different words. Sometimes a conclusion begins with the words 'In conclusion', but this is not mandatory, and is often overused (Oshima & Hogue, 1999). It is more common to begin a conclusion with the helpful words: *'This essay has ...'* and go on to sum up the main points.

5 Summary

This chapter has looked at the various parts of the essay, in particular, the introduction, body and conclusion formats. An example of a postgraduate-level essay is provided on the website. It is an authentic essay written by an international student from Asia.

6 Essay-writing checklist

Use the following checklist to help you determine the strengths and weaknesses of essays.

	Strong	Weak
Overall content		
• Understanding of topic/issue	☐	☐
• Evidence of research	☐	☐
• Analysis and synthesis of material	☐	☐
• Originality	☐	☐
• Connection with other areas (e.g. the workplace)	☐	☐
• Clarity and cohesion of arguments and points	☐	☐
• Length of text	☐	☐
• Use of diagrams, tables and graphs if appropriate	☐	☐

	Strong	Weak
Introduction		
General statements	☐	☐
• Thesis statement	☐	☐
• 'Funnel' structure	☐	☐
• Length	☐	☐

	Strong	Weak
Body paragraphs		
• Sequencing of paragraphs	☐	☐
• Topic sentences	☐	☐
• Supporting sentences	☐	☐
• Relevance of all points	☐	☐
• One main idea per paragraph	☐	☐
• Linking of points within paragraphs	☐	☐
• Length of paragraphs	☐	☐

	Strong	Weak
Conclusion		
• Restatement of thesis statement	☐	☐
• Summary of main points	☐	☐
• Final comment	☐	☐
• Absence of new points	☐	☐
• Length	☐	☐

	Strong	Weak
Language, fluency and cohesion		
• Grammar	☐	☐
• Sentence structure	☐	☐
• Vocabulary (accuracy and formality)	☐	☐
• Conciseness	☐	☐

	Strong	Weak

Referencing and citations

- Acknowledgement of all sources
- Paraphrasing, summarising and quoting
- Use of critical review language
- Format of in-text citations
- Bibliography/reference list
- Appendices

Presentation

- Fonts, margins, spacing
- Spelling and punctuation
- Capitalisation
- Titles

14 Writing a Literature Review

1 Introduction

A literature review normally forms part of a research thesis. However, it can also stand alone as a separate document. It is usually expected that you 'review the literature' in writing an essay or report, although this kind of literature review is much less extensive and wide-ranging than that expected for a doctoral thesis. However, the academic skills required for reviewing the literature in an essay or thesis are much the same. This chapter will help you to understand what it means to 'review the literature'.

> A literature review is the presentation, classification and evaluation of what other researchers have written on a particular subject. It is not simply a 'shopping list' of what others have said, however. It is organised according to your *research objective*, *research question*, and/or the *problem/issue you wish to address*. Without this, the literature review is a useless compilation of what other scholars have said and done. With the research objective, the literature review forms a focused and carefully structured outline of what others have done in the area that you are concerned with investigating.

2 What is a literature review?

Literature reviews are written to provide other people, e.g. fellow students or staff, with information about current, or relevant literature in a particular field of study. They are usually considerably more extensive and detailed than an annotated bibliography or a reading log (see chapter 10, section 7, 'Annotated bibliographies').

In postgraduate research, a literature review is a substantial work. It addresses major texts in the chosen area of study and relates and discusses their content as well as commenting on the effect of the noted research or theories. A literature review usually eventually forms a major chapter, or sometimes several chapters of a higher-degree thesis.

A literature review for a postgraduate student will consist of a number of article reviews where the student compares article 'A' with articles 'B' and 'C'. It is important to note that these are not outlined separately like an annotated bibliography, critical review, or reading log.

A literature review summarises, interprets and evaluates existing 'literature' (published material) in order to establish current knowledge of the subject. The purpose for doing so relates to ongoing research to develop that knowledge. A literature review has multiple purposes. It should:

- define and limit the problem you are working on;
- place your study in a historical perspective;
- avoid unnecessary duplication;
- evaluate promising research methods;
- relate your findings to previous knowledge and suggest further research.

A literature review must do more than describe. Rather, it may:

- compare and contrast different authors' views on an issue;
- group together authors who draw similar conclusions;
- criticise aspects of methodology;
- note areas in which authors are in disagreement;
- highlight exemplary studies;
- highlight gaps in research;
- show how your study relates to previous studies;
- show how your study relates to the literature in general;
- conclude by summarising what the literature says.

The literature review may, in addition:

- resolve a controversy and/or identify disagreements;
- establish the need for additional research;
- define a topic of inquiry;
- outline theory and list relevant hypotheses;
- note methodological deficiencies in other studies;
- take up recommendations for future research;
- outline a practical problem that needs resolution.

3 Why do a literature review?

The literature review is a 'stand-alone' review. It must be understandable to someone who has *not read* the literature you are reviewing. You must demonstrate your ability to identify an issue for inquiry and discuss the issue in a meaningful way for readers considering the same question. Readers should learn not only what has been said about the issue but what you *think* about what has been said. You will summarise, but you will also begin to develop your own ideas on the topic, i.e. a thesis statement. This means that you will also interpret and evaluate the material you are reviewing. This thesis will form the central part of your research essay or report.

There is no point in reinventing the wheel. Research is not useful unless it does something new or different. To do something new or different requires that you are aware of what has been done already by others. A literature review is, therefore, written to uncover a 'gap' in the research. New research moves on from the literature review to try to fill this gap.

> ## The conversation metaphor for research
>
> Think of the process of doing research on a topic in this way:
>
> - the **general area** is a particular 'conversation' among academics in the field of study;
> - the **specific area** is derived as a result of your focusing in on a particular part of the bigger 'conversation' (a sub-set of a larger conversation);
> - the **gap** is your noticing that something needs to be said in the conversation (which has not been said before, or which needs addressing in more detail);
> - the **research question** involves asking something that precisely addresses what needs to be said (the 'gap');
> - the **thesis statement** is your suggested or tentative answer to this question.

The literature review involves the second and third parts of this process. It is more focused than an outline of the general area of scholarship, but it is less detailed than your research question and your thesis statement.

> The literature review has two main sections (though they are not formally identified as such):
>
> 1 an outline of what others have done in the particular area that you are concerned with; then a narrowing to the 'gap' in the research;
> 2 a presentation of the 'gap' in relation to the work of others.
>
> The research questions and thesis statements are then precisely stated before you start the rest of the research project.

The relationship between the research question and the literature review

It is necessary to review the literature in order to eventually arrive at a research question and a thesis statement. The reverse relationship is necessary too. In order to review the literature properly, it is necessary to look at it in light of your proposed research question – otherwise, (a) you won't know what research is useful to read; and (b) the review will be a useless collection of unshaped ideas.

> **Note:** The research question and thesis statement *guide the process of writing a literature review,* but they are not formally stated until the end of the review. But, equally, the literature review is *necessary in order to finally arrive at a sound research question and thesis statement.*

4 The aim of a literature review

Your objective in writing a literature review is *not* to do the following:

- list as many articles and names as possible;
- try to refer to every piece of literature in the area (this is not possible, anyway).

The literature review is a highly *considered* list. You make reference to published literature only where necessary. It is only necessary when this literature:

- agrees with your thesis or research statement;
- disagrees with your thesis or research statement;
- *partly* agrees or disagrees with your thesis or research statement.

Use your research question and proposed thesis statement to guide your reading of the literature. Literature that does not have a bearing on these areas is discarded.

Using a research question and thesis statement to guide the research

You need to have in mind a rough statement of what you propose to accept or defend before you can begin to write your literature review – and preferably before you read the literature. As you read, you will need to refine and change this statement.

Often it is hard to tell if a particular writer agrees, disagrees or partly agrees with your position on a topic. In reading an article, one is often confused about where writers stand on an issue. This is usually not because the writer is unclear in their message, but because you have not developed a clear enough **thesis statement** yourself. To avoid this problem, use the 'Yes-BUT' approach to reading as discussed in chapter 13.

5 Writing a literature review

In writing a literature review, you need to demonstrate your ability to recognise relevant information and to synthesise and evaluate it, according to the tentative guiding research questions and thesis statements you have developed.

Your reader wants to know: (a) what literature exists; but also (b) your informed *evaluation* of the literature. To do this you need to demonstrate that you can do the following:

Seek information: you need to show that you can scan the literature efficiently, using manual or computerised methods to identify a set of potentially useful articles and books.

Appraise information critically: you need to show that you can apply principles of critical analysis to identify those studies which are unbiased and valid. Your

> readers want more than just a list of articles and books. They want evidence you have thought about it *critically.*
>
> **Summarise and critique**: in addition to providing fair summaries of the main points of articles, you need to show where you agree and disagree with others.

It is usually a bad sign when every paragraph of your review begins with the names of researchers: 'Smith said ...', 'Jones said ...', etc. (see chapter 10 on the language to use to avoid this problem). Instead, organise your review into useful, informative sections that present themes or identify trends (Taylor, 2008).

> A literature review is not just a summary, but a *conceptually organised synthesis* of the results of your search. It must:
>
> - **organise information** and relate it to the thesis or research question you are developing;
> - **synthesise results** into a summary of what is and is not known;
> - **identify controversy** when it appears in the literature;
> - **develop questions** for further research. (Taylor, 2008)

How to present and report information

1 Grouping information
In reviewing literature, you will need to refer to what others have done. Group this information in different ways. (Notice the difference in tenses in the examples below):

> **Difference of approach**
>
> - 'While Jones (2002) argues ... Smith (1999)... <u>claims</u> that ... .'
>
> **From distantly to closely related**
>
> - 'Smith (1999) and Jones (2001) both <u>showed</u> that ... . However, Hutchison (2002) <u>demonstrated</u> that ... .'
>
> **Chronologically**
>
> - 'Early marketing theory owes its development to ... . Many studies <u>contributed</u> to ... for example, Jones and Smith (1986). Hunt (1987) <u>was recognised for</u> ... but later Jamison (1999) <u>showed</u> that ...'.

2 Reporting information
Use different ways of reporting data, so that your literature review is not monotonous.

Information-prominent:

Research <u>indicates</u> that ... (Becker, 1997, p. 9) **(present tense)**

Weak author-prominent:

Research <u>has shown/</u>Some <u>have argued that/</u> ... (Becker, 1997, p. 9). **(present perfect tense)**

Author prominent:

Becker (1997, p. 9) <u>argues</u> that ... **(present tense)**

Another way to cite information is to use 'critical review language' (see chapter 10):

- According to Becker (1997, p. 9)
- In Becker's view ... (Becker, 1997, p. 9)
- Becker's point seems to be that ... (Becker, 1997, p. 9)
- Becker rejects the idea that ... (1997, p. 9)
- Becker questions the idea that ... (1997, p. 9)
- Becker investigates the idea that ... (1997, p. 9)
- Becker undermines the position that ...(1997, p. 9)

Example of a literature review (excerpt)

In the literature, it is recognised that a dichotomy exists between agricultural and business marketing because the marketing management approach is not prominent in agricultural marketing theory. Bateman (1976) suggests that agricultural marketing has traditionally incorporated everything that happens between the farm gate and the consumer, therefore encompassing areas which 'the purist' may not consider marketing. While analysis of government intervention and policy form the focus of agricultural marketing theory, studies of the objectives and decisions confronting individual businesses are central to business marketing theory.

Muelenberg (1986) also identifies the gap existing between the two disciplines. He notes that agricultural marketing theory has not adopted the marketing management approach of business marketing theory or examined competitive strategy in the same way as business literature. According to Richardson (1986), the marketing management approach (which he refers to as the agribusiness concept) has 'gained very little acceptance ... and no significant analytical or research results' in the area of agricultural marketing (p. 100). However, it appears that parts of agricultural marketing theory seem to be moving towards the marketing management approach.

Breimyer (1973) was the first to identify an agricultural marketing school of thought focusing on business marketing theory, and this school of thought seems to be growing more prominent. For example, Watson (1983) acknowledges that during the 1970s a minor paradigm shift occurred in agricultural marketing with a move towards business marketing. He notes how successive editions of Kohl's agricultural marketing textbook (1972 and 1980) have changed to describe the marketing concept. Muelenberg (1986) points out a number of agricultural marketeers who have partially incorporated the marketing management approach, but mainly focus on the behaviour of agribusiness companies (e.g. Bresch, 1981; Yon, 1976), rather than individual farm firms.

Ritson (1986) argues that agricultural marketing theory should focus on government policy, because in European agriculture, parts of the marketing mix which would normally be undertaken by individual businesses are controlled by the government. In some countries, marketing boards have exclusive control of the price, place and promotion of agricultural products. These organisations supposedly carry out many marketing management practices on behalf of business, including farm firms.

Although central control or government intervention may limit the marketing options available to individual businesses, farm firms still have some control over their marketing mix and production decisions. The presence of government intervention or marketing activity does not preclude or excuse individual business firms from any marketing activity or strategic process associated with the marketplace. In business marketing theory, the external environment has a major influence on the marketing activities of most firms.

The apparent differences between agricultural marketing and business marketing theories may not present a problem because both disciplines examine issues which are likely to require different theories and techniques for analysis. *However, concern must be expressed at the failure of researchers to comprehensively examine the marketing strategies undertaken by individual farm businesses.* Businesses in the agricultural sector include farmers and other often larger and more sophisticated agribusinesses, such as input suppliers and merchants. Business literature contains published articles examining the marketing strategies of large agribusiness companies; *however, little research appears to reach down to the farm business level.* (McLeay & Zwart, 1993)

(Notice the 'gap' in the example provided (the italicised passages). Notice also how the research begins by focusing on the main topic area and then narrowing down to the gap in the research. The writer will then go on to formally state the research question and outline their thesis statement.)

6 How do I begin a literature review?

1 Finding a topic and narrowing it down

As noted in a previous chapter, the first thing you need to do is to narrow your topic down until you have a good research question. Lecturers seldom give students 'narrow' essay topics. They are more likely to give students 'broad' topics to see which students are able to narrow them down for themselves. Narrowing the topic is your job (for more information, see chapter 12).

2 Choosing a controversial area

A good topic is controversial and has a great deal of difference of opinion. It should be a 'warm' topic, not a 'hot' or 'cold' one. This will ensure that there is a great deal of published material from which you can choose, but not an excessive amount. This will make the research process easier.

3 Designing a research question

Put limits on your search by designing a good research question.

7 Starting the review

1 Finding resources

Find and review – as a general rule – between 15 and 50 journal articles or chapter-length sources on your question. The rest of your selection can come from relevant chapters in books, internet articles, professional, high-quality magazines, and so on.

> **Note:** Be highly discriminating in your selection of resources. Don't choose articles that are too difficult for you to understand, or articles that are too general or poorly focused. Use secondary articles if the primary articles are incomprehensible to you. Let your research question and your abilities in reading English guide your selection.

It is best to use 'refereed' journals. These have been 'peer-reviewed' by experts in the particular subject area. When professional academics submit papers to journals, these undergo a peer-review process (for an explanation, see the chapter on the library, especially the second on journal articles, on the website). This is to ensure the quality and originality of the material to be published. Newspapers and popular magazines do not always contain content that is suitably unbiased, impartial and well researched. They often contain opinions rather than arguments. The language of peer-reviewed papers will be harder, but peer-reviewed papers are representative of the kind of material you will have to read as part of your postgraduate course. You should therefore get used to reading 'academic' texts as soon possible.

2 Write a summary and critiques

The next step is to write a critical review (see chapter 10) for each article. A good approach to reading the literature is the 'Yes-BUT' approach outlined in chapter 13.

Once you have written a critical review for each article you need to combine and assemble them in a coherent way. Your literature review should do the following:

- delete minor details;
- combine similar or related ideas;

- paraphrase accurately;
- reflect the author's emphasis;
- recognise the author's purpose;
- identify a clear and common topic;
- identify a main idea;
- stay within appropriate length;
- exclude personal opinions.

A good review will also:

- combine similar or related details into categories and provide a label or heading for those ideas;
- select the main idea, or key points provided by authors when they are explicitly stated;
- determine the main ideas when the author is not being explicit.

You want to end up with one document that combines relevant information from the relevant critical reviews already completed on each of the articles found on your topic. See the diagram below.

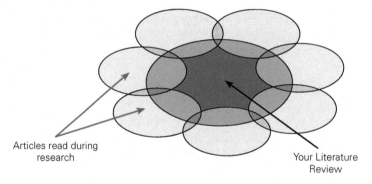

Articles read during research

Your Literature Review

● 8 Writing taxonomies

Writing a literature review involves considerable skill. Designing a **writing template** for a literature review might be helpful. Attempts have been made to outline writing taxonomies for graduate students that use predictable writing structures. These show nested part–whole relationships between ideas and support for ideas using common linking phrases (Rochecouste, 2005). Designing taxonomies such as these might be used to help shape a literature review. An illustration of this is given below.

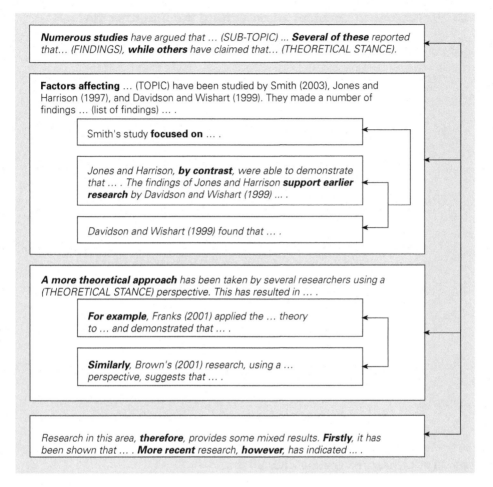

Numerous studies *have argued that … (SUB-TOPIC) …* **Several of these** *reported that… (FINDINGS),* **while others** *have claimed that… (THEORETICAL STANCE).*

Factors affecting … (TOPIC) have been studied by Smith (2003), Jones and Harrison (1997), and Davidson and Wishart (1999). They made a number of findings … (list of findings) … .

Smith's study **focused on** … .

Jones and Harrison, **by contrast**, *were able to demonstrate that … . The findings of Jones and Harrison* **support earlier research** *by Davidson and Wishart (1999) … .*

Davidson and Wishart (1999) found that … .

A more theoretical approach has been taken by several researchers using a (THEORETICAL STANCE) perspective. This has resulted in … .

For example, *Franks (2001) applied the … theory to … and demonstrated that … .*

Similarly, *Brown's (2001) research, using a … perspective, suggests that … .*

Research in this area, **therefore**, *provides some mixed results.* **Firstly**, *it has been shown that … .* **More recent** *research,* **however**, *has indicated … .*

(Based on Rochecouste, 2005)

Notice in the example that the review begins with a sub-topic. This example therefore forms part of a literature review on a larger topic. The larger topic might be, for example, *the role of television in influencing criminal behaviour in children.* (The research question might be, e.g. *Does television have a negative impact on the attitudes of children towards crime and criminal behaviour?*) The sub-topic might be, for example, whether violent cartoons have a direct causal impact on anti-social behaviour in the home. The empirical work by Smith, Jones and Harrison, Davidson and Wishart and Franks and Brown has been outlined and compared in the template above. A distinction is made between *research findings* on the impact of violent cartoons on anti-social behaviour, and the *theoretical literature* on the topic. Both have been given separate sections in the structure of the review. Within each section, the views of the writers are compared. A final section sums up the overall position of the writers on the sub-topic.

9 Factors to consider when writing the literature review

A literature review can be understood as an integrated and synthesised collection of critical reviews (see chapter 10).

The following list outlines some important issues to consider when writing your literature review.

- The length of your literature review does not determine the quality. Often a shorter literature review is better than a longer one.
- You cannot cover all previous research in your area, so be selective and specific. Narrowness in focus is the key. If you have too many points to cover, rework your review so that it articulates fewer things in more detail.
- The literature that you choose should be *directly relevant* to your chosen area of research.
- Have a general idea of your overall research aims. You will probably use your review of the literature for your research essay. What is your essay topic? Does the literature address this topic? What do you want to argue? (What is your thesis statement?) Does the literature link to your thesis?
- When you write your review, ask yourself: 'Is this literature relevant to my aims?' It may help to write down and clarify your aims several times. These aims may change as you review more and more research.
- Have specific critical questions in mind when you write your review and make sure you answer those questions.
- Make sure that your review has evidence of active, analytical thinking (see 'Critical review language' in chapter 10).

10 Literature review checklist

Before you submit your literature review to your supervisor or lecturer, consider the following questions (Taylor, 2008):

- Do I have a specific thesis, problem, or research question which my literature review helps to define?
- What type of literature review am I conducting? Am I looking at issues of theory? methodology? policy? quantitative research (e.g. studies of a new or controversial procedure)? qualitative research (e.g. studies determining criteria for allocating health-care resources)?
- What is the scope of my literature review? What types of publications am I using, e.g. journals, books, government documents, popular media? What discipline am I working in?
- How good are my information-seeking skills? Has my search been wide enough to ensure I've found all the relevant material? Has it been narrow enough to exclude irrelevant material? Are the number of sources I've used appropriate for the length of my paper?

- Is there a specific relationship between the literature I've chosen to review and the problem I've formulated?
- Have I critically analysed the literature I use? Do I just list and summarise authors and articles, or do I assess them? Do I discuss the strengths and weaknesses of the cited material?
- Have I cited and discussed studies contrary to my perspective?
- Will the reader find my literature review relevant, appropriate, and useful?

⬤ 11 Summary

This chapter has outlined a strategy for preparing a literature review. It is important not to become 'lost' in the literature. To avoid this, you need to have a strategy such as that suggested here.

Literature reviews are critical to major research projects for a number of reasons. They give both you and the reader confidence that the scholarly groundwork has been done. Good research does not reinvent the wheel. A literature review ensures that the topic being investigated is a new and legitimate one, and/or that you are making an advance beyond what others have done. However, presentation of this literature is critical. The literature review should not be written in the form of a 'he said', 'she said', but a carefully synthesised record of what others have done that has been shaped to suit your own purposes.

15 The Final Polish: Editing and Proofreading

1 Introduction

Would you take seriously a book or article full of careless errors? Of course, at university, lecturers are keen to see the quality of the content of your work: the facts, the ideas, the argumentation. But your success as a student is fundamentally affected by your ability to express yourself in a clear, accurate and persuasive manner. In the workplace, the situation is no different.

Lecturers and employers may not always talk about such things as grammar, spelling, punctuation and presentation. But they notice them. And they will look harshly on work that does not meet acceptable standards of style and literacy. Thus, editing and proofreading are skills that you will need to take very seriously. Writing cannot just be handed in for assessment without editing and proofreading it first. Native speakers who have no trouble in writing often make mistakes. Most would never fail to edit and proofread. Yet, sometimes international students hand in work that is clearly sub-standard. Why?

Partly, this occurs because of poor planning and time management. However, I think this neglect also results from not understanding the importance of editing and proofreading. Hence, this chapter outlines this skill and provides some practical tips for editing and proofreading well.

2 Why edit and proofread your work?

There is no substitute for the academic content in a piece of work. But lecturers assess students' work based on other factors, including style and literacy. Style and literacy incorporate such things as:

- grammar and syntax
- layout and presentation
- expression
- spelling
- punctuation

Some people think that editing and proofreading are synonyms, i.e. two words meaning the same thing. This is not true. They are different procedures entirely:

> **Editing** refers to the close reading and rewriting of a version of the text that is approaching completion. It involves, for example, improving expression by deleting redundancies or improving argumentation. Among other things, editing involves improving the *sense* of the material.
>
> **Proofreading** involves checking the final version of text for mistakes that may have been missed during the editing process (e.g. spelling, punctuation, capitalisation, noun–verb agreement errors). With proofing you are not looking for the sense or meaning of the material at all. In fact, as I will suggest, you can proofread best by reading everything backwards, from the last line to the first line!

Editing and proofreading your written work prior to submitting it for assessment is crucial. Neglecting these stages is like, for example, leaving one wall unfinished despite endless preparation involved in painting a house! Here are some important editing and proofreading tips:

1 Allow enough time
Don't start to edit and proofread your work as soon as you have finished writing. Put aside your work for a while, maybe for a week or so (the longer the better), before you begin the checking process. This ensures that you can look at it with 'fresh' and critical eyes.

2 Vary your editing activities
If you are running short of time, you might try drafting one chapter or section of an essay or report while editing or proofreading another. This will ensure that you stay interested in what you are doing whilst also keeping the whole project moving along.

3 Print your work before editing and proofreading
Looking at your work after you have printed it can be valuable, particularly when proofreading. Looking at your work on paper can uncover presentation mistakes, language mistakes, even content mistakes you may never have noticed otherwise.

4 Edit with problem areas in mind
If English is not your first language, it is possible that you frequently make particular language mistakes in your work. Perhaps you often make mistakes in relation to some of the following areas of grammar: verb tenses, subject–verb agreement, articles, prepositions and use of pronouns. Perhaps you tend to write sentences that are too long and complicated. Perhaps your paragraphs tend to lack focus. The more awareness you have of mistakes that often appear in your work, the more successfully you will be able to address them when editing and proofreading.

5 Research-editing skills

Take some time to look at some of the many style manuals before you begin, so you know what to look for when editing and proofreading. AGPS (2002) and Gibaldi (2008) are very good, as are Strunk (2008), Ritter (2003) and Turabian (2007). These texts will be in your university library. Taking time to read such manuals now will save you time later. Reading these texts before you begin university can be part of your strategic planning (see chapter 2).

6 Familiarise yourself with departmental requirements (for essays and reports)

Many university departments produce a 'style guide'. If they don't give you one, show the initiative and ask for one. How do they want you to cite references? Is there a preference for footnotes or endnotes? Which referencing system should you use? How much can you quote from a text? Is it OK to use bullet points when explaining something or is prose format preferred? Do they demand writing in the third person for my subject or can you use first-person pronouns? Which tense should you use? Do they ask for headers and/or footers?

7 Familiarise yourself with university requirements (for theses)

If you are writing a major piece of work such as a Ph.D. thesis, find out how the university requires your written work or dissertation to be formatted: How should tables and charts to be presented? What margins are required? What spacing do you need? How should you present the bibliography? Are there guidelines for how you should order and arrange the various chapters or sections of your work? Finding this out now saves time later, as you can set up a template to use for your assignments.

8 Recruit help

Everyone needs help in editing and proofreading their written work, including professional writers: Ernest Hemingway rewrote *The Old Man and the Sea* something like one hundred times before he was satisfied with the text. We are usually 'too close' and too familiar with our own writing to see mistakes or to recognise better ways of making an argument. As a result, asking for assistance to help you with your proofreading and editing is not 'cheating' but makes good sense. This might involve:

- asking a friend or family member to read your text;
- swapping your work with colleagues or other students (forming a study group);
- engaging a paid, professional editor, at a cost of between £15 (AUS$25) and £125 (AUS$200) per hour. (Note that paying a professional editor is *against* some university regulations, and students can be disqualified for using editors whilst completing a course of study. The Learning Skills Unit of your university may be the only professional assistance allowed. However, using an editor to improve your writing skills in your preparation period before commencing your university studies is perfectly acceptable.)

Note for thesis writers: It is usually not enough to rely on the comments of your supervisor, even if they are willing to edit and proofread your work. After they have finished reading your work for content, they are usually also too familiar with the material to see any errors, meaning they are not in any better position than yourself to offer editorial comments! You must ask for feedback from **independent** readers who are not familiar with the project. These individuals do not have to work in your subject area – in fact, sometimes it helps if they do not know the subject matter (as they read it for mistakes, not content) – but it does help if they have experience of writing a dissertation themselves.

9 Read your work aloud

Reading aloud, ideally to others but also just to yourself, is a great way to focus attention on your work. Reading aloud often makes you aware of instances in which sentences are too long and complicated, grammar or vocabulary problems are present, sentence structures are unclear, or arguments are unclear and lack logical structure. Remember: if your work is not clear enough for someone to follow it when listening, do not consider it clear enough for a person to understand when reading. Reading your text aloud can often help you simplify your sentences, and thereby make your writing clearer, more accurate and more persuasive. You may also consider asking others to read your text to you.

10 Get help from as many sources as possible

The more people you ask for help as part of this process the less likely it is that there will be errors in the final version. You will be amazed by how several people reading the same text will notice different errors!

11 Planning and being strategic

Don't waste time proofreading a chapter of a thesis or an essay before you have finished writing it. Resist the temptation to fiddle about with formatting. Only do this kind of polishing when the essay or thesis chapter is finished to your (and your supervisor's) satisfaction. Only proofread the *final* printout, otherwise small errors can turn up between editing the penultimate (the second to last) version and printing the ultimate version!

12 Edit forwards but proof backwards

During the editing process you are checking for *sense,* so read as you would normally. But when proofreading you are looking for residual errors, not sense. A good strategy is to try reading each sentence independently, starting with the final sentence in the last chapter and working backwards from there. It's tedious, but will help you to spot mistakes. Try reading each sentence *aloud.* This also helps. Reading sentences aloud helps you write clear and readable sentences (see the 'student test' in chapter 12).

13 Use a macro- and micro-editing technique

As well as asking others for help, you can also help yourself by using both **macro-** and **micro-editing**. Try to follow the steps suggested below, proceeding from macro-editing to micro-editing and not the other way around. This will ensure that you won't miss anything.

● 3 Editing and proofreading: macro-editing

Below are things to consider when macro-editing a chapter of a dissertation or thesis. Most of these also apply when editing an essay or a report.

Edit for purpose and logical development
Check each chapter's introduction, conclusion and the separate sections. Do you do what you say you are going to do? Do you summarise the main point(s) in the conclusion? Does the 'thesis' of your thesis or essay come through clearly in each of your chapters? Is the main point clear or does your writing indirectly 'go around' the main point? (This is very common with international students' writing.)

Edit for cohesion
Check the links between your paragraphs. Does the material 'flow' from one paragraph to another? Is there a topic sentence in each paragraph? Are you using 'signpost' language to guide the reader, for example, 'Given this point...', 'Firstly...', 'Secondly...', 'Thirdly...', 'In conclusion...'? Do you use numbered points or sub-sections? Are these consistently cross-referenced throughout?

Edit for sense
Make sure each sentence is meaningfully clear and precise. Does it say *exactly* what you want it to say, or is it vague or ambiguous? Look out for redundancies ('completely surrounded', 'absolutely perfect', 'serious crisis'), tautologies ('a comparative study covering both aspects'), empty expressions ('in regard to', 'in terms of', 'reflected in'), vague words ('aspect', 'factor', 'significant') or empty modifiers ('huge', 'very'). Such expressions are the mark of a poor writer, and yet we all write words and phrases like these sometimes.

Edit for repetition
Check your chapters for unnecessary repetition of concepts and ideas. Note that it is very common for students to repeat things when they have not done enough research and they have *nothing much to say!* The remedy is to do more research and to eliminate the repetition.

Edit for acronyms and jargon
'Jargon' means specialist terms in a particular discipline, e.g. 'imprint page' is a term used in the publishing industry. Words and phrases such as these must be explained unless their meaning is obvious to your reader. Acronyms are expressions like UNESCO (United Nations Educational, Scientific and Cultural Organization), ANZ (Australian and

New Zealand Bank), NAFTA (North American Free Trade Association), etc. These must to be explained clearly in their full written form when they are first used, i.e. on the first occasion you use them, write: 'Association of South-East Asian Nations (ASEAN)'. After that, you may write the acronym: ASEAN.

Edit for grammatical errors

Besides the mistakes mentioned in chapter 9, the common grammatical errors made by international students can be easily corrected. They include the following: English articles, compound nouns; lack of a subject or verb in the sentence; errors of noun–verb agreement; plural–singular verb mistakes; pronoun–noun agreement; the misplacement of the modifying verb; tense errors; apostrophe usage in possessive expressions. The remedy for overcoming such errors is to make sure you have done lots of practice with a good ESL book, such as Murphy (2004) and Vince (2003).

4 Editing and proofreading: micro-editing

Layout: main text

View each page one by one. Check for formatting: are all paragraphs indented by the same amount? Are paragraphs that follow on conceptually from a quotation *not* indented? Is the text justified (aligned to both margins)? Are the margins OK? Is spacing between words consistent? Is spacing between sections consistent? Is page numbering sequential and in the correct font? Are the headers and footers consistent throughout? Do any words appear alone on new pages? Does the layout have 'orphans' or 'widows' which make the layout look messy? (An 'orphan' is a specialist term for a word or very short line that occurs by itself at the bottom of a page, without additional text. A 'widow' is a word or very short line that occurs by itself at the top of a page.)

Layout: title page and preliminary pages

Check that all relevant information is listed on the title page in the correct order. The text should be centred, and there should be no page number. Ensure that your name and discipline appear in the correct form. For essays, list your student number and your tutor's name. These are important for university departments to identify student work.

The same checks should be performed on the preliminary pages (table of contents and list of tables).

Layout of the bibliography

Are all the references there? Check them against the text. Does the layout follow the style manual or discipline journal? Is the punctuation the same? Is the layout in strict alphabetical order, listed *by surname* of author or title (if no author)?

Layout of tables and graphs

Are these in the right place, i.e. close to the text where they are mentioned? Are they labelled correctly and is the source identified? Do they appear in the list of tables at the beginning of your work?

Edit references in text

Check the accuracy and spelling of all citations and reference details against the original. Check that ellipses (...) are used correctly (see chapter 5). Make sure that the use of ellipses does not result in misleading information being quoted (information cited must be true and accurate to the author's intended meaning). Check that reference style is consistent throughout. Check that quotation marks are used consistently.

Edit the bibliography

Make sure that the *full* details of all items are supplied: full name(s) of author(s)/editor(s), publisher and place of publication, editor(s), date of publication, volume numbers, edition, inclusive page numbers (for journals).

Edit fonts

Check usage of all emboldened, underlined and italicised passages for consistency. Make sure you haven't overused italics or any other special formatting convention.

Edit for spelling

Use a spellchecker, but remember it has limitations (see the famous 'Pome' below, attributed to Jerrold H. Zar). The 'pome' has 15 errors and yet the spelling 'checker' seems to approve it. See if you can find them all.

> **Spell Chequer Pome**
> I have a spelling checker,
> It came with my P.C.
> It clearly marks for my revue
> Mistakes I cannot sea.
> I've run this poem threw it
> And I'm shore your please to no
> Its letter perfect in it's weigh
> My chequer tolled me sew.

Edit for punctuation

Make sure you do not use commas, full stops, semicolons and colons indiscriminately. The way you use them will sometimes determine whether you are saying what you really want to say. Compare these two sentences:

> *A woman without her man is nothing.*
> *A woman: without her, man is nothing.*

You may laugh at the example, but lecturers often find worse mistakes than this in students' work. Bad expression at this level of study often creates obscurity. Be careful. You are expected to be reasonably literate before entering university. It is also expected that you demonstrate this familiarity with language in your essays. Failure to do so can influence grades. Check your work once or twice then check it carefully again! There are many free worksheets available on websites covering the topic of punctuation. I provide one on the website for this book.

5 Summary

This chapter has outlined a strategic method for editing and proofreading your work. Editing and proofreading are not the same things. Editing and proofreading effectively are also difficult, especially with your own work. You must follow a strategy to ensure mistakes are not missed. Both macro- and micro-editing techniques were outlined and recommended.

6 Editing and proofreading checklist

Use this sheet to help you to plan, write, edit and proofread assignments in terms of:

- content;
- text structure;
- paragraphs;
- grammar;
- sentence structure;
- vocabulary;

- expression;
- spelling and punctuation;
- presentation;
- tables, graphs and illustrations;
- referencing and citations.

Content
Have I addressed all elements of the task?
Have I demonstrated sufficient understanding of the topic and issue?
Have I used a sufficient range of sources?
Have I referred to ideas from other sources critically?
Is my central argument clear?
Are my supporting points clear?
Is sufficient evidence provided to support my points?
Does my text fit the word limit?

Text structure

Have I structured my text in the accepted manner? For example:

- essay: introduction, body, conclusion, references

- report: front matter, abstract, introduction, literature review, methodology, procedure, results, discussion, conclusion, recommendations, appendices, references

- Have I structured each of these sections in the accepted manner?

- Have I avoided unnecessary repetition of concepts and ideas?

Paragraphs

- Are paragraphs sequenced logically?

- Does each paragraph contain a topic sentence?

- Do all following sentences in the paragraph support the topic sentence?

- Does each paragraph contain only one main idea?

- Are linking words used (e.g. 'given this point ...', 'first ...', 'second ...', 'in conclusion ...')?

- Are paragraphs of appropriate length?

- Are titles used where necessary?

Grammar

Have I checked for grammatical errors? These may involve:

- verb tenses

- subject–verb agreement

- plurals

- articles

- prepositions

- pronouns

- word forms

Sentence structure

Are most sentences in the active voice?

Do most sentences begin with the subject?

Are sentences short and clear enough?

Does sufficient sentence variety exist?

Vocabulary

Is my vocabulary clear, accurate and formal?

Do I refer to subjects themselves instead of overusing pronouns such as 'it', 'they' or 'them')?

Do I explain all technical terms and abbreviations when first used?

Do I avoid overuse of abbreviations?

Expression

Is my writing as clear and concise as possible? Does it avoid:

redundancies, (e.g. 'absolutely perfect', 'completely surrounded', 'serious crisis')

tautologies (e.g. 'A comparative study covering both aspects')

empty expressions or 'waffle' (e.g. 'in terms of', 'reflected in', 'with regard to')

vague words ('factor', 'some', 'significant', 'aspect')

empty modifiers (e.g. 'huge', 'very')

slang and informal terms

Spelling and punctuation

Is the spelling correct?

Is the punctuation correct?

Presentation

Have I checked the presentation? This will include:

- font size and type
- indentation
- justification of paragraphs
- margins
- spacing
- section and page numbering
- headers and footers
- capitalisation
- italicised, emboldened or underlined words (don't overuse)
- wording and fonts of titles

Tables, graphs and illustrations

Have I checked that tables, graphs and illustrations are:

- positioned properly?
- referred to directly?
- titled and labelled correctly?
- cited appropriately?
- included in the list of tables or illustrations?

Referencing and citations

- Are all sources acknowledged?

- Are citations formatted correctly?

- Are ideas from other sources paraphrased or summarised adequately?

- Are my positions on ideas from other sources clear?

- Are quotation marks used for direct quotes?

- Is the reference list complete and accurate?

- Is referencing consistent?

Part VII

Being Heard: Speaking for Assessment

16 Giving a Paper and Presenting in a Tutorial

● 1 Introduction

This chapter outlines a number of things relevant to the skill of speaking. It will be recalled from chapter 1 that at university you are being assessed on what you *say* as well as what you write in assignments and exams. Assessment of your spoken contributions takes the form of participation in tutorials as well as more formal presentations in class. This chapter outlines some suggestions for both of these areas.

● 2 Tutorials

What are tutorials for? You might think you already know the answer to this question, however, it is worthwhile reflecting on it. How does a tutorial differ from a lecture? What are the aims of a good tutorial? Are there different kinds of tutorials? How do you contribute in a tutorial? This section will discuss these things in detail and provide you with some skills so you are able to experience success in tutorials.

1 Lectures and tutorials

While lectures are the recognised means of transmitting content, tutorials are the mainstay of the academic system. Lectures are an impractical way to discuss the material presented. Tutorials balance this by emphasising *discussion* over the delivery of content. Where lectures are, by nature, formal, tutorials offer the opportunity for free and informal discussion and a freedom to pursue your queries and concerns. In tutorials you are able to ask questions, make mistakes, contribute to discussions and learn. As noted in chapter 1, at postgraduate level there is often no separation between tutorials and lectures but only a longer session which combines elements of both (often called a 'seminar').

Tutors can be, to some extent, friends as well as academic mentors, though note that they are professionals and may choose to keep a professional distance from their students. Relationships are hard to build in a lecture theatre, but they are possible, and even desirable, during a tutorial. You can make lifelong friends during tutorials.

Importantly, tutors *model the thinking processes* needed in a subject. Watching a tutor thinking out loud during a class when trying to answer a question or problem can be stimulating and instructive (even exciting) for students.

The aims of tutorials

Tutorials help you to link together what you have heard in lectures and what you have read in textbooks, and give you an opportunity to *discuss* ideas with your fellow students as well as the tutor. Discussion is critical. Mini-lectures are not tutorials (although a good tutorial may have a segment of 'mini-lecture' as part of a range of other activities).

A good tutorial is highly interactive. It provides an opportunity for discussion, debate and critical reflection, and engages students in the subject content through analysis of the course material being studied. Tutorials give you a collegial and supportive environment where you can make mistakes (and learn from them). Tutorials can help you:

- sort out ideas;
- clarify problems and misunderstandings in your work;
- improve your verbal communication skills, oral presentation skills and debating skills;
- develop closer contact with others in the tutorial group.

2 Are there different kinds of tutorials?

In a word, 'yes', but they all should exhibit the features mentioned above to some extent. Tutorials can be:

> **Problem-based**: These tutorials are focused on problems that require answers, i.e. there are set questions to answer each week and the tutorial is based around these. Alternatively, the 'problem' might be a case study in which students are required to identify issues and make practical recommendations.
>
> **Issue-based**: There may not be questions or even model answers in some tutorials but, instead, topics for general discussion. These might be based on the readings for each week, or the lecture material. It is important for you to have the confidence to be able to offer insights and opinions about these topics, and to be critical of other ideas presented (including the ideas of the tutor!). Tutorials like these build important skills in verbal fluency and aim to create verbally articulate graduates.
>
> **Activity-based**: Some tutorials require more than discussion and problem solving. They can involve presentations by members of the tutorial group, role plays, games, formal debates or other activities. For example, some tutorials involve computer simulations involving mock companies, in which students are required to test various models.
>
> **Mixed**: These are a combination of all the above types.

The type of tutorial is dictated by the subject, the skills and objectives of the tutor, the imagination of the tutor and their willingness to be creative. While there is a certain amount of content that must be covered in a tutorial, the way this content is covered is at the discretion of the tutor or the lecturer in charge.

Assessment in tutorials: a strategy for participation

It is important to note that in tutorials you are being assessed on your participation. This mark will be *in addition* to your other assessed work.

How tutorials are assessed depends on the tutor or the type of tutorial. Some tutors keep a logbook with each student's name and allocate points for a 'good comment', 'excellent comment', or (a zero mark) for 'no comment' at each tutorial. They then add up the marks at the end of semester. Other tutors form a global judgement of your contribution only at the end of semester.

Be aware: It is very easy to lose significant marks from poor or insufficient tutorial participation.

Many students from non-English-speaking backgrounds are too worried or shy about their English to contribute in tutorials. This problem tends to *get worse during the semester*. In the first tutorial, students might be too scared or intimidated to say anything. As the semester goes by, it becomes harder and harder to contribute. Fairly soon, the entire semester has passed and the student has not contributed anything! This results in a fail for tutorial contributions.

One solution is to force yourself to:
- ask a simple question in week 1;
- ask a more complex question in week 2;
- make a comment on an idea in week 3;
- argue against an idea in week 4...

In this way, confidence builds quickly. See below for language typically used in tutorials.

Preparing for tutorials

As noted, tutorials are part of your assessed work for a subject. Attendance is not optional. That said, it is important to do more than simply 'attend'. You need to **speak, argue and critique** (both criticise and agree with) the information discussed in the tutorial. To do this, it is important to do **the pre-tutorial reading** assigned for each week. If you don't, you will not be able to understand the conversation or participate in it.

3 Taking part in tutorials

When you are sitting in a tutorial, you may be nervous about opening your mouth to say something. The expressions below may help you participate in tutorials more effectively. It is a good idea to memorise these expressions and practise, rehearsing them with friends.

1 Introducing ideas
- I'd like to start/begin by saying that …

- I want to suggest a few points here/by way of introduction ...
- I have a couple of points to contribute/add ...
- First of all, I'd like to talk about ...
- By way of an introduction, I'd like to define the topic ...
- I want to cover the following points ...
- This is how I intend to approach the topic: firstly ..., etc.
- What I want to suggest is ...
- My main point is that ...
- I want to claim that ...
- I suggest the following ...
- I think that...
- In my view a couple of things need to be mentioned ...

2 Asking for clarification
- Am I right in thinking that you ...?
- Is you point that ...?'
- Let me/Can I paraphrase what I think you are saying: ...?
- Sorry to interrupt, but did you just say that ...?
- Is what you are saying ...?
- Would you mind repeating ...?
- I am a little unclear about the point made by X. Is it being suggested that ...?
- I'm not clear what you meant by .../when you said ...?
- Am I right in thinking that you/believe .../consider ...?
- Is what you're saying that ...?
- I'm not sure I understand (correctly) what you said about ...?
- Could you please explain what you meant/by ... when you said ...?
- I don't understand what you mean by .../when you say ...?
- Did you mean that/think that ...?
- Do you mean that/think that ...?

3 Giving clarification
- The point I'm/making is that .../trying to make is that ...
- What I'm/saying/trying to say/is ...
- All I'm/saying/trying to say/is ...
- What I/mean is .../meant was ...
- What I was/driving at .../getting at is ...
- What I said was ...
- My main claim is simply that ...
- My main idea has been misunderstood. All I am saying is that ...

4 Disagreeing with someone
- Brad's point is interesting, however ...
- Brad's idea does not seem quite right to me. I'd say that ...

- There is another way of looking at the issue ...
- I'd suggest that Brad's point is not quite on the money/not quite accurate. I think that ...
- I disagree with Brad's point for a number of reasons: ...
- Brad's approach is only one way to see this issue. There are other approaches. One is ...
- That's interesting Brad, because I read/understood the point/issue in a totally different way. I thought...
- Can I suggest that Brad might be wrong about that?
- Can I make some critical comments/remarks on what Brad has just said?

5 *Concluding ideas*
- To sum up, ...
- To wrap up ...
- To finish ...
- To end this presentation, I want to suggest that ...
- Two remarks by way of summing up/concluding ...
- I just want to suggest the following by way of ending this contribution ...
- In conclusion ...
- My final point is that ...
- That is all I have to say for the moment, but I would welcome your comments in the group discussion.

For some of the above examples I acknowledge the use of ELBC (Academic Communication Skills) Booklet (1994).

4 Ground rules for tutorial conduct
The following 'ground rules' for conduct have been listed in an unpublished paper by Philip Bartle and expanded on in another context (Davies & Sievers, 2006). They are useful reminders of the purpose of many kinds of 'issue-based' tutorials. They may not be appropriate for 'problem-based' tutorials.

1 Expectations
Ideally, the tutor is a co-learner along with the students. Tutors are not experts (though they will naturally know more than the students). Tutors might give very little content for the student to assimilate, though they often provide the framework for content. Everyone in the tutorial learning environment is responsible for content. The tutor guides the discussion as a facilitator and students are assessed on skills in reasoning, verbal fluency, debating and argument, not just content acquired.

2 Mutual respect
Progress in a tutorial is assessed by means of good argument. Argument is used here in the sense of 'arriving at conclusions by means of valid deductions', not in the sense of a

'fight'. Students should give mutual respect to each other's ideas and views without being judgemental. Often, it is from wild, fanciful speculation that real progress in academic ideas is made. But this speculation needs to be grounded in good and clear reasoning.

3 Disagreement

Almost anything said in a tutorial can be criticised. This means that everything said can and should be disagreed with if good arguments can be made against the ideas presented. It is important that all students have an opportunity to make their disagreements forcefully. Class discussions should be open to disagreement from anyone at any time.

4 Tolerance

While disagreement in class is encouraged, so is tolerance of others' views. Contradictory opinions will often be voiced, and the tutor's role is to moderate and elicit these views. Students should be tolerant of perspectives that they do not necessarily share, and should equally be free to answer them in a calm and rational manner.

5 Openness

Allowing for new ideas to enter the discussion is vital for personal and intellectual progress. Students should not be hostile to developments in the discussion, even if they disagree with them. An open mind is essential for understanding knowledge. Allow all ideas in and then sift and challenge them in a spirit of open and friendly debate.

6 Not understanding is OK

Students should feel free to clarify any point that they are unclear about. One of the first stages in being knowledgeable is to first be aware of your own ignorance. There is nothing wrong with saying you do not understand, and there is nothing wrong with asking for clarification again and again (if necessary). If you do not understand something, it is very likely that others in the group will also be confused. In many Asian cultures, this attitude to learning – asking for continual clarification or help – might be interpreted as 'losing face'. This is not the case in a western learning environment. Indeed, asking for clarification or help shows a clever student who is willing to be engaged in the learning process, and a highly critical and intelligent one.

7 Changing positions

When debating ideas, you do not have to keep the position with which you started. As new information and ideas are presented, you should feel free to change your views. Indeed, real education consists of a progressive development of your opinions on things. However, as a matter of courtesy, always signal or indicate to the class when you wish to defend something that is different from what you defended before. For example, you can say something like this: 'I was thinking before that ... However, I am starting to agree with Brian's point about .... Now I think that ...'.

8 Participation

Sometimes it is good to listen to a debate without participating. Silences in a discussion are also instructive if they allow time for reflection and gathering your thoughts. Participation can be both direct and indirect, i.e. by means of group work. All students should be encouraged to actively contribute when they have something to say, or sit and listen when they do not. There is no requirement for students to feel they have to 'talk for the sake of it'.

9 Debate

The purpose of debate is to encourage and stimulate reflection, not to win a contest. The skills we wish to foster in a tutorial arise from contemplative activity among peers, not accumulative gain by point scoring. Debates should be conducted in this spirit.

10 Communication

Students should certainly feel encouraged to provide enlightened contributions to discussions from the perspective of different cultures and languages as often as they can. This is a way in which students from non-English-speaking backgrounds can advance a discussion and thereby educate the tutor as well as the class. As I have noted elsewhere, using examples from prior work experience in assignments is a very good way of improving your grades. It is also a good way of advancing discussion in class. At the same time, local examples should be explained in class for international students. If they are not explained, students should ask for clarification.

11 Negotiation

There is nothing wrong with compromising your ideas, or negotiating, if someone else has a better idea or argument. Nor is there anything wrong with coming to a better understanding by adopting aspects of your opponent's position as part of your own, if this can be done coherently. This is the aim of tutorials.

12 Curiosity

Be curious and you will learn something new. Martin Luther King said that 'Nothing in all the world is more dangerous than sincere ignorance and conscientious stupidity.' The default position in a tutorial is that 'everyone in the class has something to learn'. No one is an expert in a tutorial, not even your tutor (as they will freely acknowledge)!

● 3 Presenting a seminar paper

Do you feel nervous about presenting in front of a group? Public speaking fills many people with fear, especially those students who don't feel confident about their English-language skills or who have rarely, if ever, presented before a group. However, presentations are likely to be a vital part of your assessment at university. In the workplace, the ability to give a presentation effectively is also critical. And, remember, if you can't present well in an interview, you probably won't get the job.

Everyone has the capacity to present well enough to get a good grade and to create an impact. As you begin to prepare your presentation, be aware that what makes presentations great is *awareness, care, effort* and *practice*. These are much more important than the inherent confidence or 'natural ability' of the speaker. And everyone can prepare well. Concealing natural nervousness is also critical. Remember this quote by comedian Jerry Seinfeld: 'People's Number One Fear is Public Speaking. Number Two Fear is Death. Death is Number Two! Now, this means, to the average person, if you have to go to a funeral, you're better off in the casket than doing the eulogy!'

Giving a seminar presentation (or 'presenting a paper') may be one of the hardest things you will ever do at university. *Everyone* gets nervous and *nobody* finds it easy, not even your lecturers. Giving a seminar presentation involves standing up in front of your lecturers and fellow graduate students and telling them about your research, or a topic that you're investigating for assessment. Depending on the subject you are studying, as a postgraduate you may have to 'give a paper' about two or three times a semester. It is likely to form an important part of your assessment at university. This part of the chapter outlines skills for success.

1 The art of public speaking

Giving a seminar paper involves the skill of public speaking. This is a very different skill from the skills we have looked at so far in this book.

Public speaking is an art and the skills needed to do it well are virtually limitless. You may not have a talent for public speaking, but you should be able to learn to do it well enough to get excellent grades. This chapter tries to discuss presentation skills. However, it should be recognised that the best way to learn presentation skills is by means of *practice* under *guidance*. This chapter is no substitute for practical training.

In writing this chapter I have benefited from Powell (1999). Other dedicated texts are available on the topic, such as van Emden and Becker (2010). To further develop your public-speaking skills, consider joining a public-speaking organisation such as *Rostrum* or *Toastmasters International*. These organisations allow for regular dedicated practice with feedback from professional public speakers.

The value of public speaking as a skill

Opportunities to practise and become competent in public speaking are rare. Outside university, it is not often that you will have the chance to practise and improve, unless you join a public-speaking society. Despite this, the skill is highly valued in the corporate world. People who can speak confidently to an audience usually advance further in their careers, compared with those who have only technical knowledge. If you just want to work in a minor role in a company, that's fine; if you want to advance in your career you need to have the confidence to speak to an audience and this skill takes time to develop.

At university, you have the chance to develop this skill through practice. This opportunity should be embraced. Don't think of your presentation as 'just part of your assessment' or 'something you have to do'. Think of it as a 'life skill' that you need to develop to succeed beyond university. Opportunities for gaining this skill outside university exist, but it is far easier to get the skills, experience and practice while you are there. In the workplace, you may lose a large contract by not presenting well to an audience, but at university you will receive feedback to help you improve next time. Above all, you get the opportunity to *practise.*

The importance of communication skills

The importance of communication skills for future employment cannot be overstated. In a recent survey of employers by Graduate Careers Australia (2006), **interpersonal and communication skills (written, oral, listening)** were ranked *far above* 'qualifications' and 'previous employment' as **the most important selection criteria** when hiring graduates (57.5%, 35.4% and 27.6% respectively). Similarly, employers regarded 'the least desirable characteristics' when recruiting graduates to be **lack of communication skills (written, oral, listening)** at first place in a list of 10 undesirable characteristics (40.2%). Poor academic qualifications were only ranked fifth in a list of 10 least desirable characteristics (15%). ('Graduate Outlook,' 2006)

Practice and experience
The other important point to note is the difference between *practice* and *experience.* This is a critical difference in relation to the art of public speaking. You can practise speaking skills at home all you like with limited success. This is not much use unless you also get experience in front of many of pairs of eyes. There is a world of difference between: (1) a practice presentation at home in front of the mirror; and (2) a real presentation where you sweat, become nervous and forget everything you want to say in the heat of the moment!

2 How to prepare for oral presentations: general guidelines
Given the importance of presentations for your future career, you need to be serious and professional. There are a number of points to consider even before the precise content of the speech is prepared.

1 Check the speaking environment
It is likely you will present your speech in a very similar room to that used by your lecturer for classes. It could be a lecture theatre or a small tutorial room. In either case you need to check the speaking environment carefully. It is one thing to use the room as a student, another to be a presenter in the same room. It is normal for speakers to think that any problems associated with the speaking location are *not their fault*. However, this is not the right attitude. As a presenter, you want your performance to be as smooth as possible. If anything goes wrong, this reflects badly on *you*, the speaker. To do well,

and to get a good mark for your presentation, you want to give lecturers the impression of being very professional. Therefore, the following checklist should be made:

Thing to check	What to check for
Speaking location	Can you move around the space allocated easily? (It is good to be able to move towards the audience and leave the podium or lectern as much as possible.)
	Is there access to all the equipment you need?
	Is there a place to put handouts and notes?
	Can you be heard from all places in the audience?
	Can you be seen from all places in the audience?
	Can you move from the whiteboard to the computer and other equipment with ease?
	Is there a podium and lectern? Are there steps in the room to negotiate?
Furniture	Is there enough seating for all members of the audience?
	Do you have access to all the furniture you need for your presentation?
	Do you need all the furniture in the room? Does it look cluttered? Will this detract from your presentation?
Equipment	Do you have all the material you need? Laser pointers? Displays? Handouts?
	Does the equipment work?
	Is the equipment/software compatible with your materials?
	Does the overhead projector work? Do you have a spare bulb in case it blows during the presentation?
	Do you have whiteboard pens that work? Is chalk needed?
	Do you know how to turn on the computer, the overhead projector, the visualiser, the DVD player, and use the slide projector, the microphone and other equipment?
	Do you know how to dim the lights?

The above checklist is a guide only and should be tailored to your specific requirements.

2 Rehearse the start of the presentation
The start of the presentation is critical. Professional speakers recommend that it is a good idea to 'script' the first few moments so you know exactly what you need to say. You must be careful of not *sounding* 'scripted', however, like an actor remembering

lines. Again, the best way to prepare for this is by means of experience speaking in front of an audience. You will soon learn how to get the balance right between over-preparation and under-preparation. The introduction is discussed in more detail below.

3 Get straight to the point
It is important not to ramble in any presentation, but especially so in an academic presentation. The audience that attends academic presentations comprises educated people who are likely to feel annoyed if you ramble incoherently from point to point. Audiences want a clear structure with 'signpost' language throughout (more on this below). They are entitled to know:

- your main **topic**;
- what you think about this topic (your central **argument** or thesis);
- the **evidence** supporting your argument.

Keep these things in focus as you prepare your presentation. They must be clear at the beginning of your talk, be regularly mentioned throughout your talk and summed up at the end. It is a common failing for first-time presenters to not be clear about these essential points.

> **Warning:** When you are nervous, you will forget what you need to say unless you are well prepared and very familiar with speaking to an audience. Many first-time speakers are surprised about how they 'rambled' because they became nervous.
>
> Nervousness can be minimised, if not conquered. The best way to deal with it is by extensive experience in front of an audience. This means taking opportunities presented to you to practice your speaking skills. *For this reason, never refuse an opportunity to speak to an audience!* You may want to avoid the opportunities (this is natural), but remember: the people who take such opportunities advance further in their careers than those who don't.

4 Talk to your audience in the right way
A presentation differs from an assignment or essay in style as well as tone. Presentations are often described as being in the style of **heightened conversation**. They are not as informal as talking to a friend over coffee, yet they are not as formal as an essay or academic paper. The language of presentations is discussed in more detail below.

5 Know the things that work
Certain things are always popular with audiences: personal experiences, dramatic comparisons, stories with a message, impressive statistics, amazing facts and diagrams or charts. Use them as much as possible, keeping in mind that your job is not to entertain but to present a compelling case for a proposition or academic issue you wish to defend. You can do this in a formal academic way while still being interesting. An academic pres-

entation is certainly not like entertaining television; however, it need not be boring either. A complex technical presentation in Finance, for example, can be enlivened simply by relating the topic to current issues in the newspapers, such as interest rates.

6 Be concise and simple in your expression

Sentences should be kept short and simple. Never *read* from a paper. Formal writing style does not translate well into an oral presentation. A suggestion for ensuring this does not happen is to follow this procedure:

- write down your speech in full (everything you want to say);
- convert these sentences into short, bullet-point phrases or words on small 'flashcards', which you can hold unobtrusively in your hand (if you hold a large piece of paper you will look like you are reading, and this is almost as bad as actually reading);
- practise your speech with the full written version and your cards until you need only your cards. Glance at the cards quickly to remind yourself of your next point;
- give your presentation with only the cards as support to remind you of what you need to say.

7 Speak naturally

Not only should your sentences be short and clear, but your expression should also be natural. Following the above procedure for simple expression will ensure that you are speaking naturally. Your role is to *communicate* with your audience (almost as if you were speaking to a friend), not to *read to* them. Don't be afraid to hesitate when you speak, as hesitation is very normal. However, make sure you pause in the right places and don't overdo it. There should not be long silences in a presentation. Equally, there should not be a rapid-fire delivery without pauses. It's a matter of balance. Practising in front of a friend who can offer constructive criticism will ensure you get the balance right.

While you may need flashcards to remind you where you are going in your speech, remember you are not an actor trying to remember lines. The balance between being formal and being natural and relaxed is not that hard to achieve *with practice*.

8 Know your audience and their needs

It is important to address the interests and concerns of your audience. If you are speaking to a class of postgraduate students or to an audience at an academic conference, the tone and focus of the presentation will be different than if you are speaking to a group of company executives. The needs of the groups are very different. The company executives may not be especially interested in the various theories and approaches in the literature, or indeed your particular views. They will want to see solutions and recommendations to a problem, and how the recommendations can be implemented. Academic audiences want to see evidence that you know what you are talking about. This means presenting the **theoretical background** to the issue or topic. You also need to identify your **research methods** and, if your presentation requires these, the **'gap'** in the literature, and the **arguments** for and against your position.

Get to know who your audience will be. What is the average age? How many men and women will be present? What do they want to know? For a good example of adapting to an audience, watch the video *Be Prepared to Speak* (Kantola, 1985). It's very old but it has lots of useful tips. A more recent version of this, which is also excellent, is a DVD called *How to Write and Deliver Great Speeches* (Toastmasters, 2007).

9 Be yourself, but learn from others

You can learn from other speakers by seeing what works and does not work. But don't feel you have to model yourself on them. Imitation can make you feel uncomfortable. You might see how other speakers use various techniques (how they stand, **gesture** and interact with the audience), but if this does not feel right for you, don't copy it. When you see something that does work well, consider adapting it so that it suits you. All good speakers borrow techniques from others.

10 Take your time

It is important that presentations are not rushed. This is one of the main errors that beginners make. They are often worried that they will 'run out of things to say', so they over-prepare information. This leads to a feeling that they have to 'cover everything' they have prepared, and hence to a rushed performance. In general, a lecture that covers *fewer things in detail* is better than one that covers too many points. The traveller's adage is applicable here: 'put out everything you *think* you need, and then take half of that'. Similarly, for presentations write down everything you *think* you need to say, and only use half of it. This is a hard lesson to learn, and even very experienced speakers occasionally make the mistake of having too much content.

11 Let your visuals speak for themselves

Detailed tables of figures and long lines of text on an overhead projector are not suitable for presentations. You will sense the audience getting bored and shuffling in their seats. Show the audience charts, graphs and diagrams, but make sure they are not overloaded with information. Think of ways to prepare information to catch your audience's attention. This might include use of some graphics. However, for academic presentations, it is better not to overdo 'fancy' things like cartoons (unless the presentation is for an undergraduate audience) and definitely avoid animations and PowerPoint transition sounds. Professionals will feel patronised by unnecessary and superficial ways of attracting attention. Clear, simple diagrams that show the minimum amount of critical information are preferred. Be warned that PowerPoint slides often look better on the screen than when projected. Be sensitive to colour contrast and font size.

12 Questions from your audience

You must anticipate questions and be prepared to answer them. Remember, *no one in the audience wants you to fail or do badly.* People understand how hard it is to speak to an audience, and they are naturally sympathetic to you as the speaker (if you are prepared and organised – they won't be sympathetic to someone who has not taken the effort to prepare well.)

No one likes silences after a presentation either, and people will feel the need to ask questions. This does not mean they are doing it just for you. When people ask a question, it is usually because they are genuinely interested in what you are saying and want to know more. Treat questions as an opportunity to get your message across better. However, you need to prepare for likely questions in advance so that you can answer them confidently. The best way to do this is to write down a list of possible questions based on the content of your speech. Think about how best to answer the questions, and rehearse those answers in the same way as you rehearse your presentation.

13 Finishing strongly
The most memorable parts of almost all presentations are the start and finish. This is similar to a musical performance or a concert. We remember the start and finish more easily than the middle section. Professional performers know this, and they often leave their most famous pieces of music until the end, or for the start. Therefore, plan the start and finish of your presentation in great detail. If you make a mistake in the middle of the presentation it is less likely to be remembered or even noticed. If you make a mistake at the start or finish, it may be the *only* thing the audience remembers. This applies to your level of confidence and style. If you look nervous at the beginning, the audience will notice and remember it; if you lose your nerve in the middle – and start and end with great confidence – the nervousness may not even be noticed. I will look at beginnings and endings of presentations in more detail below.

3 Getting started: how to make an impact
1 The introduction
The introduction is critical. The experts on public speaking recommend that you consider the level of formality expected in the talk first. Look at the two variations in introduction language on the next page:

Only you can tell which is more appropriate for your purposes. In general, the formal variation in style and register would be more suited to clients at a company or an academic conference. The second thing to consider is the structure of the introduction. Experts on public speaking recommend the following structure:

Attention-getter
Statement of context
Statement of purpose/aim
Statement of justification
Outline of presentation

Formal	Less formal
● Can I suggest we begin? Thank you very much ...	● OK, let's get started/get going.
● Good morning, everyone ladies and gentlemen.	● Morning, all.
● I represent ... and I'd like to welcome you to today's presentation on ...	● Good to see you here.
● My name's ...	● I'm ...
● My role in the company/My paper today ...	● Today I'm going to ...
● In today's presentation/paper I am going to outline ... – present ... – overview ... – argue ...	● In my session today I will ... – cover ... – tell you ... – look at ...
● At the end of the presentation there will be ample time for questions, so I suggest that you raise them then.	● I am happy to take questions as we go along.
● I'd like to begin by demonstrating why this product .../I'd like to start by outlining my conceptual model.	● Ok, let's begin.

(based on Powell, 1999)

This is a common structure that we have seen throughout this book. It's used in essay introductions, verbal responses to questions and – as we shall see in chapter 17 – when speaking to lecturers. The move from the general to the particular is a natural progression and it certainly seems right to an audience. It is recommended that you do not deviate from this format unless you have very good reasons.

2 The attention-getter
The attention-getter is important for a presentation but not for a written document such as an essay or report. There are several means by which you can get the attention of the audience:

● an interesting fact or surprising statistic;
● an anecdote or story;
● a picture or diagram.

Relating your central message to a topical issue also works well. If you were to give a rather dry academic presentation on a topic in Finance, for example, you might consider relating your topic to an issue in the media (e.g. rising interest rates, government policies on home mortgages) before you move on to discuss the academic detail.

3 The context or background

The context or background is very important for academic seminars. It follows immediately from the attention-getter. In order to appreciate the value of your research, the audience needs to know what others have done on the topic. They need to have confidence that you know what you are talking about. The best way to do this is to first outline what *others have done*. Obviously, in an introduction this must be very brief. Expressions such as the following are recommended:

- 'This presentation *follows on from* work by Smith, who *has looked at X and Y* in some detail. Smith *has shown that* ... He *has also found that* Z. ... Today, *I am going to* ...'
- 'We *will be looking at X* in this paper. *I will be basing this on* the work of Harrison ... *as it can be seen* from the following graph, Harrison *showed that* Y ... . My presentation today *will use but also criticise* the ideas of Harrison in a number of ways ...'

4 The statement of aim or purpose

This statement should be short, sharp and very focused. It should follow on immediately from your attention-getter and context. In fact, the start of your presentation to the statement of aim should be no longer than a few minutes. The following examples are typically used for stating the aim:

- 'This paper will *argue/outline/present/look* at the/*discuss/overview/*... (see the examples of critical review language in chapter 10 for other suitable verbs).'
- 'The *main point* of this presentation is to ...'

5 The statement of justification

Once the statement of purpose is clear, you could then follow it with a statement of justification (i.e. an explanation of why the work you are doing is *needed*). Language such as the following is advised:

- 'This work is *important* because ...'
- 'One of the *critical reasons for doing this work* is that ...'
- 'I believe that *this research is necessary* because ...'

The statement of justification is optional, but often very useful for corporate presentations where you are, in effect, 'selling' something: a product, a service or a way of implementing something. It is sometimes useful for academic presentations too (though the context or background, if done well, should be sufficient).

6 The outline

After the statement of justification, it is critical to outline the rest of the presentation in short, sharp sentences. This is necessary to help the audience follow your talk and give them confidence in you as a speaker. The audience needs to know that there is **clear**

structure in your presentation. It is unpleasant to listen to someone give a rambling presentation with no clear sense of direction. The following examples show how you can give an outline of your presentation.

- The presentation has *five parts: Firstly* I will **give** an account of ... *Secondly,* I will **look** at ... *Thirdly,* I will **outline** ..., *Fourthly,* I will **show** ... *Finally,* I will **make** recommendations about how to ... *Then* I will **conclude** by showing that ...

It is a good idea, and shows good fluency, to change the verb used for each part of the outline (as indicated in **bold**).

It is customary to end the outline section of the introduction with an invitation to ask questions at the end of the presentation:

- 'I will be happy to answer any questions at the end of my presentation.'
- 'At the end of my presentation there will be time to ask questions, so please leave questions until then.'

Confident and experienced presenters sometimes invite the audience to interrupt with questions during the presentation. However, for beginners, it is sometimes difficult to respond without losing track.

It is important to emphasise that while the five sections mentioned above are important, and should be covered in the order suggested, they should not take long to complete. In fact, the introduction should be no longer than about **five minutes in total** (less than 5–10 per cent of the total presentation length).

4 Signposting
In the body of the speech, *do exactly what you said you would do in the outline.* Do not deviate from this structure at all without good reason. A good reason to deviate would be if a question asked during a speech led to a useful animated exchange with your audience. In general, however, audiences expect to be told what the speech is going to cover, and they expect the speaker to cover the ground they outlined at the start.

A commonly given adage about public speaking is: 'Tell them you are going to tell them [**introduction**], tell them [**body** of speech], then tell them what you told them [**conclusion**]'. This is, indeed, good advice. You do not want to leave your presentation open to criticism that you did not cover what you said you would. Of course, it is important not to be too ambitious in what you set out to do. The earlier remark about timing and content (10, Take your time) needs to be followed.

Signposting language is vital during the body of the presentation. You can do this by using simple phrases as 'signposts' to guide your audience through the presentation. Typical phrases used in presentations include: *Moving on to my second point ... Going back to what I said earlier ... Now let's move on and discuss X ... To wrap up ... To conclude ... Let me just expand on that third point before continuing ... To elaborate ... Just to digress for a moment ... Summing up ... Now let me recap my five main points ....*

5 Techniques for oral presentations

Michael Powell has helpfully identified the many techniques that good presenters use. These techniques are studied by experts in public speaking and used deliberately. They include:

- 'chunking'
- repetition
- reversal
- rhetorical questions
- tripling

This section summarises these techniques below.

1 Chunking

Chunking involves emphasising key words and phrases to increase the impact of your speech. You need to be able to stress and pause at the right places.

The ability to 'chunk' is important for an academic as well as a commercial presenter. No one likes listening to a monotonous, flat delivery that does not allow time for stress and pauses. Stress and pauses are critical for emphasis and help convey meaning as well as maintaining audience interest. Pausing helps both the speaker and the audience. The speaker needs pauses to allow them to remember what they are going to say next. The audience needs pauses in order to *process* what is being told to them. It is far harder to listen to a speech than to read something.

When it is appropriate to pause? What words do you need to stress? This will depend on your subject and the message you want to convey. You will be able to tell the best places to pause and stress by practising your speech in front of a **critical audience of peers**. If you are 'speaking too fast', this usually means that you are providing not enough pauses and emphasis. Another useful technique is to record the speech.

Activity:
Emphasis and stress

One of the best ways to tell if your delivery is right is to tape your entire speech using some kind of recording device and then listen back to it *critically. Imagine you are in the audience.*

No one likes the sound of their own voice in a tape recorder. However, when playing back the recording try to ignore this issue (you cannot do much about your tone and accent) and listen for the delivery. Are there enough pauses? Is the flow of ideas easy to follow? Often quite long pauses are needed, especially if the information is complex and technical.

Re-record the speech and this time make sure that certain key words are stressed and pauses are provided after important points.

2 Repetition

Repetition of words or ideas in a written assignment is a bad thing. It shows a lack of content or an inability to structure ideas. In presentations, repetition can be a very effective technique. However, it is important not to overdo repetition, and generally, only one or two (not multiple) repetitions works best. It is also important to *repeat ideas*, and not just words. Using different words to repeat an important point can give the audience a second chance to process the information in highly complex and technical presentations. Equally, it is important to always bring the audience back to the central point of the presentation using language such as: *I want to suggest that 'bridging the gap' is an important idea ..., To 'bridge the gap' is about ..., 'Furthermore, to truly 'bridge the gap' it is important to ...,* and so on.

3 Reversal

A similar device to repetition is reversal of ideas. Consider the famous lines from a speech from President J. F. Kennedy:

> *Ask not what your country can do for you. Ask what you can do for your country.*

The spoken words generate an immediate impact. Of course, academic presentations are not the same as political speeches. However, the technique is useful to consider when preparing an academic speech. Consider the following example from Finance. Which version do you prefer? Which one would you prefer to listen to?

- The expectations hypothesis of the term structure implies that that the yield spread between the long rate and short rate is an optimal predictor of future changes of short rates over the life of the 'long bond'.
- The expectations hypothesis of the term structure needs to be considered for its influence. **[pause]** What kind of influence does the term structure have? **[pause]** It implies that that the yield spread between the long rate and short rate is an optimal predictor. **[pause]** The spread is a predictor of future changes of short rates over the life of the 'long bond' **[pause]** Both the short rate and the long rate are equally affected. **[pause**) And they influence the long bond in the same way. **[pause]** In what ways are they affected? **[pause]** The long rate ... while the short rate ...

Considered as an oral presentation, the second version is much more interesting because it repeats and reverses important ideas. It also provides rhetorical questions (see below). This repetition and reversal provide emphasis and reinforcement of information.

4 Rhetorical questions

Sometimes a good way of introducing an emphatic statement is by beginning with a rhetorical question. A rhetorical question is a question with a pre-prepared answer:

So what can be concluded from this examination of Freud's ideas in the context of modern-day Psychology? Well, it is clear that Freud's theories still have some relevance. ... Today I am going to ...

The important thing to note is that rhetorical questions are never left 'dangling' without an answer. *The speaker has to immediately answer the questions if they are asked* (unless, of course, it is answered by a member of the audience). However, it is critically important to *prepare* an answer. Don't assume that the audience will answer your questions. Usually, the audience does not respond during a presentation and this can leave an awkward silence. Have an answer ready.

Have a second look at the example from Finance given earlier. Two rhetorical questions are asked which are immediately answered by the speaker. The technique of rhetorical questions has the effect of smoothing the flow of the presentation, and making the content easier to follow. Rhetorical questions are not to be used in written assignments, but they are very effective in speeches.

5 *Tripling*

Good presenters often chunk important points in threes. It is a curious feature of the human brain that items grouped in threes have more impact than items grouped in twos, fours or fives. Abraham Lincoln used this technique in the Gettysburg address:

We cannot dedicate – we cannot consecrate – we cannot hallow – this ground. Government of the people, by the people, for the people.

This technique is commonly used in commercial presentations, especially those used to sell something. It is also effective in academic presentations but should not be overused. It works well with indicator words like 'firstly', 'secondly' and 'thirdly'. Again, which of the following is more effective?

- The expectations hypothesis of the term structure implies that the yield spread between the long rate and short rate is an optimal predictor of future changes of short rates over the life of the 'long bond'.
- This paper will **firstly** look at the expectations hypothesis of the term structure, **secondly** show how the yield spread between the long rate and short rate is an optimal predictor of future changes of short rates, and **thirdly** show how this impact occurs over the life of the 'long bond'.

If a fourth point is added to the second version it may become far too complex to process aurally. Three points seem 'just right'. Often you will need to rewrite you material to ensure that you keep to the 'rule of threes'.

6 The conclusion

The conclusion is *almost* as important as the introduction. It is the last thing that the audience will hear before they have time to ask questions. Therefore, the conclusion will remain in the memory of the audience more than any other part of the presentation. It is critical that the conclusion reinforces the main idea (or thesis). Don't frustrate the audience. Make sure to remind them of your main point. If you fail to do this you will leave them uncertain about what your presentation was about.

The conclusion should do **the reverse** of the introduction: it should 'fan out' from the main point to some general speculative remarks to close the presentation.

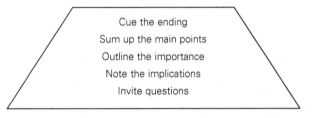

Cue the ending
Sum up the main points
Outline the importance
Note the implications
Invite questions

The following kind of language should be used for the **first part** of the conclusion:

- 'Let me conclude by reminding you of my main point …'
- 'To sum up, I have argued in this paper that …'
- 'In summary, I want to claim in this paper that …'
- 'In conclusion, today I have given reasons to suggest that …'
- 'And now to conclude. Today I have made the following point …'

The following language should be used for the **second part** of the conclusion:

- 'I covered the following points during my presentation … *firstly*, … *secondly*, … etc.'.
- 'In making this argument, I presented several ideas for discussion. *First* … *second* … etc.'
- 'In this paper I made several claims in order to support my central thesis. The *first* was …' the *second* … etc.'.
- 'I now wish to conclude. This presentation has covered *four main points: first* … *second* … etc.'.

The numbering here may seem excessive, but it is better to be overdone than under-done, and typically, students forget to do it.

The third and fourth parts of the conclusion can be dealt with in a number of ways. You can finish by looking at:

- additional research that would be worth doing by others that would assist in understanding the material you have presented;

- additional research that *you* intend to do to follow on from the material presented;
- the wider importance of your work for other researchers/academic scholarship or for society at large;
- an illustration/video/diagram that sums up your work clearly.

As these are the final significant points you will make before finishing your presentation, it is best if this section is thought about carefully and presented with some impact. Consider the use of diagrams, pictures, graphs, tables or short video clips.

The following language should be used for the fourth part of the conclusion:

- 'This work has a number of implications: *first ... second ...*'
- 'I'd just like to end by looking at where this research can go in the future ...'
- 'In the future, I intend to follow through with what I have presented here by ...'
- '*Lastly,* let's look at the following diagram and see how my work fits in with the aims of the present paper.'
- '*Finally,* as it can be seen in the following table ...'

And end with a variation of the following for the final part of the conclusion:

- 'Thank you for listening to my presentation. I would now like to invite questions.'
- 'Thank you for your attention. ... Are there any questions?'
- 'Thank you for your attention. ...I welcome any questions.'

It should be noted that while there are several distinct phases during the conclusion, the conclusion should not be drawn out. It should be no longer than about 5 per cent of the length of the total presentation. There is nothing worse than a presenter saying: 'in conclusion' and then not concluding quickly! You should move quickly and seamlessly though each of the stages. You are probably feeling very happy to be at the end of your presentation, but resist the temptation to draw the ending out too long. Short, sharp and crisp is best.

7 Dealing with questions

When a member of the audience asks you a question, it's a good idea to comment on it before actually answering it. Powell has noted four basic types of question.

(a) Good questions

These are intelligent, appropriate questions that deserve an answer from you. First, thank the person for asking the question. Then comment on the question before answering it. Questions like these help you to get your message across to the audience better.

(b) Difficult questions

These are the questions that you can't or prefer not to answer. It is best to answer questions like these honestly and say you do not know the answer. Offer to find out the answer and get back to the questioner with the answer, or turn the tables and ask the questioner how *they* would answer the question. This promotes engagement with the audience, but it should be done politely.

(c) Unnecessary questions

You have already given this information, but it is possible that the questioner misheard you. Tell the questioner that you covered this information earlier, repeat the information briefly, and continue.

(d) Irrelevant questions

Sometimes people ask irrelevant questions. Thank them for their question anyway. Tell them that the question is not appropriate in the context of your presentation (give a reason). Kindly suggest that you might discuss this matter privately over coffee.

> **Note:** At university, you are graded on your answers to questions as well as on the presentation itself. When people ask you questions, listen carefully. Avoid the temptation to **interrupt**. Take a moment to think and then *comment* on each question before you actually answer it. You can start by using phrases introduced in chapter 16, such as: *'Let me paraphrase what I think you are saying. You are saying .... Have I understood you correctly?'*

8 Before the speech

Your seminar presentation usually follows the completion of a research essay or other major assignment. Therefore use the essay preparation time as a time to also collect ideas for the presentation that (normally) follows. They need not be exactly the same ideas.

Nervousness

Being nervous is absolutely normal. Nervous energy is vital for doing a good job. Use your nervousness to your advantage, but control it so that you don't *look* nervous. The best ways to control your nerves are as follows:

- Practise public speaking as often as you can whenever you are given the opportunity to speak to an audience. Practise your presentation in front of friends or family several times and ask them for their comments.
- Don't think of yourself as 'nervous'; think of yourself as being 'excited by the opportunity to speak'. This small change in attitude makes a big difference in your level of general preparedness.
- Recognise that no one in the audience *wants* you to fail. People in the audience know what it is like to present to an audience and are *naturally* sympathetic to you.

- Go early to the presentation venue and get used to the location. Imagine your audience looking at you and smiling. Use *positive imagery* to assist you to overcome nervousness.
- Prepare carefully by structuring your presentation carefully.
- Beforehand, practise breathing deeply and slowly. Some people find that it helps to go for a slow walk before the presentation.
- Remind yourself that the audience consists of other students who also have to give a seminar. Many are your friends.
- Remember that public speaking is a specialised skill that you need to practise if you are going to improve.

The finer points

There are some general points to remember when giving presentations. These are as follows:

- When you practise in front of your friends, make sure that you sound 'natural' and not too rehearsed. Your delivery should almost be 'conversational' in style. Use prompt-phrases on flashcards instead of whole sentences. This will ensure that your speech is not stilted and mechanical-sounding.
- Dress appropriately so you feel confident. You do not want your choice of clothing detracting attention from your talk.
- Use gestures for emphasis.
- Use constant **eye contact** which ranges across the entire audience.
- Use connector language to mark out the parts of your speech.
- Smile occasionally (very important!!!) but don't grin all the time.
- Recap important points using different language.
- Ask rhetorical questions and involve your audience to some degree (but keep control, as you are the presenter).
- Use pauses for emphasis and do not speak too fast (you will be nervous and this will make you 'race' – control it).
- Use short sentences (it's not an essay).
- Use examples which your audience can relate to.
- Use surprising facts and statistics to gain interest.
- Don't hide behind the equipment. Gain the confidence and interest of your audience by walking towards them a little and moving around a bit (but don't pace nervously).
- Don't walk in front of your PowerPoint slides.
- Make sure that you summarise your main points in concluding. Do not just say: 'Well, that's it' and walk off! Start by saying *'In conclusion ...'* or *'To sum up ...'*, and then follow this cue with a list of points covered in the presentation: *'I have outlined four main types of topographical modelling in this presentation ... These were ... '*
- Conclude appropriately by asking for questions.

- If you don't know the answer to a question, tell the questioner that it is an interesting question and that you will find out the answer and get back to them about it.

The most important – and memorable – parts of a speech are the introduction and conclusion. Practise them!

5 Presenting a tutorial

You may be asked to prepare something for a tutorial or to run a tutorial. This could involve a formal presentation. Alternatively, it might involve **leading a discussion**. A good way to do this is to base your 'discussion' on an appropriate reading. It is suggested that this involve the following stages:

1 Choosing a topic for discussion
First choose a topic for discussion that the rest of the group is likely to have an interest in. You might assess their interest in various topics first. Alternatively, your tutor might allocate a topic for you.

2 Choosing a reading
Second, choose a text for the class. The reading material could be an article in a newspaper or a journal. (It is a good idea that it is not too long and not too complex!) Alternatively, it might not be a reading but a segment of a video. Whatever the medium, it is important to have a *focus* for the discussion to follow.

If it is a reading, make a copy for each member of the group and give it to them to read at least a day or more before the discussion is to take place. Ideally, it is best to give it to students at the *previous* tutorial, and then remind them to read it a few days before.

3 Consider the learning method
Consider some kind of *active learning method* to engage the tutorial audience in the topic, for example, a class debate. There are many different methods you could use here, limited only by your imagination. (Consider, for example, role plays, interactive games, tests, and so on.)

4 Beginning the tutorial
Begin the session by summarising the key points of the article, or even better, 'eliciting' the key points from the audience (this involves some teaching skills). Sum up the evidence or arguments for the key points with diagrams, graphs, flow charts and/or tables. Ask for comments and criticism on the information provided from your audience. (Ideally you will have pre-prepared responses to typical questions in advance.)

5 Other important considerations

When leading a discussion you should be aware of the following important points:

- Make sure you cover everything in the reading or material under discussion. You *are* being assessed on your contribution to the class (whether this has been mentioned or not). Therefore if you miss something crucial it reflects badly on you – and it is, after all, your tutorial.
- Don't think of the opportunity as 'something you have to do'. Think of it as an opportunity to become the 'class expert' on a particular topic. Be adventurous in your preparation for your class. This preparation will be reflected in your class grade later on. Other students in the class may not prepare well. Don't be tempted to follow suit (to avoid being 'different'): do something highly professional. Your audience, and your tutor, will appreciate it. Set the gold standard for the class.
- Make sure that everyone in the group contributes to the discussion.
- The main aims of the task of running a tutorial are to elicit comments on the following aspects of the reading/subject matter of the class:
  - What is the author's opinion of this issue?
  - What are her/his main arguments?
  - What evidence does the author give to support her/his contentions?
  - Is this evidence sound? Are there flaws in the data presented?
  - Is the article balanced in its presentation of the issue or does it use unreasonable devices to persuade the reader?
  - What are the group members' opinions of the issue?
- Make sure that the comments made in the discussion are understood by all group members and rephrase comments that are unclear to check for meaning.
- Keep the discussion moving along. Make sure that the discussion does not become irrelevant or repetitious. Finish the discussion within the agreed time limit.
- Be aware of your audience and make clear, unbiased and logical comments. Try to communicate in a way that everyone will understand.
- Make notes during the discussion in order to provide a written summary of the main ideas discussed at the end of the class for later distribution to your tutor and other students.
- Give a written record of the material presented in class to your tutor. This will impress them greatly. They will use this to remind them of your tutorial presentation when they assess your contributions in class.

Everyone participating in a tutorial is expected to 'give and take', which means that they should listen carefully to what is being said as well as giving their own opinions and playing an active part in the discussion.

● 6 Summary

This chapter has outlined some skills for public speaking for assessment and presenting a tutorial. Some international students enter university with a fear of speaking in class. This is a great pity. The importance of class-based participation cannot be overestimated. When you talk in a tutorial you will find yourself not only expressing ideas, but also forming, refining and even rejecting them. Skills in oral communication and verbal fluency can be learned if they are practiced conscientiously.

During your postgraduate study you will be required to give presentations. It should be noted that public speaking is a complex skill and takes considerable practice and experience in front of an audience. It is hoped that the advice given in this chapter will assist you in your preparation.

● 7 Presentation checklist

Use this sheet to help you plan and assess presentations in terms of:

- overall content
- introduction
- body
- conclusion
- delivery
- visuals/equipment
- language

Overall content
Appropriateness for audience (depth, detail, scope)
Accuracy and relevance of points
Strength of argumentation
Level of interest
Use of supporting examples, explanations, definitions, facts, figures, anecdotes
Length

Introduction

- Introduction of self (and other presenters if necessary)
- Attention-grabbing starter (anecdote, quote, question, amazing facts, etc.)
- Introduction of topic and presentation of relevant background information
- Statement of main argument, focus or purpose
- Overview of presentation sequence
- Request for questions to be asked at the end (if desired)

Body

- Clear and logical sequence
- Language for transitions

Conclusion

- Language to indicate impending end of talk
- Restatement of main purpose or argument
- Summary
- Memorable final comment
- Invitation of questions and ability to manage them
- Statement of thanks

Delivery

- Body language: posture, gestures for emphasis, movement

- Position: not in front of visual support or behind desk or other equipment

- Voice: pronunciation, volume, fluency, expressiveness, pauses, speed

- Eye contact: constant and ranging across entire audience

- Use of notes

- Use of humour (if at all)

- Enthusiasm

- Confidence

- Friendliness

- Dress

- Interaction with audience

- Ability to manage questions and disruptions

Visuals/equipment

- Timely issuing of handouts

- Visuals: clear, attractive, professional, consistent in design, relevant, referenced

- Appropriate references to visuals in presentation

- Audio-visual equipment, checked and ready before presentation

- Use of equipment (whiteboard, overhead projector, computer, visualiser, screen)

Language

- [ ] Accurate vocabulary
- [ ] Accurate grammar
- [ ] Explanations of technical terms
- [ ] Appropriate level of formality
- [ ] Clarity of sentences and language
- [ ] Conciseness

17 Speaking to Your Supervisor or Lecturer

● 1 Introduction

A supervisor is an academic who provides individual assistance to students completing research projects. Supervisors are sometimes designated to students and there is no 'choice' (this decision is made be made by your head of department or by a committee). If you are required to choose a supervisor some good advice for doing this is provided in Wisker (2008). This chapter is about dealing with a supervisors and lecturers when you need to speak to them individually.

● 2 Dealing with your supervisor, lecturers and tutors

You will often need to see your lecturer, supervisor or tutor about something. What do you do? Lecturers are just people. However, you may be intimidated by them at first because you are unfamiliar with their culture and the expectations they have of you. Lecturers usually make themselves available to students during 'consultation hours'. These are dedicated periods during each day or week which fall outside lectures.

In a western culture, lecturers might have a more 'direct' approach to communication than you are used to. Lecturers in western countries expect you to take the initiative in the conversation and be *assertive and direct* in what you want to say. Make your point, ask your questions, listen to their response and thank them for their time. In English-speaking countries it is not rude to come directly to the point in a meeting, rather it is expected.

● 3 Preparing for a meeting

Your supervisor or lecturer will expect you to take the lead in the discussion, if you want to see them about something. Therefore prepare carefully for the meeting. Here are a few suggestions on how to prepare for a face-to-face meeting.

- If you are a graduate student doing a research degree and you have a regular meeting with your supervisor, review any reading you have done since you last met. Be prepared to give a brief account of it, especially of any of the problems it may have raised in your studies to date. Express yourself simply and clearly: 'Last time we met you asked me to read Henderson's work on critical literacy. I have done that and have written a summary of his ideas that I want to discuss with you.'

● Make a list of all the problems you have encountered and be prepared to discuss them. If the purpose of the meeting is to discuss something you have written, reread your copy of the work so that it is fresh in your mind.

● If you want to see the lecturer about a matter he or she spoke about in the lecture, be sure that you have read the recommended reading for that lecture first.

● Take with you a written list of the points you want to raise with your lecturer, tutor or supervisor. Organise them in a logical order with the most important at the top. This way, if your supervisor or lecturer is too busy to consider all your points, you will at least receive advice on the most important things.

● After you have greeted your supervisor or lecturer, summarise in one or two sentences what you have done since the last time you saw him/her and then immediately raise your most important point that you wish to discuss: 'Since we last met I have clarified the main procedures involved in the experiment I am going to conduct. What I wish to see you about now is the best way to write and distribute the survey instrument.'

● Take notes during the discussion. This shows you are paying attention and want to learn. It will also ensure that you do not forget anything important and have a record of the meeting.

● **4 How to behave and what to say**

Be direct and forthright in your questions and responses to lecturing staff. *Look into their eyes,* not at the wall or ceiling. Don't be indirect or unclear about what you want. This may seem very rude to you but it will be highly appreciated by lecturers. Look confident and relaxed. Take your time and don't rush. If you are not confident in your English fluency, pause a lot and allow yourself plenty of time to say what you need to say.

● Begin by saying: 'Thanks for seeing me. I appreciate your time. I want to see you about ..., This is what I need to know ...'

● List the topics briefly from the **most important** to the **least important**.

● Then elaborate on each point in turn.

● Stop after each point for comment or reaction from the lecturer.

● When the lecturer has concluded his or her comments, move to the next point using a transition word, e.g. 'Thank you. Now the second thing I needed to clarify is X.'

- Conclude the meeting by asking any follow-up questions that may have arisen from the lecturer's comments.
- Thank the lecturer again for their time, smile, and leave the meeting.

We saw this 'inverted funnel' approach – moving from the general point to specific points or evidence – in chapter 1, and again in chapter 12. We also saw it in chapter 16. It is a useful structure for writing and oral presentations of information that seems very 'natural' and logical to western people.

Naming norms in addressing staff

Note that there are sometimes different naming traditions in different western countries. As a general rule, in the UK, academic titles are used, i.e. Dr/Professor [Surname] (**Note:** it must be **the surname** and not the given name. Because surnames are used in the first position in many Asian languages, many Asian students get this wrong). In the USA this is also generally expected unless advised otherwise. In Australia, academics can be more informal and insist on first names being used. In this case, the academic title can be omitted. However, only do this if the academic has *previously insisted* on being addressed using their first or given name only. They might say, for example: 'My name is Dr Robert Harris, but please call me 'Bob'.

Note that it is generally unwise to use other titles, especially those for women, e.g. *Mrs* (married), *Miss* (unmarried), *Ms* (either married or unmarried; can represent a wish to identify marital status as irrelevant). These titles can be a source of irritation for the recipient if used incorrectly.

---

5 Summary

This chapter has attempted to give you confidence in addressing academic staff in western tertiary institutions. Communication styles in the teaching and learning context do differ (Hofstede, 1986). This is especially so with Asian and western communication styles. With some practice and guidance, these forms of communication can be developed, and this will give you much more confidence in asking questions of academic staff. Indirectly, these skills will assist students in the globalised workforce where western communication styles still predominate.

Part VIII

Want to Go Further?

18 Writing a Research Proposal

1 Introduction

After you have completed a postgraduate coursework degree you may be wondering: 'What's next?' You may be inspired by your postgraduate studies enough to think about a graduate-level research degree. If so, the next step is to complete a research proposal and to consider a doctoral degree or Ph.D. The next two chapters provide some suggestions for students considering these options.

2 What is a research proposal?

A research proposal is a short document (usually 3–7 pages) written to inform others of a *proposed* piece of research, usually a master's or doctorate by research thesis, but it can be work for a corporate purpose. University students usually write research proposals for academics who may eventually supervise the work based on the proposal.

A research proposal can be rejected as 'unsuitable' or 'poorly designed', and a piece of research can be rejected on the basis of the proposal – so the proposal is obviously an important document. It is worthwhile spending some time getting it exactly right. This will also save you time in the long run. A well-designed proposal forms the outline of the thesis, or major project, to follow. Ideally, the proposal can be mapped on to various parts of the final document.

3 What things are included in a research proposal?

The following things must be included in any proposal:

- an introduction or background to the research problem or issue (including the 'gap' in the current research – the latter is *most* important);
- a research question and – if possible – a thesis statement answering the question;
- the justification for the proposed research, i.e. why the research is being done and why it is needed;
- a preliminary literature review (covering what others have already done in the area);

- the theoretical framework used in the proposed research;
- the contribution of the research to the general area;
- the proposed research methodology used;
- a research plan and outline;
- a timetable of proposed research;
- a list of references used in preparing the proposal.

The following things may *also* be included in the proposal:

- the limitations of the research (what the research is *not* intended to do – i.e. the 'scope' of the research);
- the resources to be used in the research (e.g. equipment, etc.),
- how the research will be evaluated or tested;
- where and how the results of the research will be disseminated or distributed;
- the background of the researcher and their suitability for the task.

In this chapter we will go though the main sections only.

1 Introduction

This should be as brief as possible (a paragraph or two). Make this part of the proposal clear and crisp. Get to the main focus quickly. You need to give a sense of the **general field** of research of which your area is a part. This needs to narrow down to the **specific area** you are concerned with, and this should lead logically to **the 'gap'** in the research that you will fill. When the gap is identified, then a **research question** can naturally be raised. The answer to this question is called the **thesis statement**. See the 'Conversation metaphor for research' in chapter 14.

Note that the thesis statement may only be tentative at this stage as the research has not yet been carried out. It is not expected in a proposal that you have an answer to your research question. This is what the thesis provides. It helps if you have a tentative answer, however. A *hypothesis* is useful for this purpose, though this might only be necessary for more empirical subjects (Economics, for example) (see chapter 7).

Further points to note:

- you should briefly outline any controversies that are in the literature without giving full details (as these are covered in the literature review section);
- you should use simple and jargon-free language, as your supervisor may not be aware of all the language in your focus area;
- the introduction must *narrow down* – not get wider. You must demonstrate how you have command of the issues in the area and that you are focusing on a particular issue;
- the introduction generally forms (roughly) **Sections 1.1 to 1.5** of the final document (see the diagram in Section 10, below).

2 Research question

This forms **Section 1.4** of the final document. Note that the research question may not necessarily be a 'question' as such, but can be a statement of a problem to be investigated. There is an example below. Note the move from general area, to specific focus area, to the gap in the research (the first italicised passage) and then to the proposed thesis statement (the second italicised passage):

- The **general area** is business marketing theory;
- the **specific research area** is marketing management concepts (especially the difference between agricultural and business marketing theory);
- the **'gap'** is the application of these concepts to the farming sector;
- the **research question** is whether the distinction between agricultural and business marketing theory is justified in the case of the farming sector (**Section 1.4** of the final document);
- the **thesis statement** is that neither agricultural marketing nor business marketing concepts are appropriate in the farming sector and that a new methodology is needed (this is what the research will provide) (**Section 1.5** of the final document).

According to business marketing theory, businesses are more likely to succeed if they utilise marketing management approaches or techniques. For example, the marketing concept, a cornerstone of business marketing thought, stresses the importance of determining the needs and wants of consumers and delivering the desired satisfaction more effectively and efficiently than competitors (Kotler, 1986). *Philosophies from marketing management have recently been applied to almost every industry from insurance to travel and hospital services, but not often to farming.* Concerns have been raised about the distinction which appears to exist between agricultural and business marketing theory (Bartels, 1983; Bateman, 1976; Muelenberg, 1986). In this research proposal the role of marketing management in agricultural marketing theory and practice is described. *It is argued that the marketing strategies of farmers are not adequately described by either the business or agricultural marketing disciplines, and a methodology for analyzing the farm business marketing strategy process is outlined.* (Adapted from McLeay & Zwart, 1993)

Note that the 'research question' in this case is really a statement of what needs to be investigated. This is a perfectly acceptable way of presenting this part of the introduction. However, it could also be phrased in the form of a question or formal hypothesis.

3 Justification for the proposed research

One page is usually sufficient for this. Perry suggests that writers need to tell the reader that the research can be justified along four main criteria:

- the size of the industry/area involved;
- the gaps in the literature demand attention;

- the unusual or improved methodology being used;
- the benefits in terms of policy and practice.

(Perry, 2003; Sekaran, 1992)

Other kinds of justification are possible, of course. The example above could clearly be justified along all criteria.

4 Preliminary literature review

This is where you provide more detail on what others have done in the area, and what you propose to do. You will need to write around 2–3 pages. You need to cover the following:

- the major issues or schools of thought;
- the gaps in the literature (in more detail than that provided in the introduction);
- research questions (for qualitative research) and hypotheses (for quantitative research) which are connected carefully to the literature being reviewed;
- definitions of key terms (when you introduce each idea, or in a definition subsection);
- questions arising from the gaps that can be the focus of data collection or analysis.

This section eventually becomes chapter 2 of the final document.

Perry suggests that potential candidates read a thesis in a similar area to get a feel for what is required in this section (see also chapter 14).

An example of a literature review

An examination of textbook definitions of business and agricultural marketing provides the most general guide to theoretical content. Although there is no generally accepted definition of agricultural marketing, it is frequently viewed as part of the economic system (Ritson, 1986; Bateman, 1976) and is widely recognised as involving the exchange process. A typical definition is given by Shepard and Futrell (1982) who state: ' ...' [passage omitted]. By this definition agricultural marketing theory focuses on the workings of the distribution system, and is typically viewed as a process that begins after produce leaves the farm gate. ... Thus production planning is frequently excluded from the marketing process. ... Although there is no universally accepted definition of business marketing, it is generally accepted that business marketing, like agricultural marketing, involves the exchange process. For example, Kotler (1972, p. 12) defines marketing as: '...'. (McLeay & Zwart, 1993)

Note how the writers are using definitions of key terms and making distinctions in this area to eventually arrive at the contribution of their own research to the debate.

5 Theoretical framework

The theoretical framework usually forms the final part of the literature review section. It describes the model that you are using in the thesis to demonstrate your point. See Sekaran (1992, ch. 3) for a useful account of theoretical frameworks.

6 Proposed research methodology

This section should be about 1–2 pages. It forms chapter 3 of the final document.

You do not have to describe the methodology used in great detail (this will be done in the final document) but you should justify its use over other similar methodologies. For example, you could explain:

- why you are using a certain paradigm or theory;
- why you are using qualitative or quantitative research;
- why you are using a case study of a specific kind;
- why you are using surveys, correlational experiments, field studies, specific statistical measurements, etc.;
- why you are using certain dependent, independent or moderating variables (see chapter 7);
- why you have chosen a sampling frame and the size of a certain sample;
- how you are proposing to have access to the data;
- how you are proposing to analyse the data (this is usually chapter 4 of the final document).

You also need to provide operational (testable – or at least well-supported in the literature) definitions of key terms used such as 'firm size', 'business marketing theory', etc. (Perry, 2003; Sekaran, 1992).

7 Contribution of the research

This forms **Section 1.6** of the final document. In this section, you outline how your research will make a *change* to an area of study. This is different from the justification of your research. The justification explains *why* the research should be done. The contribution section explains how what you will do will lead to certain outcomes. You need to outline:

- the importance of the research outcome(s);
- the practical or theoretical nature of the outcome(s).

The outcome could be the extension of a theoretical model to a new area; it could be testing a theory in a new area of biological science, or it could be something practical like the development of a checklist for managers, for example. The limitations of research section, if you have one, can go in this section. This will become **Section 1.7** of the final document.

8 Research plan and project timetable

The research plan or outline can be discussed in conjunction with a research timetable. However, note that they have a different function.

The **research plan** or outline simply lists what will be covered in each chapter or section of the proposed document. This helps you as well as the reader:

- it gives you a framework on the direction your proposed document will take;
- it shows the reader that the project is well-organised and achievable in the time available.

You need only provide one or two lines for each. This becomes **Section 1.7** of the final document.

The **project timetable** should indicate the weighting of each part of the proposed document (in percentage terms), the topics covered, approximate word limit and – importantly – the approximate length of time it will take to complete them. You might consider providing a graph for convenience.

Chapter	Topic	%	Words	Months
1	Introduction	5	3,500	3
2	Literature review	30	21,000	6
3	Methodology	20	14,000	4
4	Data analysis	25	17,500	5
5	Conclusions and implications	20	14,000	6
TOTAL		100	70,000	24

(Based on Perry, 1994; Phillips & Pugh, 2010)

Note that:

- the timetable is approximate only and things always take longer than you think!;
- allow extra time at the start and finish of the project;
- the timetable does not commit you to anything (though obviously it helps if you can follow it).

9 List of references

This must be provided in the usual scholarly fashion. It helps to convince your reader that your proposal is worth pursuing if you can identify literature in the field and demonstrate that you understand it. It makes a very strong impact if you can identify where there is a research 'gap' in the literature (that your proposal hopes to fill). This is your contribution to the scholarly 'conversation'.

In-text references should be provided for all sections of the proposal with the exception of the research plan and timetable.

10 Relationship between the proposal and final project

Note finally that while the proposal can be mapped on to the final document, much work needs to be done. The proposal merely provides a 'shell'. The research thesis, or final document, fills in the details. Parts of the proposal are not required in a final document (for example, resources and evaluation, and timetable). The order and arrangement of each document is slightly different, also, as the diagram shows.

Proposal	Thesis/final project
1 introduction	1 introduction
1.1 general area 1.2 specific topic 1.3 gap 1.4 research question 1.5 thesis statement	1.1 general area 1.2 specific topic 1.3 gap 1.4 research question 1.5 thesis statement 1.6 contribution 1.7 thesis outline/limitations
2 literature review	2 literature review
3 theoretical framework	3 methodology
4 methodology	4 data analysis
5 contribution	5 conclusions and implications
6 research plan and timetable	6 references
7 references	7 appendices

Note: Variations in the above are possible.

4 Summary

Research proposals usually form the first stage of the process of beginning a higher degree by research. However, they can also be requested by lecturers from students who are writing large theses for master's-level work, or sometimes in corporate contexts. The skills needed in doing a research proposal are also valuable for outside the university in the corporate world. A research proposal is similar to what is sometimes called, in industry, a 'scoping brief'. It outlines the aims and plans for an intended piece of work before the researcher begins the work itself. This enables others to pass judgement on the likely benefits of the research. It is also useful for the researcher to get feedback on the proposed research before they begin. This saves time and misdirected scholarly effort. A research proposal is typically followed by a confirmation report, which is a much longer document of around 20 pages (see chapter 19).

19 What Next? Completing a Ph.D.

1 Introduction

There are already many excellent books on writing a Ph.D. and doing postgraduate research, such as Phillips and Pugh (2010) and Stevens and Asmar (1999). There are other texts dedicated to Ph.D. writing: Dunleavy (2003) and Williams et al. (2010, 2011). This final chapter does not try to replicate these other, more dedicated texts. The purpose of this chapter is to give an honest appraisal of the value and benefits of doing a Ph.D. Many postgraduate students never go on to complete a Ph.D., but they are required to write large theses as part of their coursework. Of course, there are differences in these tasks, but they are differences in *degree* not *kind*. A Ph.D. is a very large thesis. The same skills are involved in smaller theses. If you enjoy your postgraduate studies, a Ph.D. may be the next logical step for you to take.

2 What is a Ph.D. and why do one?

The Ph.D., or Doctor of Philosophy, is not the highest level of academic achievement in the university system. There are higher doctorates – D.Litt., D.Sc. (these are awarded as 'honorary' degrees for a substantial body of published work). However, the Ph.D. degree is the ultimate achievement for most students. Indeed, it counts as admission to a fairly select 'club'. Having a Ph.D. is a necessary condition for becoming an academic in universities – though it is not a sufficient condition (you need publications too).

Despite its importance, the completion of a Ph.D. is only the *beginning* of your academic career. Even if you do not pursue an academic career, the Ph.D. is a valuable experience for many reasons:

- it demonstrates a very high level of academic scholarship;
- it demonstrates that a student has the skills to produce a major piece of written work by themselves;
- it demonstrates a very high level of information literacy skills.

A Ph.D. normally takes between three and four years' full-time study. It is not uncommon to spend five years on a Ph.D., and some people take longer than this (though most university deadlines are three years with a *possible* extension to a fourth year). Part-time students can take seven years or sometimes longer. Some students never finish, and abandon the project. A Ph.D. is, above all else, a test of *dedication*.

A doctoral degree is *usually* done entirely by research with a supervisor (or supervisors) as the main advisers for the project (see chapter 17). Some Ph.D.s involve additional coursework subjects, concluding with a smaller research project.

In both cases – research alone or coursework and research – the supervisor(s) may help in directing you to literature in the area, but you mainly work alone, with occasional meetings with your supervisor(s). These meetings can be weekly, monthly or irregularly (at the discretion of the supervisor). Of course, the supervisor's role is critical (see chapter 17).

3 Positives and negatives

On the positive side, doing a Ph.D. can be a very liberating, rewarding and life-changing experience. The process of completing one can teach you advanced skills that are intrinsically valuable – research, writing and critical thinking – and being a Ph.D. student means that you are engaged in 'real' – often 'cutting-edge' – research, which can be exciting and stimulating. As the culmination of a university career, it has no equal. Recall the table in section 5 of chapter 1, where a distinction is made between *reproductive, analytical* and *speculative* knowledge. Doing a Ph.D. is very much at the speculative end of this continuum. It is an opportunity for good students to make their own contribution to knowledge. The Ph.D. student has gone beyond analysis of other people's ideas; they are *adding* new ideas to cutting-edge debates. This can be a very exciting process.

Nevertheless, there are negative points to take into account. Consider your options carefully before starting one. A Ph.D. is not for everyone. Nor is it necessarily a guarantee of getting a good job. Doing a Ph.D. can be a very lonely and isolating experience. A measure of your ability to complete one is having completed a previous piece of research (for example, an honours thesis or a master's by research) or if you are very confident in your ability to 'see the project through' to completion. There are no prizes for *unfinished* Ph.D.s.

> An important point is this: if you are *fascinated* by your proposed topic it is **likely** that you will be able to complete it. Over and above all – the Ph.D. is a test of **dedication.**

4 What does a Ph.D. involve?

A normal research Ph.D. requires you to:

- work largely alone on the Ph.D. project for 3 or more years full time (seldom less than 3 years – often much longer). A supervisor guides you in the early stages;

- make a substantial *original contribution* to the literature in this area (the 'thesis');
- argue convincingly for this 'thesis' with normal conventions of academic scholarship;
- prepare the thesis for formal submission as a doctoral degree.

During your candidature you will be expected to attend and contribute to departmental seminars, and to present one or more seminars yourself. You may even be required to present a paper at an academic conference, and/or to publish papers from your research in international journals.

At the end of their candidature, the student needs to produce a sizeable document (resembling a bound book) of between 80,000 and 100,000 words: 80,000 is usual, 100,000 is usually the maximum length (though there are variations in different countries.) This document has to be carefully argued, researched and documented. It must contain evidence of careful scholarship. The thesis is then examined independently by professionals in the field (usually highly-published academics) that are normally external to the university. These professionals prepare written reports on the thesis. No 'grades' are awarded. They either:

- reject the thesis;
- accept it subject to *major revisions* (requiring rewriting and re-submission);
- accept it subject to *minor revisions* (requiring a sign-off by internal examiners);
- accept the thesis without changes.

From a Ph.D. handbook:

The University expects its doctoral graduates to have the following qualities and skills:

- an advanced ability to initiate research and to formulate viable research questions;
- a demonstrated capacity to design, conduct and report sustained and original research;
- the capacity to contextualise research within an international corpus of specialist knowledge;
- an advanced ability to evaluate and synthesise research-based and scholarly literature;
- an advanced understanding of key disciplinary and multidisciplinary norms and perspectives relevant to the field;
- highly developed problem-solving abilities and flexibility of approach;
- the ability to analyse critically within and across a changing disciplinary environment;
- the capacity to disseminate the results of research and scholarship by oral and written communication to a variety of audiences;
- a capacity to cooperate with and respect the contributions of fellow researchers and scholars;

- a profound respect for truth and intellectual integrity, and for the ethics of research and scholarship;
- an advanced facility in the management of information, including the application of computer systems and software where appropriate to the student's field of study;
- an understanding of the relevance and value of their research to national and international communities of scholars and collaborators;
- an awareness where appropriate of issues related to intellectual property management and the commercialisation of innovation; and
- an ability to formulate applications to relevant agencies, such as funding bodies and ethics committees.

(*PhD Handbook*, 2011; your university will have a similar institutional guide. See also 'Questions to Consider when Writing a PhD Thesis' 2007.)

5 The process of completing a thesis

The process of completing a Ph.D. has several stages. The main ones are:

- the proposal stage;
- the confirmation stage;
- the thesis-writing stage.

There is often a data-collection stage (depending on the thesis area). If you have to collect data, this occurs after the proposal has been accepted and after confirmation has been granted, but before you write the thesis.

1 The proposal stage
During the proposal stage, you have to:

- write an initial research proposal to demonstrate that the project is worth doing (see chapter 18);
- have the proposal examined by several academics within your department and, sometimes, prepare a verbal 'defence' – sometimes called a *viva* – of the project in front of an audience of peers (if this is not done at this stage, it is certainly done at the confirmation stage).

If the proposal is accepted, you have to write a document that satisfies the requirements of confirmation.

2 The confirmation stage
The confirmation stage must generally occur within twelve months of enrolment. It requires you to complete a sizeable document (the exact size varies but usually around 20 or more pages). In this document, you must expand on the initial proposal by:

- reviewing much of the previous literature in the general area of your proposed topic;
- finding a sub-topic in this general area;
- finding a 'gap' in the research area that needs further investigation;
- proposing a plausible 'thesis' that explains or accounts for this gap.

The thesis must be advanced in enough detail for the reader to gain an appreciation that you have a clear grasp of their topic area and a potentially unique approach to the topic. You must submit the confirmation document to a panel of lecturers in the department. It is then reviewed and detailed comments are given to you by the supervisor(s). You must also prepare a formal presentation (complete with slides) to an audience of peers in a departmental seminar.

It is easy to underestimate the importance of the seminar. In fact, it is crucial. The academics attending the seminar will have read the confirmation document and prepared questions that you will have to answer on the spot. If the confirmation document is considered poor or inadequately argued, these shortcomings will be exposed publicly in an audience of peers. (Staff are generally pleasant in doing this, though it can be very hard from the candidate's point of view.)

While the aim of the seminar is to be encouraging, its purpose is also to expose weaknesses in the proposed thesis. This process can be nerve-racking. Practising and preparing the seminar well before the due day is crucial. Support services in your university can offer advice in this and provide forums for you to practise your presentation. It is important to know the subject area well, prepare answers to expected questions and be clear about what your proposed thesis will do (that has not been done in the existing literature). Confirmation of the admission to the Ph.D. is granted after one year providing satisfactory progress is maintained, and all requirements have been met.

3 The data-collection stage
This stage can be long, tedious and tiring. Depending on the kind of project it is, it might involve frequent trips overseas collecting data, doing endless interviews, or collecting data from surveys. It might also involve doing empirical or statistical tests, 'crunching numbers', and drawing lots of diagrams, graphs and tables (although not all theses involve this; some are more 'theoretical' in nature). This data will be under close scrutiny from your supervisor throughout the process. He/she will make suggestions for ways to improve your data collection and evaluation.

If the thesis is a theoretical piece of research, the data-collection stage will involve endless hours of reading academic papers and books, and trying to find a 'gap' in the research literature.

Regardless of whether the thesis is qualitative or quantitative, pure or applied, theoretical or empirical (see chapter 7), the data-collection stage must always be done in conjunction with wide-ranging reading of relevant journal articles that cover related theoretical and empirical advances. Data alone are never enough; they must be supplemented by a good grounding in theory.

4 The writing-up stage

For some kinds of theses, namely analytical projects, the writing-up stage takes the entire duration of the thesis. For others, it consists of a shorter period of time after finalising data collection and analysis. In both cases, the process is often fraught with difficulties for reasons such as those listed below:

- things often take longer than you expect (getting responses to surveys; finding resources from overseas libraries; analysing the data and drawing reliable and valid conclusions);
- shaping and refining one's thesis or argument is rarely easy and takes many attempts (consider using an argument-mapping approach, as outlined in chapter 8);
- sorting out the various chapters and sections is time-consuming;
- integrating and responding to comments from supervisors and colleagues takes lots of thinking and writing time;
- editing and proofreading the final document is very hard to do as you are too close to your own work. However, there are some tips that can help (see chapter 15).

These difficulties are to be expected. After all, you are, in effect, writing your first book! A key thing to remember is to allow more than enough time. For all postgraduate study, planning and organisational skills are critical (see chapter 2). Good information-management skills are especially important when writing a Ph.D. (see chapter 3).

6 Twelve tips for the writing-up stage

The following tips come from personal experience and are noted in similar documents about writing a Ph.D.:

1 Never read something without writing a summary of the ideas and what you think about them. Doing this in the form of a Critical Review helps (see chapter 10).
2 Make sure you also keep a citation record and a search log, as references are easy to forget, and you may need to find a reference years later (see the website for a bonus chapter on **information literacy**).
3 Write a Table of Contents with headings and sub-headings of how your proposed thesis will look. This will take several iterations as things change and take shape (but the process of doing it helps you enormously).
4 Write one-page summaries of the various sections and pass them around to colleagues for feedback (they are more likely to read a short summary than an entire chapter).
5 Start anywhere on your thesis. You don't have to write the introduction first. Often the Methodology section is the best place to start because it is easier to write.

(Always write the abstract last as it can be the hardest section to write; (see chapter 11).

6   Don't stop writing something until you have reached a 'pick-up' point. You can commence something new when you start again. It's easy to forget what you were trying to say or argue if you stop mid-stream (even if it is only to make a cup of coffee).

7   Set attainable sub-goals rather than writing a whole chapter/section in one hit (i.e. 'I will write section 3.2 today').

8   When trying to organise your chapters and sections, put all your tables and diagrams in a logical order. Pretend you are explaining the ideas to a friend who is uninformed about your area of research. What order would be best? Then, design section headings and chapter headings based on the order of the material.

9   Work on a draft of one chapter while editing another and doing preliminary research for another. In other words, keep the project moving along by spreading your efforts on different tasks.

10   Form a work group of other Ph.D. students to work on drafts. You don't have to be working in the same fields or discipline areas (in fact, it is often better if you are in different areas).

11   Commit yourself to a writing routine in the same place (if you constantly change study location you will be distracted).

12   Write something on a daily basis.

The last tip – *write something on a daily basis* – is the most important. There are several good reasons to do this:

- You can always fix, change, improve, or reject something later on. Regular writing ensures you have something to improve on and/or reject.
- The process of writing helps your thinking. It helps you get a sense of what you want to do. (A philosopher once said: 'There is no such thing as an unexpressed thought'). Getting something on paper is a critical part of getting clear about an issue or problem. Many students make the mistake of viewing the writing-up as not part of the research, but rather as something done after the research is complete. This is especially the case when they've done some comprehensive empirical work. Yet research is only of value when it is communicated, and if you can't communicate your ideas and findings effectively, then you don't really know what you are talking about. In short, the write-up *is* the research!
- Regular writing helps you to feel that the project is progressing, and lets your supervisor know you are moving forward (the psychology of this for you is important – even if what you actually produce is not used in the final thesis).
- You can't produce something good in a hurry, no matter how clever you are.
- You can't make better something that has not yet been written. You can, by contrast, always improve on something that is ill-formed, disorganised or unclear.

- Think of the task in manageable terms: 200 quality words a day = 1400 words a week = 5600 words a month = 50,000 in nine months!

At this rate, the process of meeting word-length requirements seems quite achievable. However, if you leave your writing-up until the last few months, it is definitely unachievable.

7 Starting a Ph.D.: is it for you?

Sometimes students ask themselves if they are 'ready' for the Ph.D. This is impossible to answer in such a book as this. However, it is important to satisfy *yourself* that you are ready for the challenge that a Ph.D. brings.

As a postgraduate learning adviser, I often used to see students who viewed a Ph.D. in terms of a career stepping-stone. This is unfortunate. The Ph.D. is not necessarily a good way to 'get a job' or to 'make money'. It is, however, a good way of joining the company of other academics, and it is a necessary condition of an academic career. But this step is not for everyone. There are other, perfectly worthy and interesting, career options for a completing postgraduate student.

8 Your existing strengths: a recap

Before you consider the challenges of further study, you might like to reflect on the skills you have acquired already, or shortly will acquire, as a postgraduate. Recall the list of skills mentioned in chapter 1. This list of skills is surprisingly long. Many students often do not pause to reflect that these skills are really *generic* or *transferable* skills that are highly suitable for *any workplace environment*. If you have read this book – and if you have assiduously practised the advice given – the following are skills you should now possess: the ability to give a good presentation; summarise and critique information; write clearly and logically; paraphrase and critically analyse; find and manage information resources; and so on.

All of these skills are highly desirable to many employers and should not be underestimated. Look at any advertisement for a job in the newspaper or on the internet. It is usually transferable skills that are mentioned. These, along with content knowledge, are what a postgraduate education should provide. With these skills you are ready for the world of work. Consider visiting the Careers and Employment Centre in your university and getting some advice on future career directions.

9 Summary

This chapter has looked at what a Ph.D. is, what it involves and why you may choose to do one. Naturally, if you have commenced a postgraduate degree, you will be inclined towards higher-degree study already and will want to know the next step. There are many other options available to you once you have successfully completed a course-work or research degree (employment, consultancy, etc). Your options will largely depend on how well you have mastered the requirements of your postgraduate studies, your level of motivation to study further as a fully-fledged researcher, and the grades you have obtained for your coursework studies. This book has hopefully enabled you to do well and to consider these options in decisions that you make for your future. Good luck!

Glossary of Terms

abbreviations used in referencing A variety of ways in which reference information is shortened to avoid repetition and redundancy

abstract/executive summary/synopsis A statement of the key information from each section of a report or research paper

academic argument An intellectual dispute with others over the truth/falsity or relevance/application of some claim to scholarly knowledge – with the aim of arriving at a more accurate version

academic expectations Skills that you are required to demonstrate to lecturers as a postgraduate student

academic tribes The rules of different academic disciplines in relation to assignment writing

acknowledgement Using referencing to show how you have used the words and ideas of others

active learning Learning by doing something for yourself and not relying on others

activity-based tutorials Tutorials where students do something in class (e.g. engage in simulations)

agreeing or disagreeing with the work of others Forming a judgement about other people's ideas or evidence

analysis phase Underlining noun phrases in an assignment to be sure you understand the requirements and answer all parts of an assignment question.

analytical Looking at both sides of a debate and coming to a conclusion about the merits of one side or the other

analytical annotated bibliography An annotated bibliography providing a line or two of analysis as well as the summary

analytical learning ('deep learning') Thinking critically about what the lecturer tells you and arriving at your own opinions based on evidence and argument

analytical reading Very careful reading when you wish to understand something exactly

analysing a case study Taking the position of a fictional manager and being given a written case to analyse and make recommendations about

annotated bibliography A summary of an article in 150 words or less

argument A series of connected statements which *lead* to a conclusion

argument map A box and arrow-type diagram showing the inference from premises to a conclusion or contention in an argument

argument phase Ensuring that there is a clear argument form, or link between premises and conclusion, which leads to a thesis statement

assertions Claims that do not lead to a conclusion on the basis of reasons, e.g. ''It's raining.' If I say this I am not *concluding* anything, I am just making a statement

assessment in tutorials Ways of gaining a 'participation mark' for students. Different methods are used for doing this

assessment procedures Rules that need to be followed when handing in assessed work

assessment tasks Activities or assignments you have to complete to successfully pass a course of academic study

assumptions Ideas which lie behind someone's view or position (may be explicit or implicit)

attention-getter Something interesting to start a presentation (e.g. a surprising fact)

attributing a view to another person Judging a person's opinion as being theirs when it is not clear, but where you have a reasonable suspicion

author prominent Putting the author's name first before a citation

backtracking Going back over what you have already read

being direct and forthright Getting to the point quickly and decisively

being vocal Being confident, and unafraid of expressing your views orally in front of other people

bias Believing in something without being willing to listen to the opposing evidence.

bibliographic citations Reference information in a bibliography or reference list

bibliography A list of documents (books, articles, etc.) that you have read and/or quoted for a specific essay or assignment.

block-style writing Ensuring that all the points or group of ideas for a position are covered before looking at the group of ideas for an alternative position.

book bibliographic details All the details necessary to identify a book precisely: the author, title, place of publication, publisher, date of publication, and if necessary, the edition number and/or the editor's name

brain-on reading Reading with a research question in mind

break-out groups Smaller discussion groups formed out of a larger class. Break-out groups normally reconvene into the larger group and present the results of their deliberations

broad skill areas General skills that are as important as content or subject knowledge, e.g. speaking skills or skills in critical thinking (*see* generic skills)

CALL number The unique identifying number of a library resource

card system of file management A simple and cheap method of file storage on cards under subject and author headings

case study A real-life empirical study where multiple sources of evidence are used

case-study report A formal document in several sections involving the description and analysis of a company with an emphasis on isolating problems and weighing specific solutions to a particular issue

chain-style writing Covering all the points or group of ideas for one position before doing the same with an alternative group of ideas

choosing a reading Deciding on what students should read in a class and handing it out before the class

chunking Putting phrases into segments by using pauses and stress in the right places

citation   Another word for a reference.

coherence (in paragraphs)   Each point supporting the main idea in a paragraph

'cold' research   A research area on which there is little current published information

company report   A formal document in several sections involving the description and analysis of a company, with an emphasis on discussion and recommendations

computer-based file management   Using a computer to do file management

conclusion indicator words   Words which indicate that a premise of an argument is to follow

conclusion   Where you sum up the findings and discussion and arrive at a point of view

conclusion (to essay)   Should contain: overview of main argument, summing up of main ideas, ending with a general statement of some kind

conclusion (public speaking)   Presentation of conclusions should follow this structure: cue ending, sum up, outline main point, look at implications, invite questions

confidentiality clause   A statement of when a report can be released for public view owing to it containing commercially sensitive information

confirmation report   A document, typically around 20 pages in length, completed as a necessary hurdle requirement for continuing a research-based doctoral programme

connector words/language   Language to guide the reader through your critical review

conserving attitude to knowledge   Repeating and summarising 'correct' information without analysing it yourself

construct   A concept used in research

construct validity   The extent to which appropriate measurement tools can be used for the concepts being studied

consultation hours   Specific times when your lecturer or supervisor is available for meetings

contact time   Time where you see lecturers and tutors and work on subject content

content knowledge   Subject knowledge in a discipline

contention   A statement asserted on the basis of reasons (also known as a 'conclusion')

context   The background or basis to your presentation

contribution to research   *See* thesis statement

conversation metaphor for research   Seeing research in terms of an exchange of ideas between experts in a specific area of interest

co-premises   Reasons in an argument that depend on each other in order to support the conclusion or contention

critically analyse   See 'critical thinking'

critical review language   Language used to show your position in relation to an idea

critical review (summary and critique)   Reading, reviewing, summarising and critiquing one article

critical thinking   Judging the merits of a view, theory or opinion by using academic argument

critiquing   Judging both the positive as well as negative points and coming to your own conclusion based on your analysis

deciphering   Reading for pronunciation and meaning of unfamiliar words

deductive argument   An argument sequence that moves from a general statement to a particular conclusion

'deep' learning   *See* 'analytical learning'

descriptive annotated bibliography   An annotated bibliography providing no more than a summary

direction words   Words used to advise a student of what to do in an assessment exercise

direct quotations   Using the exact words of someone else to support a point being made (inverted commas and a citation are necessary)

discussion/analysis   Where you analyse or interpret what was discovered

drawing a conclusion using the work of others   Basing a conclusion on other people's ideas or evidence

editing   Checking writing for meaning or sense

editor   A person who compiles and coordinates papers in a book

elaborate   Give more details

electronic databases   Computer-based catalogues of resources, usually in specific discipline areas

ellipses   Dots showing deliberate omission of part of a quotation

empirical report   A formal document in several sections involving the description of the use of a scientific methodology and/or procedure

endnote system   Similar to the footnote system, but the citation information is found at the end of each document

essay-style report   A formal document written in introduction–body–conclusion format involving the statement of a key thesis, the discussion of arguments for and against a point of view, and arriving at a conclusion

explanatory footnote   Using a footnote to mention marginally relevant information or to explain something in more detail.

extending attitude to knowledge   Where students themselves begin to pose their own speculative questions and make original contributions

extensions   Request to lecturers to hand in work late (usually only for medical reasons)

external validity   The extent to which the data can be applied beyond the circumstances of the case to more general situations

eye contact   Deliberately ranging your eyes to look at different parts of the audience, to show confidence and to get attention

file management or information management   A system which allows you to store and retrieve scholarly information quickly and efficiently

fixed commitments   Time when you are committed to attending something (also called 'contact time')

flashcards   Small cards hidden in your hand and used to remind you of presentation content

focusing   Where your eyes concentrate when reading (it is recommended that this is done at the top of letters)

footnote system   A method of referencing where all information is placed in the text at the bottom of the page. A reference list or bibliography is also provided at the end of a document.

forming alliances   Using the arguments and evidence of other writers to support your own view on an academic issue

free periods   Time when you have no fixed commitments (also called 'non-contact time')

front matter   Preface material prior to a book or report

generalisability   The extent to which a research study can be generalised to new and different situations

generic skills   Skills that are independent of subject or discipline-based knowledge or subject matter

gesture   Use of your arms and hands for emphasis and to show confidence

ground rules of conduct   Ways to think about the process of learning and engagement with others in a tutorial

groupwork   Assignments done with other students where the workload must be shared

Harvard system (author–date)   A method of referencing where minimal information is placed in the text (surname, year, page number) and the remainder is found in the reference list or bibliography at the end of a document

heavy noun phrases   Long and complex noun phrases

heightened conversation   Style of speaking in-between formal and informal

'hot' research   A research area where there is an overwhelming amount of published information of which one has to keep abreast on a daily basis

hypercritical   Excessively and unfairly critical

hypothesis   A hypothesis is a testable statement that relates two or more constructs

hypothetico-deductive   Moving from observation to hypothesis to theory and then deducing or predicting further observations from the theory

ice-breaker   An activity designed to get people talking and meeting one another

imaginary audience test   Pretending that your writing is being read or listened to by (e.g.) high school students; i.e. an intelligent but general audience

inference   A logical move from premises to conclusions in an argument

in-text citations   Citations in the text (usually in the text itself but may be at the 'foot'/bottom of a page or the end of document)

independence and self-reliance   Depending only on yourself, and not friends, lecturers or family, to complete something

information desk librarians   Librarians who offer initial advice on library services and general information

information literacy   Knowing where to find and retrieve relevant information and where to get help if you need it

information prominent   Putting the information or idea before the citation.

inter-library loan   A facility where items from other libraries can be retrieved for your use (usually for a small fee)

intercultural differences in communication styles   Cultural differences in how we relate to each other in face-to-face situations

internal validity   The extent to which different methodological tools can be used to triangulate data

introduction (to essay)   Should contain: general area, specific area, gap in research, research question, tentative thesis statement and outline of essay to follow

introduction (public speaking)   Presentation of introductions should follow this structure: attention-getter, statement of context, statement of aim, statement of justification, outline

inverted funnel (approach to speaking)   Moving from the general point or main point to specific details before concluding

issue (of a journal)   A bound collection of papers in a journal that appears regularly

issue-based tutorials   Tutorials where issues are discussed and criticised

issues phase   Listing all the main things you need to cover for each part of an assignment and elaborating on what needs to be determined for each

joint author   A joint author writes in collaboration with another, or several other writers

journal abstracts   Books that list the abstracts or summaries of the contents of journal articles as well as the publication details

journal bibliographic details   For an article you need: author of the article, title of the article, title of the journal, volume number, year, issue number and inclusive page numbers (i.e. starting page of article to ending page of article)

journal indexes   Books that list the publication details of journal articles

journal   A publication that appears regularly (e.g. monthly, weekly, quarterly or daily)

justification for research   A statement of why your research is important or interesting

laying down time   Having a rest from working on a particular assignment to allow you to see the mistakes when you return to it

leading a discussion   Being in charge of a tutorial discussion

lecture   Formal one-way delivery of academic material by a lecturer to an audience of students

lecturer-directed model of learning (lecture) (also known as 'teacher-centred' learning)   Where students sit and listen to lecturers who impart information

light noun phrases   Short noun phrases

limitations   Where the problems associated with the report methodology or procedure are mentioned

literature review   The presentation, classification and evaluation of what other researchers have written on a particular subject

'lukewarm' research   A research area which is not too 'hot' nor 'cold' (i.e. where there is a good deal of recent published research, but not an overwhelming amount)

macro-editing   Editing from presentation and page formatting down to in-text references, bibliography and the use of font.

methodology   The analytical approach used to analyse your data or evidence

micro-editing   Editing from the paragraph-level coherence down to the sentence-level grammatical errors

mixed tutorials   Tutorials with elements of problem, issues and activity-based tutorials

naming norms   Conventions of how personal names are used

negative case-analysis method   The rejection or refutation of a hypothesis

objections   statements used to reject a contention or conclusion in an argument

objectivity   The extent to which a research study is independent of the researcher's opinions, biases and predictions

operationalised   (in research) A hypothesis or claim that is testable

originality   Different ways in which a student can make a contribution to a topic

outline   A summary of the major parts of a speech

overview of main points   A summary of the main ideas in an essay, case study or report

pagination   This is another way of saying page numbers. Single pages are written as 'p. 7' and multiple pages are written as 'pp. 3–16'

paper   Another word for essay or report, written by a professional academic, or student

paraphrase   A version of a text written in different words from the original including all details, and often involving a further elaboration of points in the original text. A paraphrase is the use of someone else's ideas in *your own* words

parsimony   The extent to which a research study is simple, narrowly focused and well-directed to its aims and objectives

participation   Active engagement in activities by speaking, commenting, arguing, criticising, taking the initiative in group activities, and so on.

passive learning   The opposite of active learning. Relying on others to 'give information' to you

peer-reviewed/refereed   A published work usually anonymously assessed by experts. Peer review occurs in several distinct stages over time

perfectionism   Great attention to detail/attempt to make something 'perfect'

phrase reading   Reading phrases, not words, and concentrating on long eye fixations on nouns and verbs

plagiarism   The intentional use of the words or ideas written by someone else

planner   A weekly or yearly timetable created to help you study efficiently and productively

point out assumptions   To make things which lie behind the ideas and evidence of others very specific when they are unstated in the writing

position   The point of view, attitude, or argument of someone on a given topic

precision and confidence   The extent to which a research study yields believable and reliable results

preliminary literature review   An overview of the literature with minimal detail given in a research proposal

premise indicator words   Words which signal that what goes before is a premise, and that what comes after is a conclusion

premises   Statements which are used to infer a certain conclusion. They are statements you argue *from* to a conclusion

pre-semester break   The period before the semester starts

presentation verbs   Words like: 'outline', 'overview', 'demonstrate'…

presenting or 'running' a tutorial   Being in change of preparing the tutorial for the week (or a segment of the tutorial)

pre-tutorial reading   Reading material that is essential to complete before a tutorial or seminar in order to understand and contribute meaningfully to class discussions

primary sources   These are sometimes called source material. It refers to original manuscripts and contemporary records, such as letters, government reports, etc.

private study   Time when you work by yourself on preparing for lectures, tutorials, exams and assignments

problem-based tutorials   Tutorials where problems are solved and answers obtained

procedure   The way in which the methodology is implemented

procrastination   Putting things off/delaying things. Making excuses and wasting time when you should be working, particularly in relation to writing for assessment

proofreading   Checking writing for residual mistakes

publication details   This is the place of publication, the name of the publisher and the year the item was published

purposeful reading   *See* 'brain-on reader'

purpose of research   The aim of a research project

qualitative research   A non-linear research process where a question is asked and refined during the research leading to tentative conclusions

quantitative research   A linear research process where an hypothesis is posed, and data is collected and tested using empirical methods

quotation   The exact words of someone else given in inverted commas with reference details provided.

reasons   Statements used to support a contention or conclusion in an argument

rebuttals   Statements used to reject an objection in an argument

recommendations   Where you state what should be done based on your findings and discussion

redrafting   Reworking a piece of assessment in order to improve it

refereed journal article   *See* 'peer-reviewed/refereed'

reference footnote   Using a footnote (at the bottom of a page) to provide an in-text citation

reference/citation   A reference (sometimes called a citation) comprises all necessary bibliographic details so that a document can be found

reliability   The extent to which an investigation produces consistent and repeatable results

repetition   Saying the same thing in the same or different words

replicability   The extent to which a research study or experiment can be repeated

report   A general term. Can be an empirical report, company report, case-study report or argumentative essay

representation phase   Drawing of a simple concept map or flow chart of the main sections of the assignment (sometimes called 'brainstorming')

reproductive learning ('surface learning')   Copying what the lecturer tells you

research   A process involving the investigation, collection of data and the evaluation of the data

research gap   What others have done/haven't done in a research area and what needs to be done.

research log   The documentation of a search history that ensures that you search efficiently and do not repeat searches unnecessarily

research methodology   The research approach taken, e.g. quantitative, qualitative, case method, etc.

research phase   Constructing a research question and search statement to assist in finding information on narrowly focused research topics

research plan   The direction of your research, i.e. its aim and purpose

research problem/issue   A problem or issue that is considered important or interesting in a given research area

research proposal   Document written to inform readers about a proposed topic of study. A research proposal is typically from 5 to 7 pages in length, completed as a necessary requirement for admission into a research-based doctoral programme

research question   A narrowly focused question designed to elucidate an area of investigation

research timetable   Your proposed timetable from commencement to the completion of your work

researchable   Something that can be researched (which is narrowly focused and which is not simply opinion)

reserve collection   A special place in the library where frequently used resources are kept (and cannot be borrowed)

residual errors   Mistakes left over in your writing in your penultimate (second last) or final version

results/findings   Where you plainly state what has been discovered

reversal (in presentations)   Saying something more than once by turning the order around

rhetorical questions   Questions that you ask the audience and then answer yourself (if they don't answer)

rigour   The logical soundness of a research methodology

routine   A regular schedule or procedure

running a tutorial   *See* 'leading a discussion'

scanning   Reading by searching for something specific and ignoring anything unrelated to that specific item

scholarship   The ability to find and use information from published sources in your own work

scripted   Sounding like everything is written down and excessively rehearsed

search strategy   A systematic process of finding academic resources

secondary sources   This refers to critical or descriptive literature of a primary source by another writer (or 'secondary author')

seminal reading   An academic article or book that is considered highly original and path-breaking in terms of the ideas expressed

seminar   A format of instruction involving a blend of lecture and tutorial

'shopping list' review   Where one person's ideas are noted, then another's, then another's, with little integration of the ideas

signpost language   Language used to guide your reader or listener

skimming   Reading and getting a general idea of the content and ignoring anything unrelated to the main point

soundness   A property of premises in an argument. A premise is 'sound' if it is true or at least plausible (believable)

speaking environment   The place where you have to present

speculative learning   Thinking for yourself by being original in various ways

'stand-alone' review   A review which summarises the literature so that someone can understand what you read, without reading it themselves

statement of aim   The main point of the presentation

statement of justification   Why your topic is important or interesting

stating the view of another person   Making someone else's voice or opinion clear (summarising their view)

stating your own position   Making your 'voice' or opinion clear (having a 'thesis')

strategic planning Adopting a planning approach that caters for longer-term goals. This might involve, e.g. planning well in advance for your studies by preparing for assignments before semester starts, meeting lecturers and discussing requirements

student involvement model of learning (tutorial) (also known as 'student-centred' learning) Where students are actively involved and tutors facilitate learning

style and literacy The level of professionalism, competence and grammatical fluency in writing

subject librarians Specialist librarians who can help you find information in your subject area

summary A shortened version of a text in different words from the original, and omitting many details.

supervisors Academics chosen to assist students in completing postgraduate research degrees

surface reading Superficial reading where everything is read but not read very carefully

taking a stand Coming to your own view about an academic issue

taking the initiative Showing that you can think for yourself and be *proactive* and not just *reactive* to situations

teacher-centred learning When the lecturer imparts information and the students take notes (i.e. in a formal lecture)

testability The extent to which a research question or hypothesis can be tested

theoretical framework The model or position taken to explain some phenomenon

thesis (a) A point of view on a topic; (b) a large paper produced for a research degree

thesis statement Your answer to a research gap

time management Using your time efficiently and productively

title page The first page in a book which has the full title and author of the book. It often gives the name of the publisher as well, and sometimes the date of publication, although this is often found on the back of the title page (the imprint page)

topic sentence The main point of a paragraph

triangulation Using different methods of analysis to check whether your conclusions are accurate

tripling Saying something in groups of three where possible for impact

truncation The use of symbols to capture a variety of different word forms in a database search

tutorial Class-based, informal discussion activity where academic thinking is modelled and trialled

tutorial language Commonly used phrases for expressing an idea, asking for clarification, criticising someone's idea, etc.

unity (in paragraphs) Having only one idea in each paragraph

university formatting requirements University or department guidelines for how to present your work

validity (arguments) A property of argument structure. In a valid argument the premises link well to the conclusion or contention

validity (research)   A measure of whether what you are testing is what you *say* you are testing (as opposed to something else); it is also a measure of whether your results can be generalised to other similar situations

variables   Things that are tested, which influence what is tested, modify what is tested, and which may appear during the process of testing

vested interest   A prior bias in the truth of some statement because there is a personal interest in it, e.g. someone can believe that red wine is good for health if they have shares in a wine company

vocalisation   Voicing words silently or aloud when you read

voicing your opinions   Giving your own ideas, or critiquing others' ideas, as part of a class discussion

volume (of a journal)   A bound collection of journal issues

wall calendar   A yearly planner placed on a wall where you can see it every day

weak author   Mentioning a range of authors before a citation.

weekly planner/timetable   A daily record of all a student's fixed commitments and study periods

writing a case study   A field work project where students are required to study a company and work on-site

'writing for a generous reader' principle   Writing in a way that assumes that the reader will make an effort to understand what you are saying

'writing for a selfish reader' principle   Writing in a way that assumes that the reader will *not* make an effort to understand what you are saying (i.e. writing very clearly)

writing stage   Following the structure of an introduction carefully using connector words and linking language.

yearly planner/timetable   A yearly record of all a student's assignment deadlines, exams and other assessment requirements

yes-BUT approach to reading   Noting where writers agree, disagree and partly agree with a hypothesis, research question or thesis statement

References

The Adventure of English (2003) video, M. Bragg (presenter), R. Bee & D. Thomas (directors), ITV (DVD 2009). http://en.wikipedia.org/wiki/The_Adventure_of_English

AGPS (2002) *Style Manual for Authors, Editors and Printers* (6th edn). Milton, Qld: John Wiley.

Arnaudet, M., & Barrett, M. (1984) *Approaches to Academic Reading and Writing*. Englewood Cliffs, NJ: Prentice Hall.

Ballard, B., & Clancy, J. (1984) *Study Abroad: A Manual for Asian Students*. Kuala Lumpur: Longman.

Ballard, B., & Clanchy, J. (1988) *Studying in Australia*. Melbourne, Australia: Longman Cheshire.

Bartlett, A., Holzknecht, S., & Cumming Thom, A. (1999) *Preparing Students for Graduate Study: To Hit the Ground Running*. Canberra, Australia: Asia Pacific Press and National Centre for Development Studies, Australian National University.

Becker, L. (2003) *How to Manage Your Arts, Humanities and Social Science Degree*. Basingstoke, UK: Palgrave Macmillan.

Becker, L. (2004) *How to Manage your Postgraduate Course*. Basingstoke, UK: Palgrave Macmillan.

Beecham, R. (2006) Annotated Bibliographies. Retrieved 19/11/07, from http://tlu.ecom. unimelb.edu.au/students/study/helpsheets.html

Bretag, T., Crossman, J., & Bordia, S. (2007) *Communication Skills for International Students*. North Ryde: McGraw Hill Irwin.

Clarke, D. (2003) Research Methods in Education. Unpublished manuscript, Melbourne.

Cottrell, S. (2008) *The Study Skills Handbook* (3rd edn). Basingstoke, UK: Palgrave Macmillan.

Cottrell, S. (2011) *Critical Thinking Skills: Developing Effective Analysis and Argument* (2nd edn). Basingstoke, UK: Palgrave Macmillan.

Currie, P., & Gray, E. (1987) *Strictly Academic: A Reading and Writing Text*. New York: Newbury House.

Davies, W. M. (2009) Not Quite Right: Teaching Students How to Make Better Arguments. *Teaching in Higher Education*, 13(3), 327–340.

Davies, W. M., & Sievers, K. H. (2006) *The Nature of Knowing: A Resource Manual for Understanding Knowledge*. Melbourne, Australia: IBID Press.

Dunleavy, P. (2003) *Authoring a PhD: How to Plan, Draft, Write and Finish a Doctorial Dissertation*. Basingstoke, UK: Palgrave Macmillan.

ELBC (Academic Communication Skills) Booklet. (1994) Adelaide, Australia: Technical and Further Education.

Ericsson, K. A., & Charness, N. (1994) Expert Performance. *American Psychologist*, 49, 725–747.

Gibaldi, J. (2008) *MLA style Manual and Guide to Scholarly Publishing* (3rd edn). New York: Modern Language Association of America.

Godfrey, J. (2009) *How to Use Your Reading in Your Essays*. Basingstoke, UK: Palgrave Macmillan.

Graduate Outlook. (2006) *Graduate Careers Australia*. Retrieved 12/10/07, from http://www.graduatecareers.com.au/content/view/full/52

Greetham, B. (2008) *How to Write Better Essays* (2nd edn). Basingstoke, UK: Palgrave Macmillan.

Grix, J. (2010) *The Foundations of Research* (2nd edn). Basingstoke, UK: Palgrave Macmillan.

Hofstede, G. (1986) Cultural Differences in Teaching and Learning. *International Journal of Intercultural Relations*, 10, 301–317.

Hurworth, R. (2003) Introduction to Qualitative Research Methods in Education. Unpublished manuscript, Melbourne, Australia.

Johnston, C. (2001) Student Perceptions of Learning in First Year in an Economics and Commerce Faculty. *Higher Education Research and Development*, 20(2), 169–184.

Kantola, R. (writer). (1985) Be Prepared to Speak: The Step-by-Step Video Guide to Public Speaking. A. Hardy (producer), R. Field (director): San Francisco, CA: Kantola-Skeie Productions/Toastmasters International.

Lewis, M., & Reinders, H. (2003) *Study Skills for Speakers of English as a Second Language*. Basingstoke, UK: Palgrave Macmillan.

McEvedy, M., & Wyatt, P. (1990) *Assignment Writing: Developing Communication Skills*. Melbourne, Australia: Nelson.

McLeay, F. J., & Zwart, A. C. (1993) Agricultural Marketing and Farm Marketing Strategies. *Australian Agribusiness Review* 1(1), 80–99.

Monash University Arts Academic Language and Learning Unit (AALLU) (2010) What Makes a Good Critical Review? Accessed 01/11, from http://arts.monash.edu.au/aallu/resources-good-crit-review.pdf

Murphy, R. (2004) *English Grammar in Use: A Self-Study Reference and Practice Book for Intermediate Students of English with Answers*. Cambridge: Cambridge University Press.

Nunan, D. (1992) *Research Methods in Language Learning*. Cambridge: Cambridge University Press.

Nutting, J., & White, G. (1990) *The Business of Communicating*. Sydney, Australia: McGraw-Hill.

Oshima, A., & Hogue, A. (1999) *Writing Academic English* (3rd edn). White Plains, NY: Longman Cheshire.

Pears, R., & Shields, G. (2010) *Cite them Right: The Essential Referencing Guide* (8th edn). Basingstoke: Palgrave Macmillan.

Perry, C. (1994) A Structured Approach to Presenting Ph.D. Theses: Notes for Candidates and their Supervisors. Paper presented at the ANZ Doctoral Consortium, Sydney University, Australia.

Perry, C. (2003) Research Proposal Structure Keyed into the Thesis Structure. Retrieved 18/04, from http://www.usq.edu.au/library/help/postgrad/research.htm

PhD Handbook (2011), Melbourne: School of Graduate Research, University of Melbourne, http://www.http://www.gradresearch.unimelb.edu.au/current/phdhbk/

Phillips, E. M., & Pugh, D. S. (2010) *How to get a PhD* (5th edn). New York: Open University Press.

Powell, M. (1999) *Presenting in English: How to Give Successful Presentations*. London: Language Teaching Publications.

Questions to Consider when Writing a PhD Thesis. (2007) http://www.gradstudies.unimelb.edu.au/phd/enrolcandid/phdhbk/phdthesis/question.html

Quinion, M. (1998, 27/10/2002) Don't understand these 2 dates. Citing Online Sources. Retrieved 20/12/03, from http://www.quinion.com/words/articles/citation.htm

Rao, V., Chanock, K., & Krishnan, L. (2007) *A Visual Guide to Essay Writing*. Canberra, Australia, Australian National University: Association of Academic Language and Learning (AALL).

Reinders, H, Moore, N., & Lewis, M. (2008) *The International Student Handbook*. Basingstoke, UK: Palgrave Macmillan.

Ritter, R. (2003) *The Oxford Style Guide*. Oxford, UK: Oxford University Press.

Rochecouste, J. (2005) Constructing Taxonomies for Student Writing. Paper presented at the European Association for the Teaching of Academic Writing. Retrieved 16/06/05, from http://eataw2005.hau.gr/pages/about.htm

Sekaran, U. (1992) *Research Methods for Business: A Skills-Building Approach*. New York: John Wiley.

Seperich, G. J., Woolverton, J., Berierlein, G., & Hahn, D. E. (eds.). (1996) *Cases in Agribusiness Management*. Scottsdale, AZ: Gorsuch Scarisbrick.

Stevens, K., & Asmar, C. (1999) *Doing Postgraduate Research in Australia*. Melbourne, Australia: Melbourne University Press.

Strunk, W (2008) *The Elements of Style*. Boston: Allyn & Bacon.

Taylor, D. (2008) A Brief Guide to Writing a Literature Review. *Writing in the Health Sciences: A Comprensive Guide, 1*(1). Retrieved 08/04/10, from http://hswriting.library.utoronto.ca/index.php/hswriting/article/view/3092/1239

Toastmasters (2007) *How to Write and Deliver Great Speeches* (DVD/Study Guide). Toastmasters International/Kantola Productions LLC.

Turabian, K. (2007) *A Manual for Writers of Term Papers, Theses and Dissertations*. Chicago: Chicago University Press.

van Emden, J., & Becker, L. (2010) *Presentation Skills for Students* (2nd edn). Basingstoke, UK: Palgrave Macmillan.

Vince, M. (2003) *First Certificate Language Practice*. Oxford, UK: Macmillan.

Weissberg, R., & Buker, S. (1990) *Writing Up Research: Experimental Report Writing for Students of English*. Englewood Cliffs, NJ: Prentice Hall.

Williams, K., Bethell, E., Lawton, J., Parfitt-Brown, C., Richardson, M., and Rowe, V. (2010) *Planning Your PhD*. Basingstoke, UK: Palgrave Macmillan.

Williams, K., Bethell, E., Lawton, J., Parfitt-Brown, C., Richardson, M., and Rowe, V. (2011) *Completing Your PhD*. Basingstoke, UK: Palgrave Macmillan.

Wisker, G. (2008) *The Postgraduate Research Handbook*. Basingstoke, UK: Palgrave Macmillan.

Yin, R. (1994) *Case Study Research: Design and Methods* (Vol. 5). London: Sage.

Index